I0818830

SERGE RAMELLI

LONDON

SERGE RAMELLI

LONDON

teNeues

LONDON

HEY WAIT! Don't just jump into the pretty photos! *How can you have any pudding if you don't eat yer meat?* (Yes, that's a Pink Floyd reference.) I have a challenge for you: I want to see if you have the answer to one of the most critical questions that humanity faces as we enter this era of—this most incredibly overused of buzz phrases—artificial intelligence.

I know, I know! Pfft—boring black words on a white page! Who even has the time to read anymore!? You just want to see Serge's indelible splashes of color, his unique framing and bold compositions, and the deeply saturated sunsets that Serge seems to magically conjure from his camera like a French Merlin pulling the sword from the stone! Ha! Just checking to see if you were paying attention. Obviously, Merlin pulled a croissant out of a hat, not a stone from a sword. Sheesh. (Hopefully, my references are like a spoonful of sugar to help the medicine go down.)

Now I know what you are thinking: "Who does this elderberry-smelling idiot think he is with this challenge? I'm brilliant! I'll answer any question in seconds! I even know the airspeed velocity of an unladen swallow—11 meters per second for the European Swallow, not African if you must know! What is the question!?"

Well, fortunately, the question is not "Where can I find a shrubbery?" my brilliant *Monty Python*–loving friend. (And no, it's also not "To be or not to be.") But please, allow me to digress, because how I frame the question for you may very well be more important than the question itself.

My first "picture" of London—if you would call it that—was actually the one I imagined while hearing the voice of my godfather in my earliest memory of him. I think I was four or five, sipping on a Shirley Temple while he spoke of his adventures in London. I remember the taste of the cherry syrup–flavored ginger ale almost as clearly as I remember how his baritone, refined British accent and the manner in which he conveyed his words made the moment feel magical. It conjured images of a faraway land filled with Arthurian legends, refined gentlemen, monuments stretching back to the Roman Empire that defied time, and perhaps a lost piece of culture that never should have been forgotten. And on top of all that, the brutal violence of the London mob.

Fast-forward 45 years, and it is now 2025. My godfather has been gone for 15 years. I have two teenage daughters. I've completed another film, traveled the world, made money and lost money, as well as people I've loved dearly. I have not only fought for my life but also fought to maintain my marriage and family in a sociopolitical psychological warscape seemingly focused on eradicating those human institutions.

Some days I'm overwhelmed with the joy and adventure of life, and on others I pontificate stuffily about the inevitable decay of all beautiful things—or some similarly poetic-sounding fluffiness. All of this is to say: like you, I find myself in a rapidly changing world that we must not only constantly adapt to but also overcome and conquer in our own ways if we wish to survive.

And this is a world where technological advance is not just supplementing but replacing human endeavor at an exponential rate, calling into question something philosophers who walked the halls of Oxford hundreds of years ago were already pondering: What does it truly mean to be human? But that's not the question I want you to answer. So what is? Hang on a moment, my cinema-loving friend—we're getting to it and this will all make as much sense as a smashed coffee cup and police bulletin board in a *Keyser Söze*–style dramatic reveal à la *The Usual Suspects.*

There I was, recently returned from a scout in London, when my dear friend Serge reached out to me to write the introduction for this new collection of photographs. I interviewed him briefly about his love of London—how he enjoyed the cosmopolitan blend of cultures and peoples he found there, his fascination with the architectural dichotomy of massive modern skyscrapers nestled among centuries-old monuments. It was very different from Paris, and it created a completely different photographic journey for him.

But secretly I wondered, *Why?* Why not just dump everything I've written before into an AI program, have it spit something out, and be done instantly—at no charge? And that's the nature of the question I have for you.

But let me put it a different way, because this is, in essence, the defining question of our time: Is there still a place for the human artist when most of the world is being convinced technology can do it better? Wait! Don't answer yet.

Let me ask you another question: Why did you buy this book? Why are you looking at Serge Ramelli's *supercalifragilistic* photographs? Why not just ask a search engine to pull up images of London—or even ask AI to create any image of London you could imagine in seconds?

Well, I decided to try this my own way: I dumped in all the articles I'd written for Serge in the past and told the AI to create an intro about London. It had it ready in five seconds. It was exactly the length it needed to be. It felt perfectly constructed. It used some of my own language. But it just felt off. I realized it was missing the two most important elements of human communication: humanity and connection. (Perhaps "artificial intelligence" is a misnomer—synthesized intelligence might be more fitting.)

The article didn't mention anything about my godfather, or how much I loved him and British culture because of him. Or what it felt like on that rainy London day when I was last by his side in the hospital. Or the *Monty Python* movies he watched with me. Or the Pink Floyd albums he played for me. Or the joy I felt exploring art in a graffiti-filled tunnel below the Eye of London. Or the taste of the crisp air in the pristine English countryside. It also didn't—and couldn't—mention that I like my martinis shaken, not stirred, because of my lifelong love for all things James Bond.

Yes, AI is the greatest tool the human race has ever invented—just as the internet was before that. And electricity before that. And the combustion engine before that. And medicine before that. And architecture before that. And so on, back to the wheel and fire, and then all the way back again when we see what comes next.

But it can't tell you how to feel about the childlike wonder we see in Serge's photographs—an eye that still waves a magic wand to discover sparkle and places to fly a kite to the highest height. The way he captures the beauty in the world and tries to put that joy into his frames to share with you. Or how he blends the angles, the colors, the moments, the compositions, and the complex architectural contradictions to encapsulate the 1,500 years of human endeavor, suffering, tragedy, and triumph that have built London from what was once just a forest by a river into one of the greatest cities on Earth, and then present it to you in a curated series of bold images with an artistic vision that is uniquely his.

So, what is it that makes you human? Is it the questions you ask, or is it the answers you find? Is it the pain you feel, or the pleasure you seek? Is it the moments of lust that overcome your logic, or your endless pursuit of eternal love? Is it the opportunities you take or the sacrifices you make? It could be one of these, or all of these, and many others unique to you.

I believe that it is our dreams, our aspirations, and our willingness to overcome the challenges of life to attain them—not just for the benefit of ourselves—but for the entire human race. And artists, true artists, are the champions of the human race. They are the dreamers of the new dreams, the eternal muse guiding us forward and ultimately connecting us to one another in a celebration of those things that make each one of us uniquely us, through the common dreams and loves we share. Just as this new volume of Serge's photographs connects us to our love for the beauty and majesty of London—and, in that way, connects us each to a better understanding of each other.

So, my friends, London is calling at the top of the dial, and even if the ice age is starting and the sun is zooming in, turn the page, take a walk with Serge down by the river, and give yourself a smile.

Darius Stevens Wilhere
June, 2025

LONDON

HEY, WARTE MAL! Spring nicht einfach in die hübschen Fotos rein! *How can you have any pudding if you don't eat yer meat?* Ja, das ist ein Pink-Floyd-Zitat, zu Deutsch: Wer sein Fleisch nicht brav aufisst, kriegt keinen Pudding. Ich habe eine Challenge für DICH. Ich will sehen, ob du eine Antwort auf eine der wichtigsten Fragen hast, die die Menschheit sich stellen muss, jetzt, wo wir in die Ära der (begrifflich so schrecklich überstrapazierten) Künstlichen Intelligenz eintreten.

Ich weiß, ich weiß! Langweilige schwarze Wörter vor weißem Hintergrund! Wer hat überhaupt noch Zeit zu lesen!? Du willst einfach nur Serges unauslöschliche Farbspritzer sehen, seinen einmaligen Kontext und seine kühnen Kompositionen, die Sonnenuntergänge in satten Farben, die Serge aus seiner Kamera hervorzuzaubern scheint wie ein französischer Merlin, der das Schwert aus dem Stein zieht! Ha! Wollte nur mal sehn, ob du auch aufpasst. Natürlich zog Merlin ein Croissant aus einem Hut, nicht ein Schwert aus einem Stein. Also echt jetzt. (Meine Anspielungen sind hoffentlich wie „ein Löffelchen voll Zucker", das „bittre Medizin versüßt".)

Ich weiß genau, was du jetzt denkst. „Was glaubt dieser nach Holunderbeeren riechende Idiot, wer er ist mit seiner Challenge! Ich bin ein Genie! Ich beantworte jede Frage in Sekunden! Ich kenne sogar die Höchstgeschwindigkeit einer unbeladenen Schwalbe (11 Meter pro Sekunde für eine europäische Schwalbe, nicht für eine afrikanische, wenn du's genau wissen willst)! WIE LAUTET DIE FRAGE!?" Nun, zum Glück lautet die Frage NICHT: „Wo finde ich ein Gebüsch?", mein genialer, Monty-Python liebender Freund. (Und nein, sie lautet auch nicht „Sein oder nicht sein".) Aber bitte erlaube mir abzuschweifen, denn in welchen Kontext ich die Frage für dich setze, ist möglicherweise wichtiger als die Frage selbst.

Mein erstes „Bild" von London, wenn man es so nennen kann, war das, was vor meinem geistigen Auge erschien, als ich (in meiner frühesten Erinnerung an ihn) die Stimme meines Patenonkels hörte. Ich war vier oder fünf Jahre alt und schlürfte einen Shirley Temple, während er mir von seinen Abenteuern in London erzählte. Der Geschmack des mit Kirschsirup versetzten Ginger Ales ist mir noch genauso in Erinnerung wie seine tiefe Stimme und sein vornehmer britischer Akzent. Die Art seiner Schilderung machte den Moment magisch. Er beschwor Bilder eines fernen Landes herauf, eines Landes voller legendärer Artussagen-Helden, distinguierter Gentlemen, alterslos wirkender Bauwerke aus der Römerzeit – und vielleicht auch eines Stücks verlorene Kultur, die niemals hätte in Vergessenheit geraten sollen. Und das Ganze wurde von ihm noch gespickt mit Geschichten über die brutale Gewalt der Londoner Unterwelt.

Wir spulen 45 Jahre vor ins Jahr 2025. Mein Patenonkel ist nun schon seit 15 Jahren tot. Ich habe zwei Töchter im Teenageralter, gerade einen weiteren Film fertiggestellt, die Welt bereist. Ich habe Geld verdient. Und auch verloren, genau wie geliebte Menschen. Ich habe um mein Leben gekämpft und darum, meine Ehe und Familie in einer soziopolitischen psychologischen Kriegszone zu bewahren, die es scheinbar darauf anlegt, diese menschlichen Institutionen auszulöschen.

An manchen Tagen bin ich voller Freude und überwältigt vom Abenteuer des Lebens. An anderen halte ich hochtrabende Reden über den unausweichlichen Verfall alles Schönen oder irgendwelche anderen kitschigen poetischen Konzepte. Was ich damit sagen will: Wie du finde ich mich in einer sich rasant verändernden Welt wieder. Einer Welt, an die wir uns nicht nur ständig anpassen, sondern die wir auf unsere eigene Art überwinden und erobern müssen, wenn wir überleben wollen.

In dieser Welt ergänzt der technologische Fortschritt das menschliche Schaffen nicht nur, sondern ersetzt es in exponentiell ansteigendem Maße. Daraus ergibt sich die Frage, die sich schon einige Philosophen, die vor Hunderten von Jahren durch Oxfords Hallen wandelten, stellten: Was bedeutet es wirklich, ein Mensch zu sein? Aber nein, beantworte die Frage noch NICHT. Geduld, mein Kino liebender Freund, dazu kommen wir gleich und es wird so viel Sinn machen wie eine zerbrochene Kaffeetasse und eine Pinnwand auf einer Polizeiwache bei *Die üblichen Verdächtigen*.

Ich war gerade von einer Recherchereise nach London zurückgekehrt, als mein guter Freund Serge anfragte, ob ich das Vorwort zu seiner neuen Fotosammlung schreiben wolle. Ich interviewte ihn kurz über seine Liebe zu London, sein Vergnügen an dem kosmopolitischen Mix aus Kulturen und Menschen dort. Über seine Faszination mit der architektonischen Gegensätzlichkeit der Stadt, in der massige moderne Wolkenkratzer mitten zwischen Jahrhunderte alten Monumenten stehen, was sich sehr von Paris unterscheidet und für ihn eine komplett andere fotografische Reise bedeutet.

Doch insgeheim fragte ich mich: „Warum? Warum nicht einfach alles, was ich bisher geschrieben habe, in ein KI-Programm hochladen und sich einen Text ausspucken lassen – auf der Stelle und kostenfrei?" Und das ist im Grunde die Frage, die ich für dich habe.

Aber lass es mich anders ausdrücken, weil dies im Kern die entscheidende Frage unserer Zeit ist: Gibt es noch einen Platz für menschliche Künstler:innen, wenn ein Großteil der Welt davon überzeugt ist, dass Technologie es besser kann? STOPP! Noch nicht antworten.

Lass mich dir eine andere Frage stellen: Warum hast du dieses Buch gekauft? Warum siehst du dir Serge Ramellis super-cal-i-fragilistische Fotos an? Warum lässt du dir nicht einfach von einer Suchmaschine Bilder von London anzeigen oder von einer KI in Sekundenschnelle jedes beliebige Bild, was du dir nur vorstellen kannst, erzeugen?

Ich beschloss, es selber auszuprobieren: Ich fütterte die KI mit Artikeln, die ich in der Vergangenheit für Serge geschrieben hatte, und gab ihr die Anweisung, daraus ein Vorwort zu London zu verfassen. Fünf Sekunden später hatte ich einen perfekt aufgebauten Text in perfekter Länge. Er verwendete teilweise meinen Sprachstil, aber irgendetwas fühlte sich komisch an. Irgendwann wurde mir klar, was es war: Dem Text fehlten die zwei wichtigsten Elemente menschlicher Kommunikation – Menschlichkeit und Verbundenheit. (Vielleicht ist „künstliche" Intelligenz" nicht der richtige Begriff; synthetische Intelligenz wäre passender.)

In dem KI-Artikel stand nichts über meinen Patenonkel. Nichts darüber, wie sehr ich seinetwegen die britische Kultur liebe oder wie sich der verregnete Tag in London anfühlte, an dem ich ihn das letzte Mal im Krankenhaus besuchte. Nichts über die Monty-Python-Filme, die wir uns zusammen anschauten. Oder die Pink-Floyd-Alben, die er mir vorspielte. Oder über die Freude, die ich verspürte, als ich die Graffiti im Tunnel unter dem Eye of London entdeckte. Oder über den Geruch der frischen Luft in der reinen englischen Landschaft. Der Text erwähnte auch nicht (weil er es nicht konnte), dass ich aufgrund meiner lebenslangen James-Bond-Leidenschaft meine Martinis lieber geschüttelt als gerührt mag.

Ja, KI ist das Erstaunlichste, was die Menschheit je erfunden hat. Genau wie das Internet vor ihr. Und davor Elektrizität. Und davor der Verbrennungsmotor. Und davor Medizin. Und davor Architektur. Und so weiter bis hin zum Rad und zum Feuer.

Aber KI weiß nichts über das kindliche Staunen, das Serges Bilder in uns auslöst. Sein Fotografenblick bringt Orte wie mit einem Zauberstab zum Glitzern und lässt den Drachen der Fantasie hoch in den Himmel steigen. KI begreift nicht, wie er die Schönheit der Welt einfängt und in Bildrahmen packt, um sie mit uns zu teilen. Oder wie er Winkel, Farben, Augenblicke, Kompositionen und komplexe architektonische Widersprüche verbindet, um 1500 Jahre menschlichen Strebens und Leidens einzufangen; Tragödien und Triumphe, die London – einstmals nur ein Wald am Fluss – zu einer der bedeutendsten Städte der Welt machten. All das präsentiert Serge uns mit seiner einzigartigen künstlerischen Vision in einer kuratierten Serie kühner Aufnahmen.

Was also macht uns menschlich? Sind es die Fragen, die wir stellen, oder die Antworten, die wir finden? Ist es der Schmerz, den wir verspüren, oder das Vergnügen, das wir suchen? Sind es die Augenblicke der Lust, die unseren Verstand aushebeln, oder unsere endlose Sehnsucht nach ewiger Liebe? Sind es die Chancen, die wir ergreifen, oder die Opfer, die wir bringen? Es könnte einer dieser Aspekte sein oder alle zusammen – und noch viele andere, die jeden von uns zu etwas Besonderem machen.

Ich glaube, dass es unsere Träume und Bestrebungen sind und unsere Bereitschaft, Herausforderungen zu meistern, um diese Träume zu realisieren; nicht nur für uns selbst, sondern zum Wohle der gesamten Menschheit. Und Künstler, wahre Künstler, sind die Vorkämpfer des Menschengeschlechts. Sie sind die Träumer neuer Träume; sie leiten uns und verbinden uns miteinander, indem sie die Dinge, die uns einzigartig machen, und unsere gemeinsamen Träume und Freuden zelebrieren. So verbindet uns auch dieser neue Band von Serges Fotografien mit unserer Liebe zur Schönheit und majestätischen Pracht Londons und lässt uns damit auch einander besser verstehen.

Also, meine Freunde: *London is calling at the top of the dial.* Und auch wenn die Eiszeit einsetzt und die Sonne reinzoomt: Blättert um, macht mit Serge einen Spaziergang am Fluss entlang und schenkt euch ein Lächeln.

Darius Stevens Wilhere
Juni 2025

LONDON

MINUTE, MINUTE ! Ne vous jetez pas comme ça sur ces belles photos ! *How can you have any pudding if you don't eat yer meat?* (Oui, je cite bel et bien Pink Floyd, mange d'abord la viande, si tu veux du dessert). J'ai une grande question à VOUS soumettre. Voyons si vous avez réponse à l'une des questions les plus difficiles qui se posent à l'humanité au seuil de l'ère de – ce terme dont on nous rebat les oreilles – l'intelligence artificielle.

Je sais ce que vous pensez, encore un foutu texte barbant imprimé noir sur blanc ! Qui lit encore de nos jours ? Vous voulez juste voir les gerbes de couleurs inoubliables de Serge Ramelli, ses cadrages exceptionnels et ses compositions audacieuses, ainsi que les couchers de soleil saturés qu'il semble tirer de son appareil photo comme par magie, tel Merlin extrayant l'épée plantée dans le rocher ! Bon, je voulais juste m'assurer que vous ne dormiez pas. Manifestement, parce qu'en fait Merlin a tiré un croissant de son chapeau, et non pas une épée d'un rocher. Sheesh ! (*J'espère que mes références culturelles aident à faire passer la pilule.*)

Je sais ce que vous pensez à l'instant, « pour qui cet hurluberlu se prend-t-il avec sa grande question ! Je suis intelligent ! Je réponds à n'importe quelle question en quelques secondes ! Je connais même la vitesse en vol d'une hirondelle non chargée (elle parcourt 11 mètres par seconde pour l'hirondelle européenne, pas l'africaine, si vous tenez à le savoir) ! QUELLE EST LA QUESTION ? Fort heureusement, la question n'est pas : « Où puis-je trouver un jardinet », mes brillants amis amateurs des Monty Python. (*Et non, ce n'est pas non plus « Être ou ne pas être »*) Mais permettez-moi de faire des digressions car il se pourrait que ma manière de cadrer la question soit plus importante que la question en soi.

Ma première « image » de Londres, si vous voulez l'appeler ainsi, s'est en fait formée par procuration. Je l'associe au tout premier souvenir que j'ai de mon parrain. Je devais avoir quatre ou cinq ans et je sirotais un Shirley Temple, tandis qu'il me racontait ses aventures à Londres. Je me souviens du goût du soda au gingembre aromatisé au sirop de cerise aussi nettement que je me rappelle comment sa voix de baryton, son accent britannique distingué et sa manière de s'exprimer ont rendu ce moment magique. Je voyais une contrée lointaine grouillante de légendes arthuriennes, de gentilshommes raffinés, de vestiges romains ayant défié le temps, et peut-être aussi un pan de culture disparu qu'on n'aurait jamais dû oublier. Le tout baigné de violence mafieuse.

Propulsons-nous 45 ans plus tard, en 2025. Mon parrain est décédé il y a 15 ans. J'ai deux filles adolescentes. Entre-temps, j'ai réalisé un film, couru le monde. J'ai gagné de l'argent, mais j'en ai aussi perdu, tout comme j'ai perdu des êtres chers. Je me suis battu pour ma survie, mais aussi celle de mon couple et de ma famille dans une ambiance de guerre psychologique socio-politique axée de toute évidence sur la destruction de ces structures humaines.

Certains jours, je déborde de joie de vivre et je suis comblé par l'aventure de la vie, tandis que d'autres, je pontifie sur l'inévitable déchéance des belles choses ou sur des sujets ronflants pseudo-poétiques. Tout cela pour dire, comme vous, que je me trouve dans un monde en mutation rapide, auquel nous ne devons pas uniquement nous adapter constamment, mais que nous devons maîtriser et conquérir chacun à sa manière si nous voulons survivre.

Or, dans ce monde, le progrès technique ne vient pas seulement en renfort du travail humain mais le remplace à une vitesse fulgurante, remettant en question quelque chose qui préoccupait déjà les philosophes qui déambulaient dans les couloirs de l'université d'Oxford il y a plusieurs siècles : être humain, qu'est-ce que cela signifie au juste ? Mais ce n'est pas là la question que je vous pose. Alors, quelle est donc la question ? Attendez encore un instant, chers amis cinéphiles, nous y arrivons et *vous aurez votre moment mug qui se fracasse par terre comme dans* Usual Suspects, *au moment où Keyser Söze est démasqué.*

Voilà où j'en étais, tout juste revenu d'un repérage à Londres, quand mon grand ami Serge m'a contacté pour me demander d'écrire l'introduction de son nouveau livre de photographies. Je lui ai posé quelques questions sur son amour pour Londres, sur sa perception du brassage culturel et social qu'il y a observé, sur sa fascination pour le clivage architectural, c'est-à-dire les massifs gratte-ciel modernes plantés au beau milieu de monuments centenaires, ce qui est à l'opposé du paysage urbain parisien et offre une expérience photographique totalement différente.

Mais au fond de moi, je me demandais, « à quoi bon ? Pourquoi ne suffirait-il pas que j'entre tout ce que j'ai écrit jusqu'ici dans un programme d'intelligence artificielle, qui me recracherait un texte instantanément et gratuitement ? » Et c'est là la question que je vous pose.

Mais permettez-moi de la reformuler parce qu'il s'agit, au fond, de la question fondamentale de notre époque : l'artiste humain a-t-il encore sa place, alors que la plupart des gens sont convaincus que la technologie peut faire mieux que lui ? MINUTE ! Ne répondez pas si vite.

Je vais vous poser une autre question : Pourquoi avez-vous acheté ce livre ? Pourquoi regardez-vous les clichés magiques de Ramelli ?

Pourquoi ne demandez-vous pas simplement à un moteur de recherche de vous trouver des images de Londres ou à l'intelligence artificielle de créer en quelques secondes n'importe quelle image de Londres sortie de votre imagination ?

Bon, j'ai décidé de tenter l'expérience : j'ai téléchargé tous les articles que j'avais écrits pour Serge par le passé et demandé à l'outil d'intelligence artificielle de créer une introduction sur Londres. Ce qu'il a fait en cinq secondes. Le texte avait exactement la longueur voulue. Il semblait parfaitement construit. Il reprenait certaines de mes expressions. Mais il sonnait tout simplement faux. Il lui manquait les deux principaux ingrédients de la communication humaine : de l'âme et une relation personnelle. (*Peut-être l'appellation intelligence artificielle ne convient-elle pas, et faudrait-il plutôt parler d'intelligence synthétisée.*)

Le texte ne mentionnait pas mon parrain ni ne disait combien je l'aimais, ni comment il m'avait fait aimer la culture britannique. Encore moins comment je me sentais en cette journée pluvieuse lorsque je lui ai rendu une dernière visite à l'hôpital. Pas plus qu'il ne parlait des Monty Python qu'il avait regardés avec moi. Ni des albums des Pink Floyd qu'il me passait. Ni de ma joie en découvrant l'art dans un tunnel bardé de graffiti sous le London Eye ni du goût de l'air vif dans la campagne anglaise intacte. Il ne mentionnait pas non plus, d'ailleurs comment aurait-il pu le faire, que je préfère mon Martini mélangé au shaker, et pas à la cuillère, moi qui admire James Bond depuis toujours.

C'est vrai, l'IA est le plus fabuleux outil jamais inventé par le genre humain. Comme Internet l'était avant elle. Et l'électricité avant cela. Et le moteur à explosion encore avant cela. Et la médecine auparavant. Et l'architecture. Et ainsi de suite jusqu'à l'invention de la roue et la maîtrise du feu, avant de revenir à aujourd'hui pour voir quelle sera la prochaine grande invention.

Mais elle ne peut pas vous parler du miracle enfantin que nous voyons dans les photographies de Serge qui semble agiter une baguette magique pour découvrir la splendeur et des endroits où faire voler un cerf-volant très haut dans le ciel. La manière dont il capte la beauté en ce monde et essaie de mettre cette joie dans ses prises de vue afin de la partager avec vous. Ou la manière dont il mêle les angles, les couleurs, les moments, les compositions et les complexes contrastes architecturaux afin de capturer les 1500 ans de labeur, souffrances, tragédies et triomphes qui ont permis d'édifier sur ce qui était autrefois une simple forêt sur les rives d'un fleuve l'une des plus formidable métropoles sur Terre, j'ai nommé Londres, et de vous la présenter dans une sélection de portraits audacieux dénotant un parti pris artistique très personnel.

Qu'est-ce qui fait donc de vous un être humain ? Les questions que vous vous posez ? Ou les réponses que vous donnez ? Est-ce la douleur que vous ressentez, ou le plaisir que vous recherchez ? Les moments de volupté qui triomphent de votre raison, ou votre quête incessante de l'amour éternel ? Les chances que vous saisissez ou les sacrifices que vous faites ? Cela pourrait être une de ces choses, ou toutes, et bien d'autres qui vous sont propres.

Je crois que ce sont nos rêves, nos aspirations et notre détermination à surmonter les épreuves de la vie pour qu'ils deviennent réalité, pas uniquement pour notre propre bien, mais pour celui du genre humain. Et les artistes, les vrais, sont les défenseurs du genre humain. Rêveurs artisans des nouveaux rêves, ces muses éternelles qui nous guident et nous amènent à nous connecter tous ensemble par les rêves et amours que nous partageons, dans une célébration de ces choses qui font de chacun d'entre nous des personnes uniques. Tout comme cette nouvelle monographie de Serge Ramelli nous relie à notre amour de la beauté et de la majesté de Londres, nous reliant ainsi à une meilleure compréhension mutuelle.

Bon, les amis, ce n'est pas tout, *London is Calling*. Même si *the ice age is coming, the sun zooming in* [l'âge de glace arrive et le soleil se rapproche de plus en plus], tournez les pages et flânez avec Serge Ramelli sur les berges de la Tamise. Souriez, c'est parti !

Darius Stevens Wilhere
Juin 2025

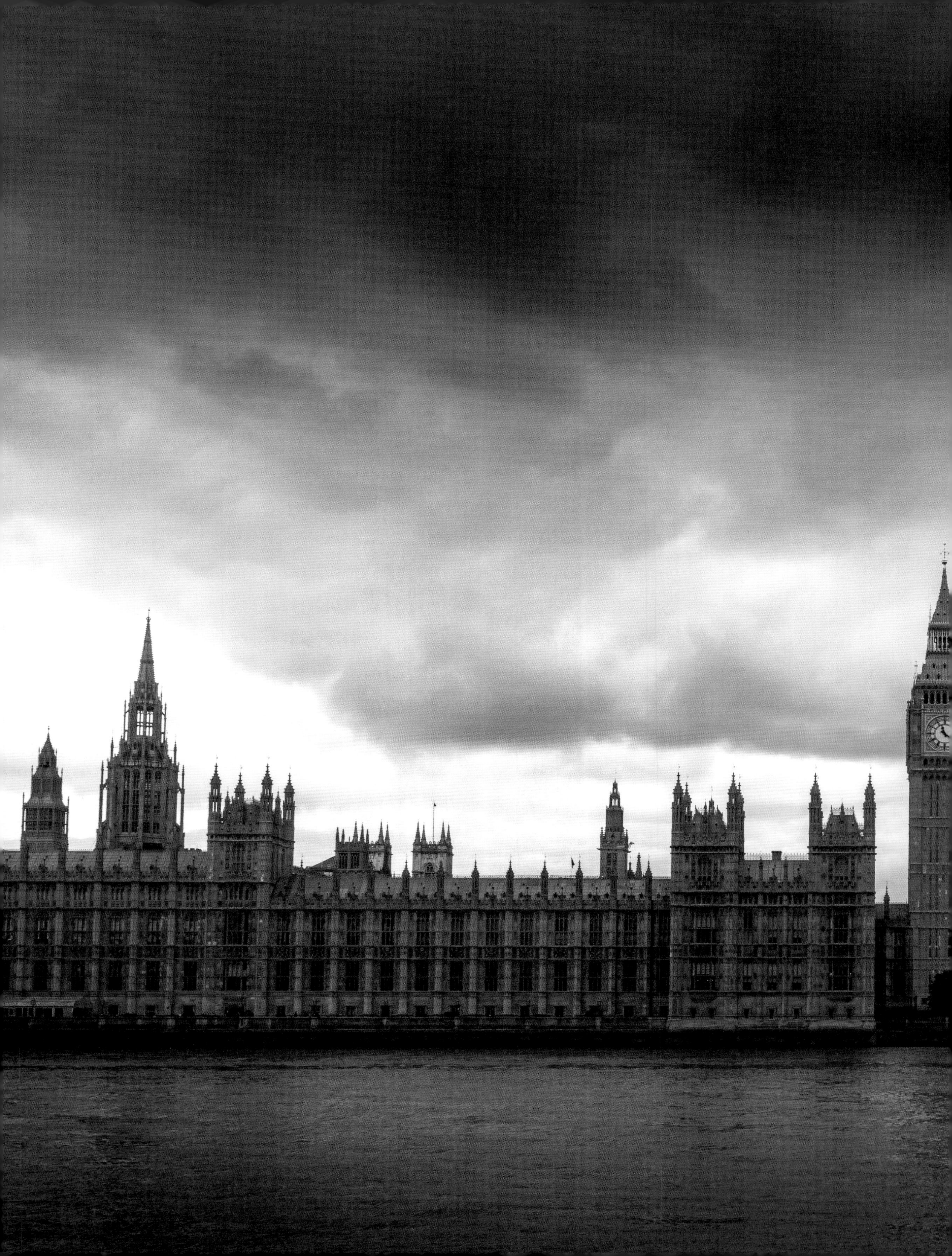

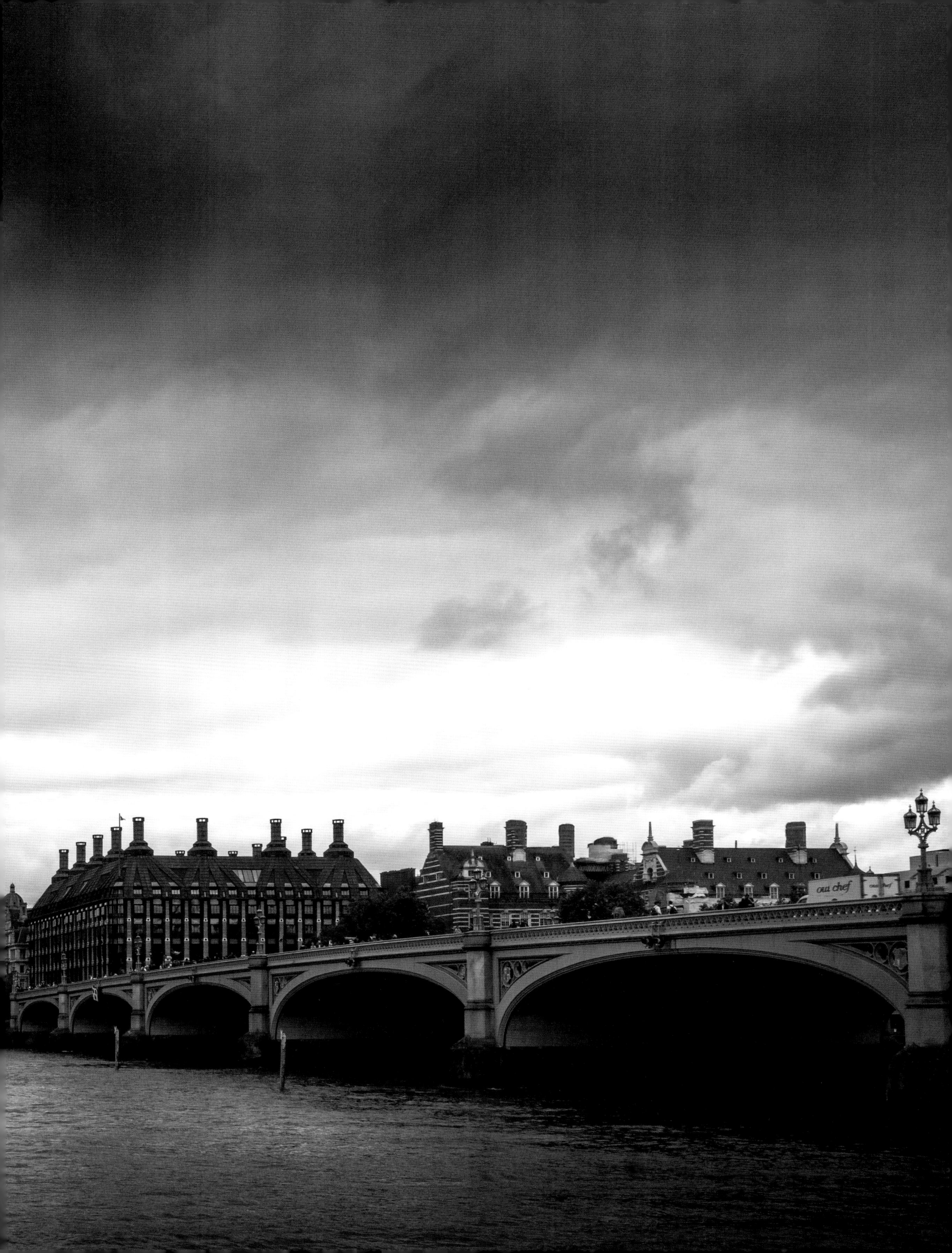
oui chef

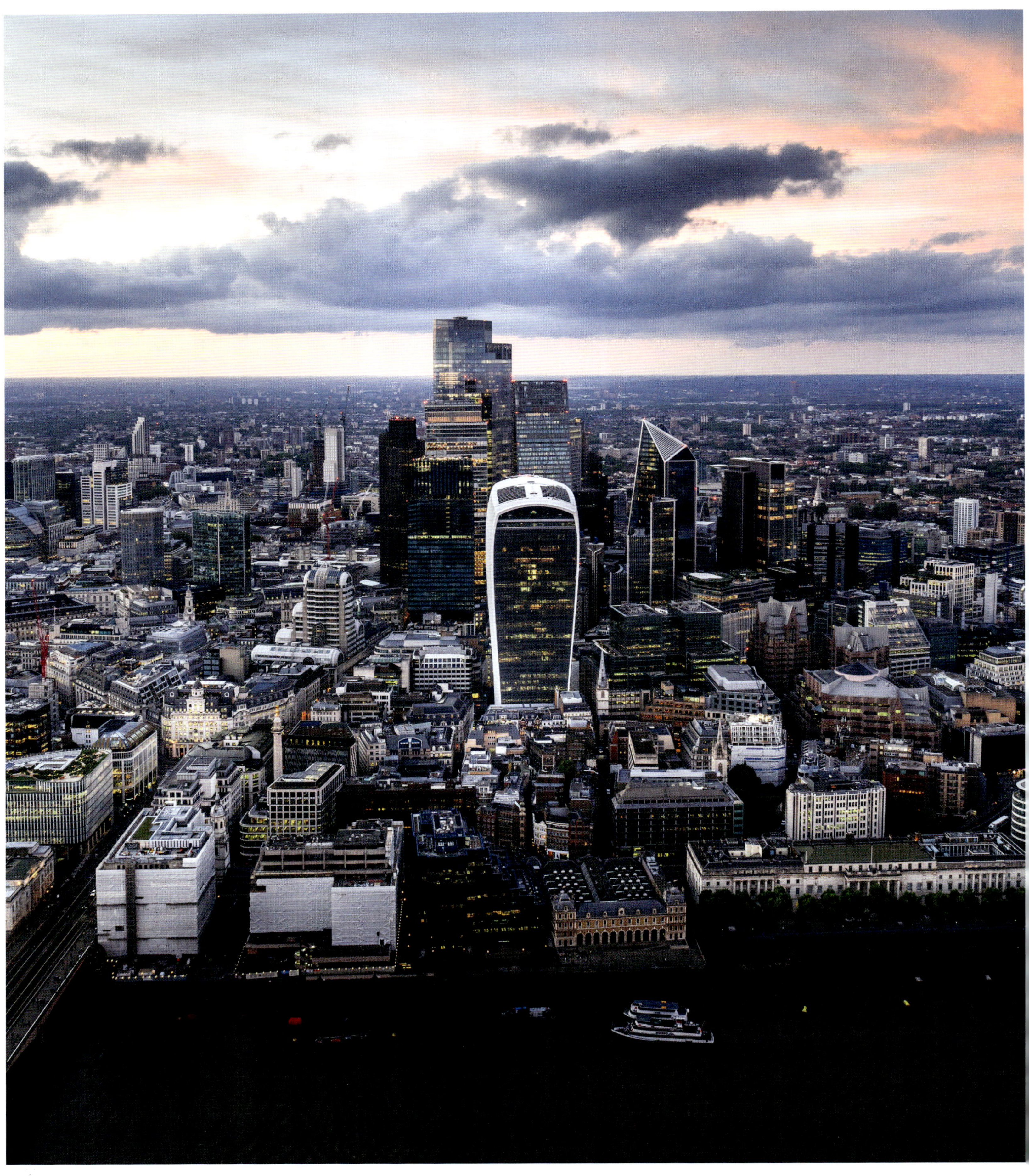

An aerial view of London's financial district, where towering skyscrapers rise along the River Thames. The City of London, the historic center of the capital, stands as a global hub of finance and modern architecture.

Luftaufnahme von Londons Finanzviertel, wo Wolkenkratzer am Ufer der Themse in den Himmel ragen. Die City of London ist das historische Zentrum der Stadt und zugleich ein globaler Dreh- und Angelpunkt der Finanzwelt sowie ein Hotspot moderner Architektur.

Vue aérienne du quartier des affaires de Londres, avec sa forêt de gratte-ciel surplombant la Tamise. Cœur historique de Londres, la « City » est un pôle international de la finance et de l'architecture moderne.

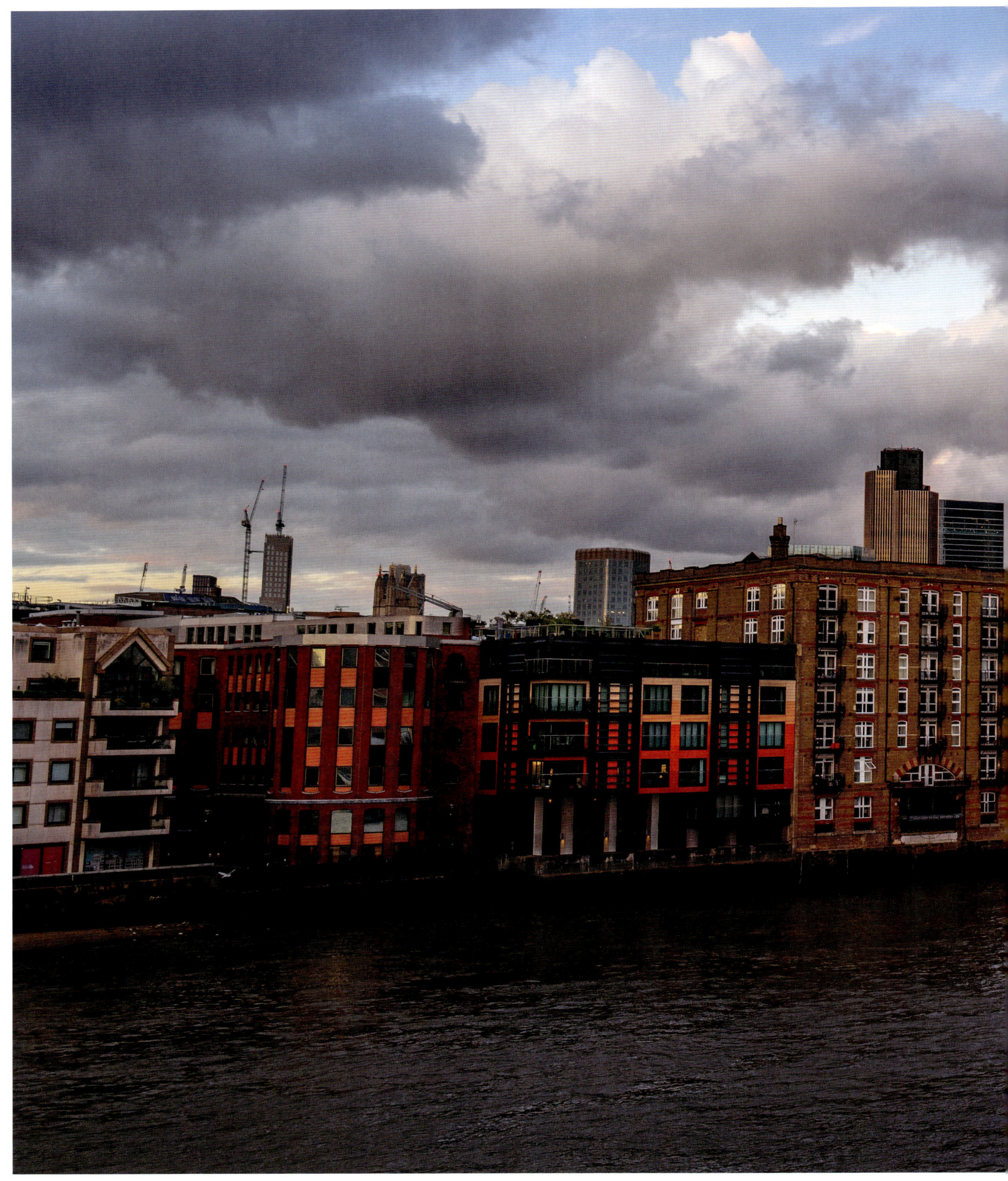

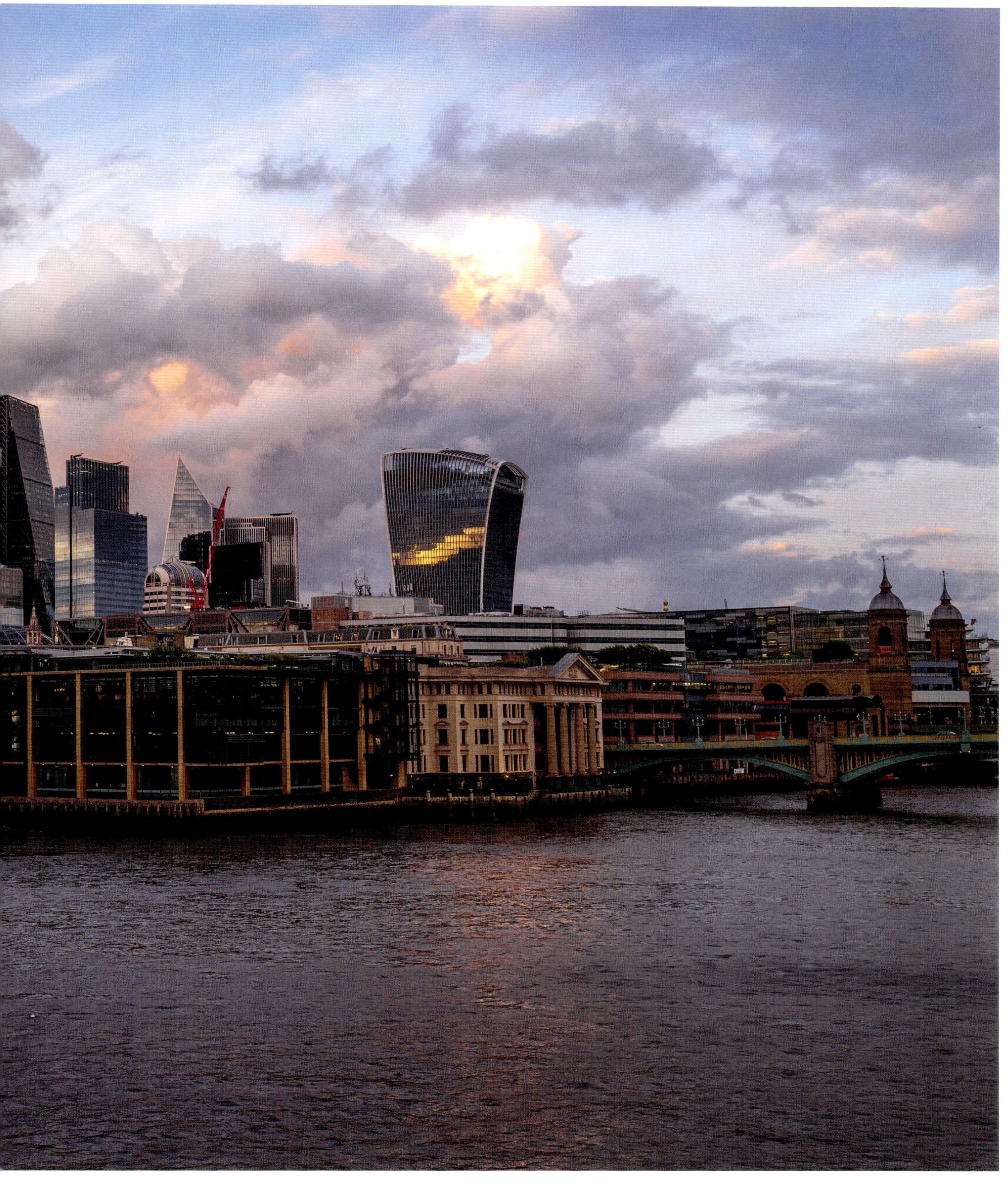

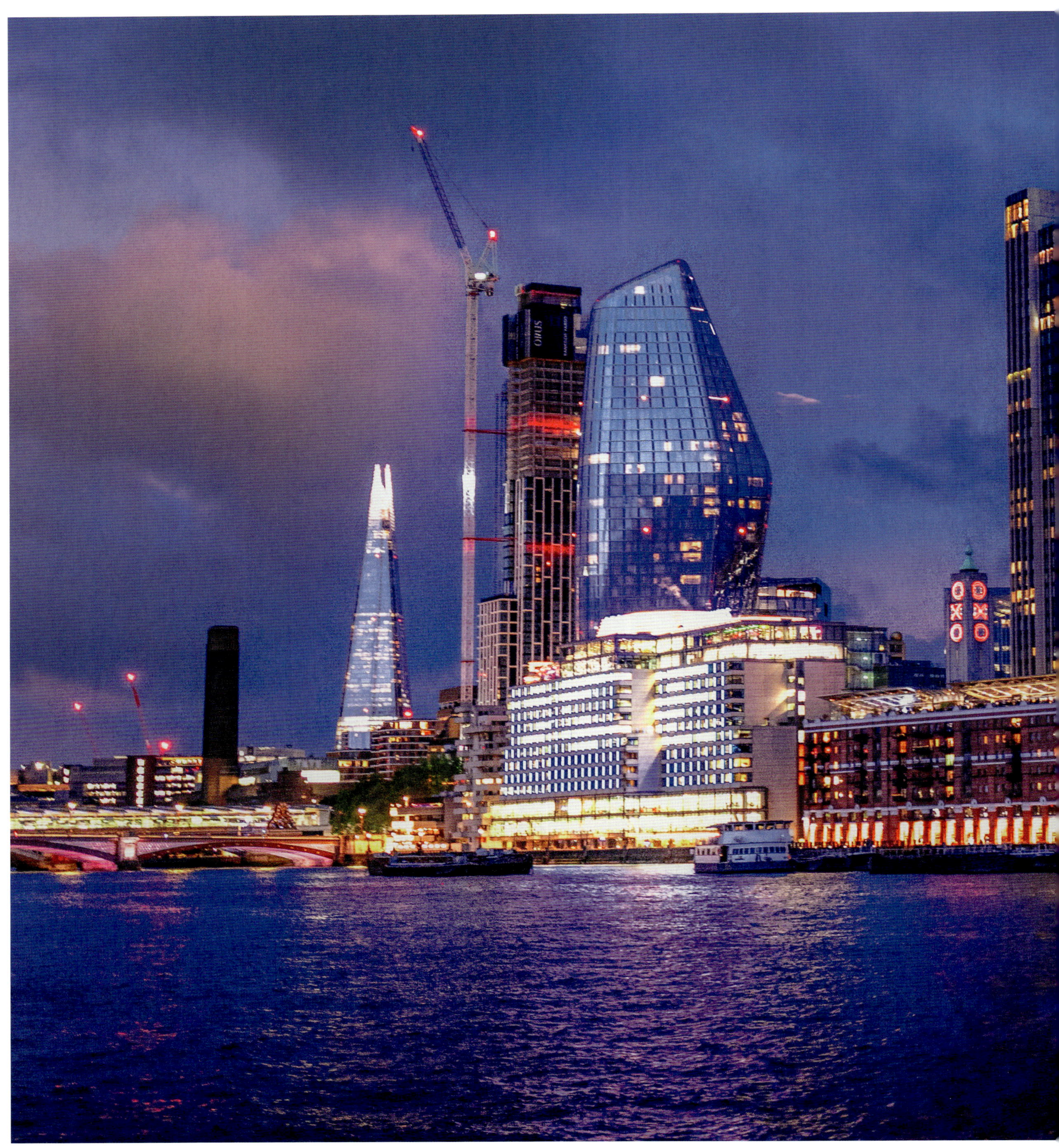

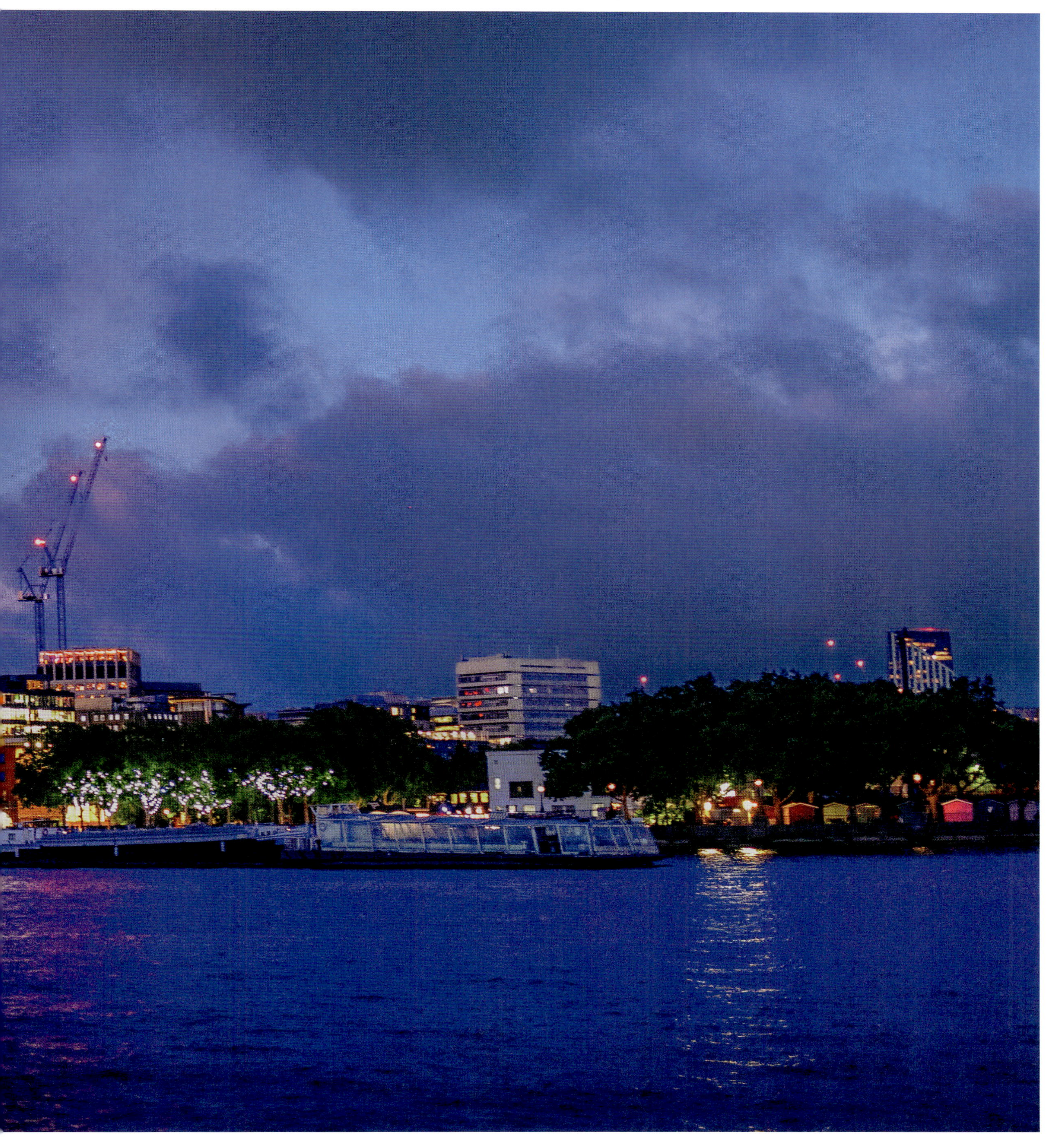

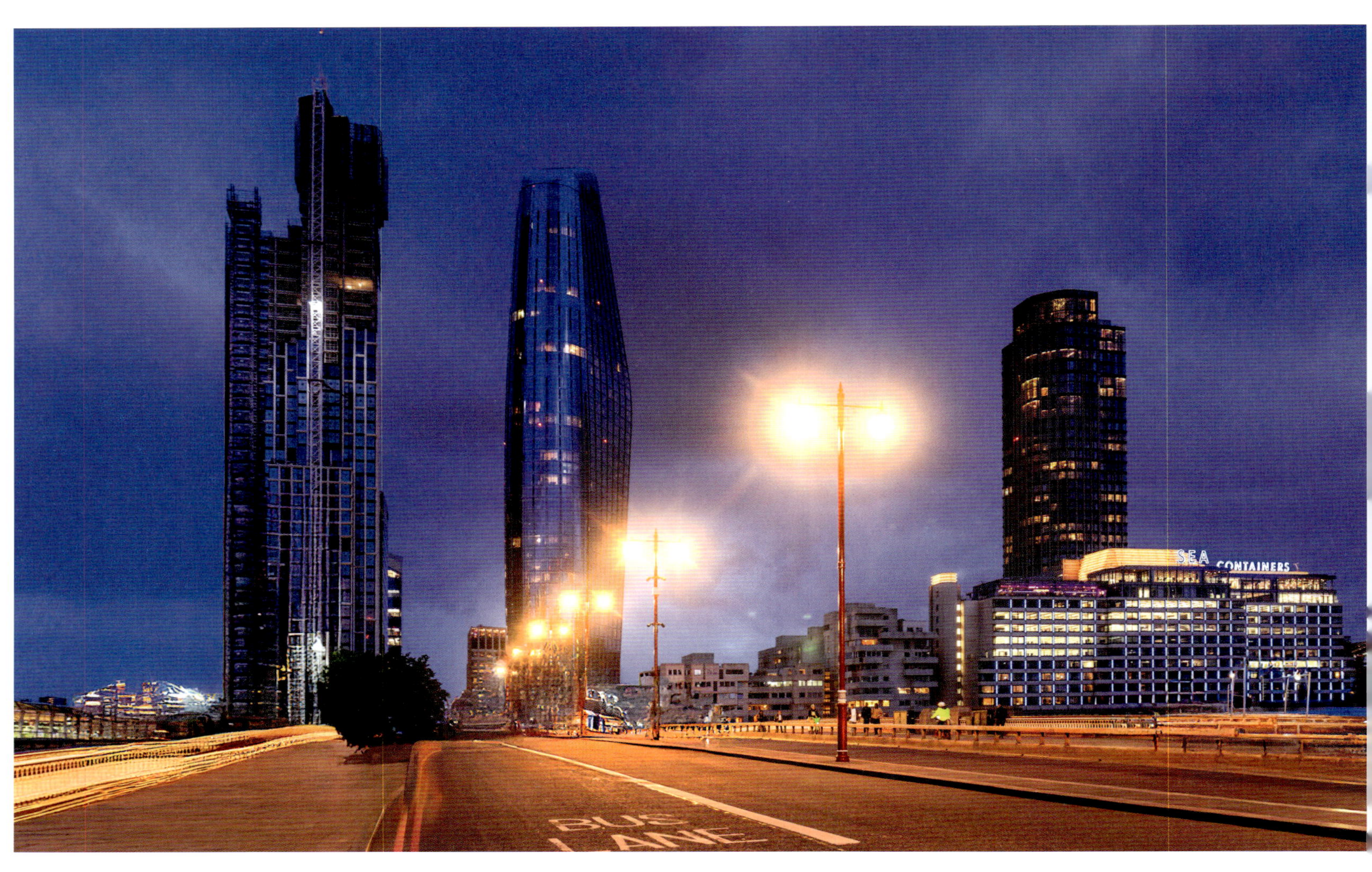
SEA CONTAINERS
BUS
LANE

Previous pages and opposite: The view toward Southwark, with Blackfriars Bridge—linking the City of London and Southwark—the iconic Shard, and brightly lit hotels and apartment buildings lining the riverfront.

Vorherige und diese Seite: Die Blackfriars Bridge, die die City of London und Southwark verbindet, mit Blick Richtung Southwark. Zu sehen sind auch der ikonische „Shard“ und die Lichter von Hotels und Apartmentblocks am Flussufer.

Cette page et la précédente : Première impression de Southwark en venant de la « City » par le pont de Blackfriars : l'emblématique « Shard » (tesson de verre) et les hôtels et immeubles d'habitation généreusement éclairés qui bordent la Tamise.

The iconic dome of St. Paul's Cathedral, framed by trees at sunset, casts a warm glow over this masterpiece of English Baroque architecture designed by Christopher Wren.

Die berühmte Kuppel von St Paul's Cathedral, umrahmt von Bäumen. Die untergehende Sonne taucht dieses Meisterwerk englischer Barockarchitektur von Christopher Wren in ein warmes Licht.

D'entre les arbres apparaît la célèbre coupole de la cathédrale Saint-Paul. Le soleil couchant enveloppe de sa lumière chaude le chef-d'œuvre du baroque anglais conçu par Christopher Wren.

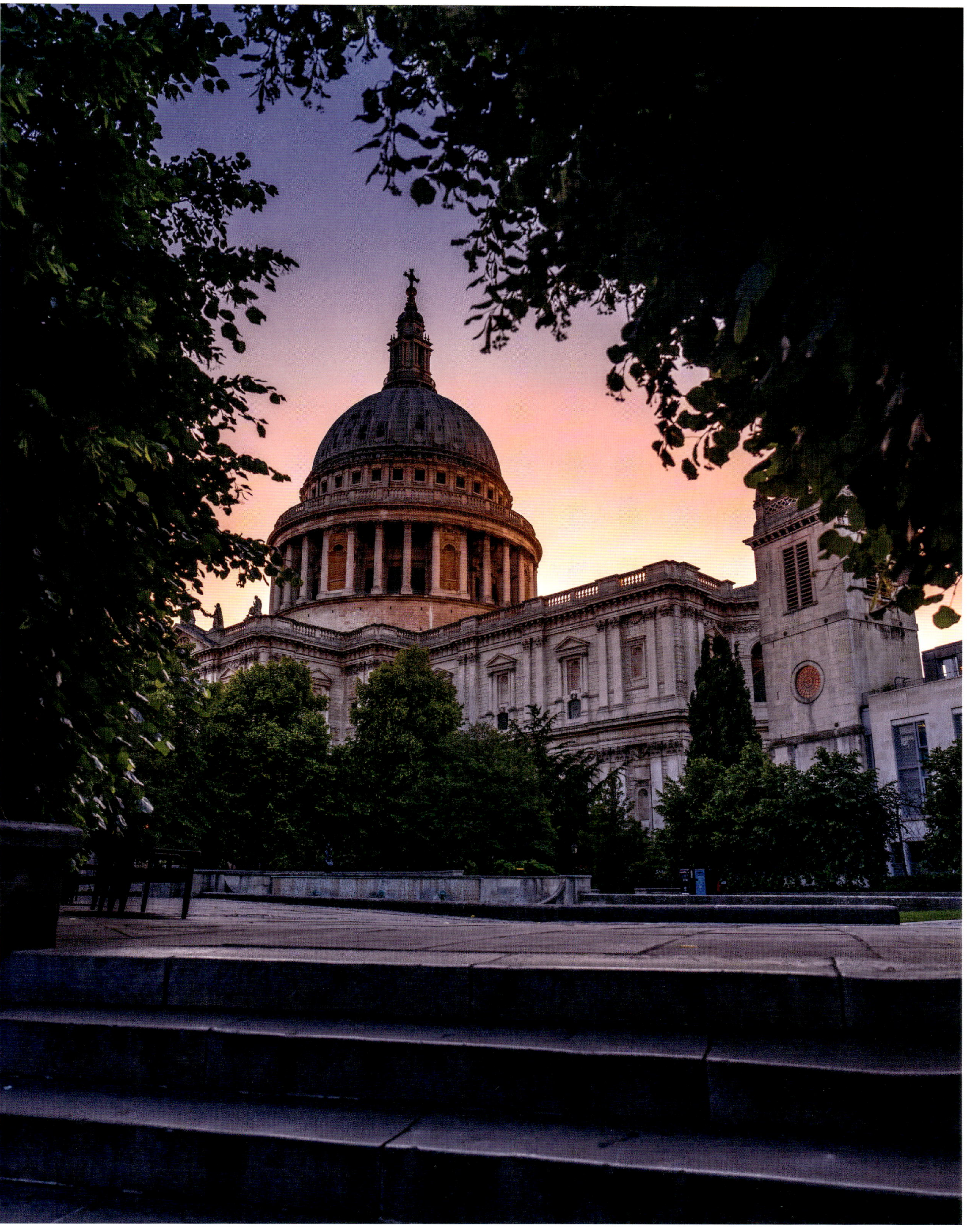

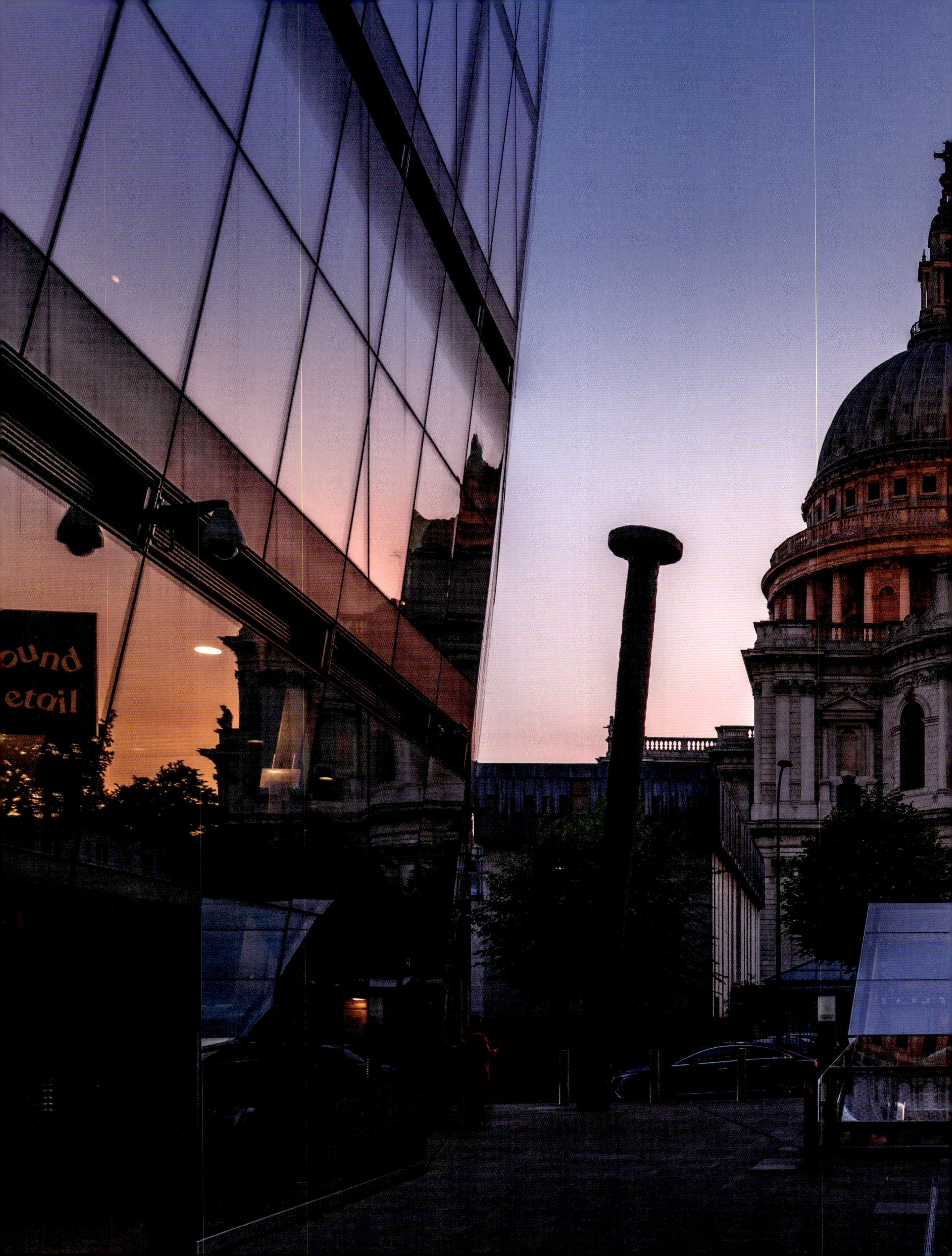
ound
etoil

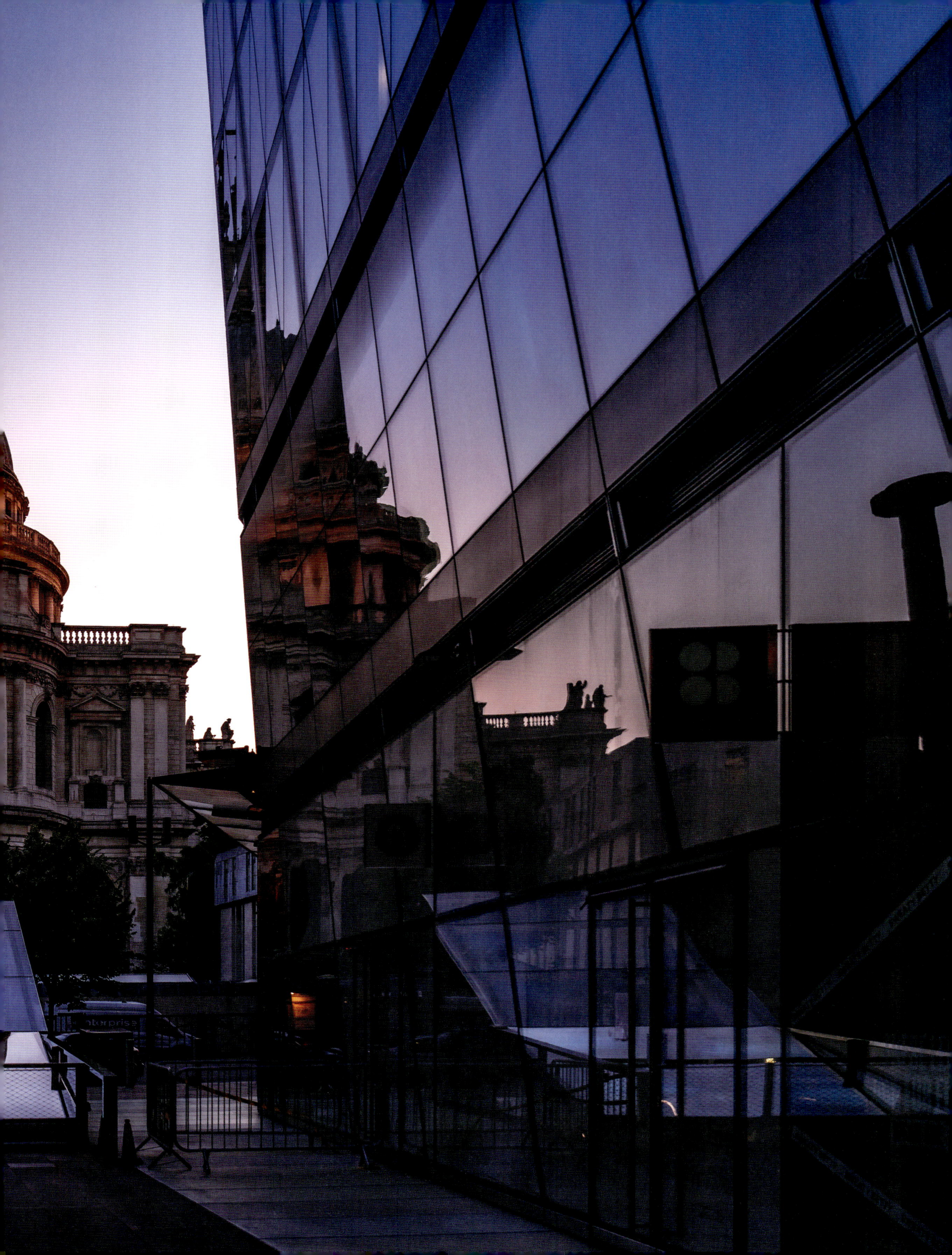

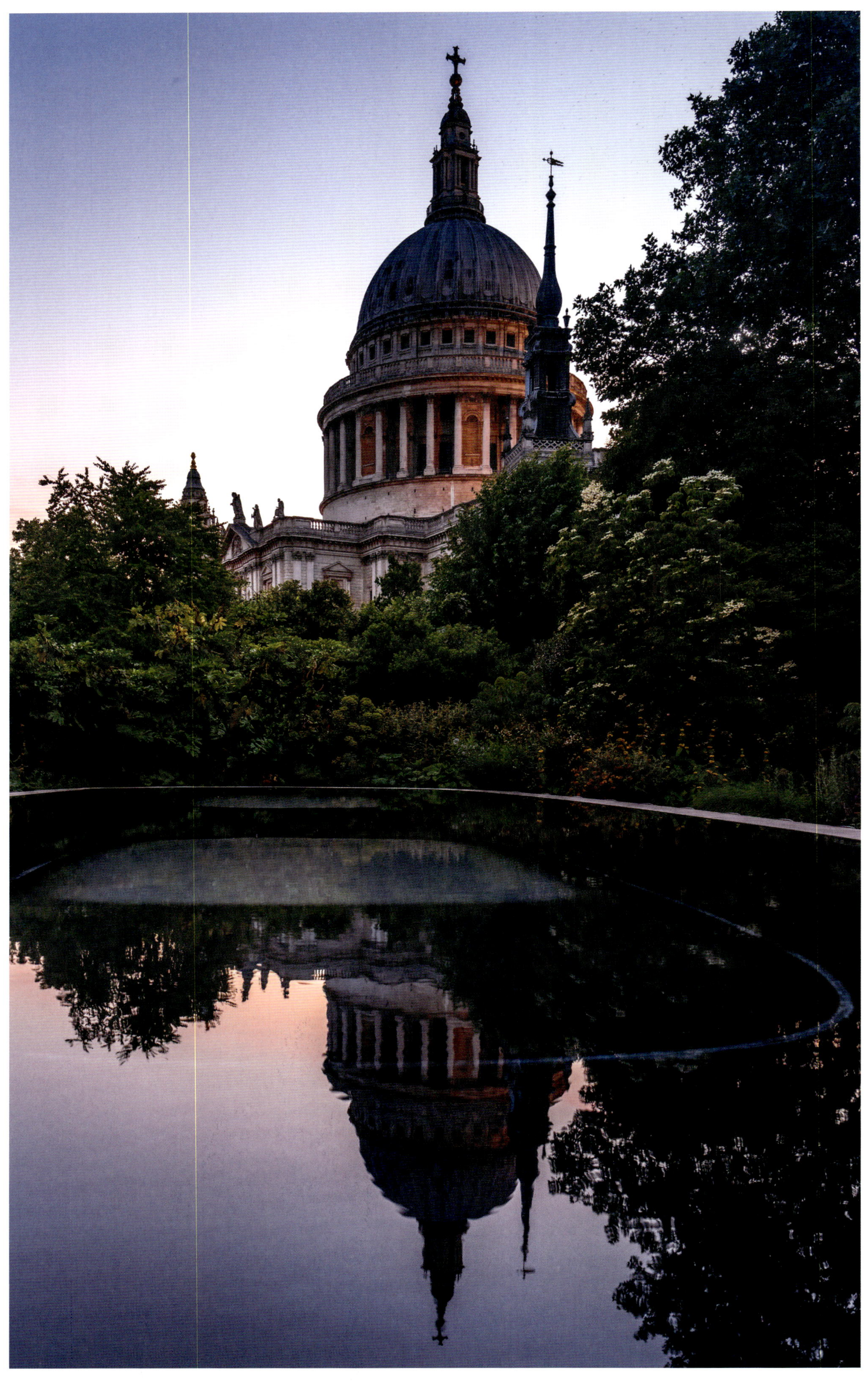

St. Paul's at dusk. The Anglican cathedral—one of the largest churches in the world—has hosted numerous state funerals, royal weddings, and other major public events.

St Paul's im Dämmerlicht. Die anglikanische Kathedrale ist eine der größten Kirchen der Welt und war bereits Schauplatz zahlreicher Staatsbegräbnisse, royaler Hochzeiten und anderer bedeutender öffentlicher Ereignisse.

Saint-Paul au crépuscule. Cette cathédrale anglicane est l'une des plus grandes églises au monde. De nombreux grands événements publics, tels que funérailles officielles et mariages royaux y ont été célébrés.

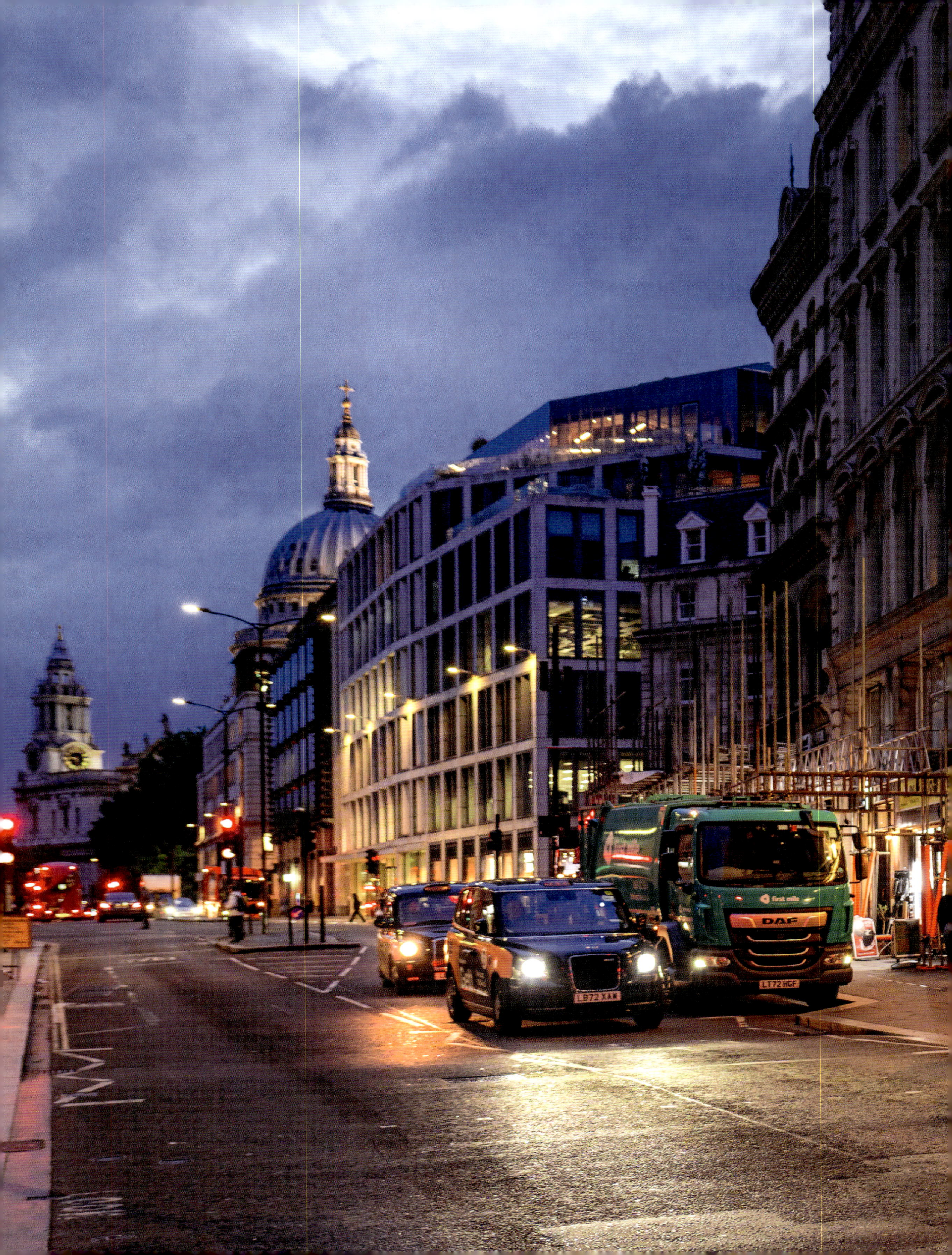
first mile
DAF
LT72 HGF
LB72 XAW

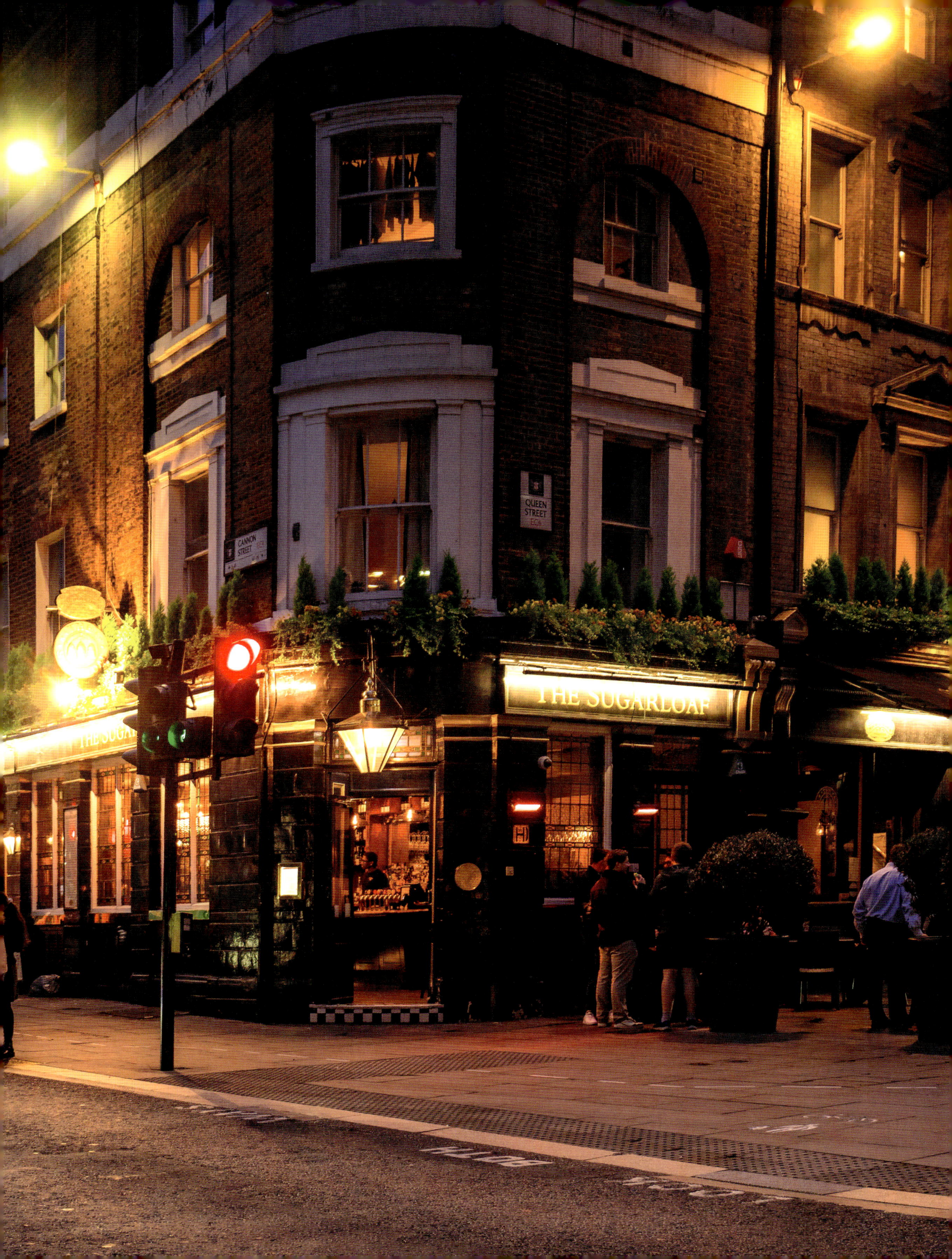
THE SUGARLOAF

Few cities offer such a strikingly seamless blend of old and new—
where traditional buildings stand beside towering modern glass skyscrapers.

Ein traditionelles Gebäude neben einem modernen gläsernen Wolkenkratzer:
Nur wenige Städte verbinden Altes und Neues auf so nahtlose Weise wie London.

Rares sont les villes où l'œil passe aussi facilement de l'ancien au moderne sans transition,
un bâtiment historique côtoyant un gratte-ciel vitré moderne.

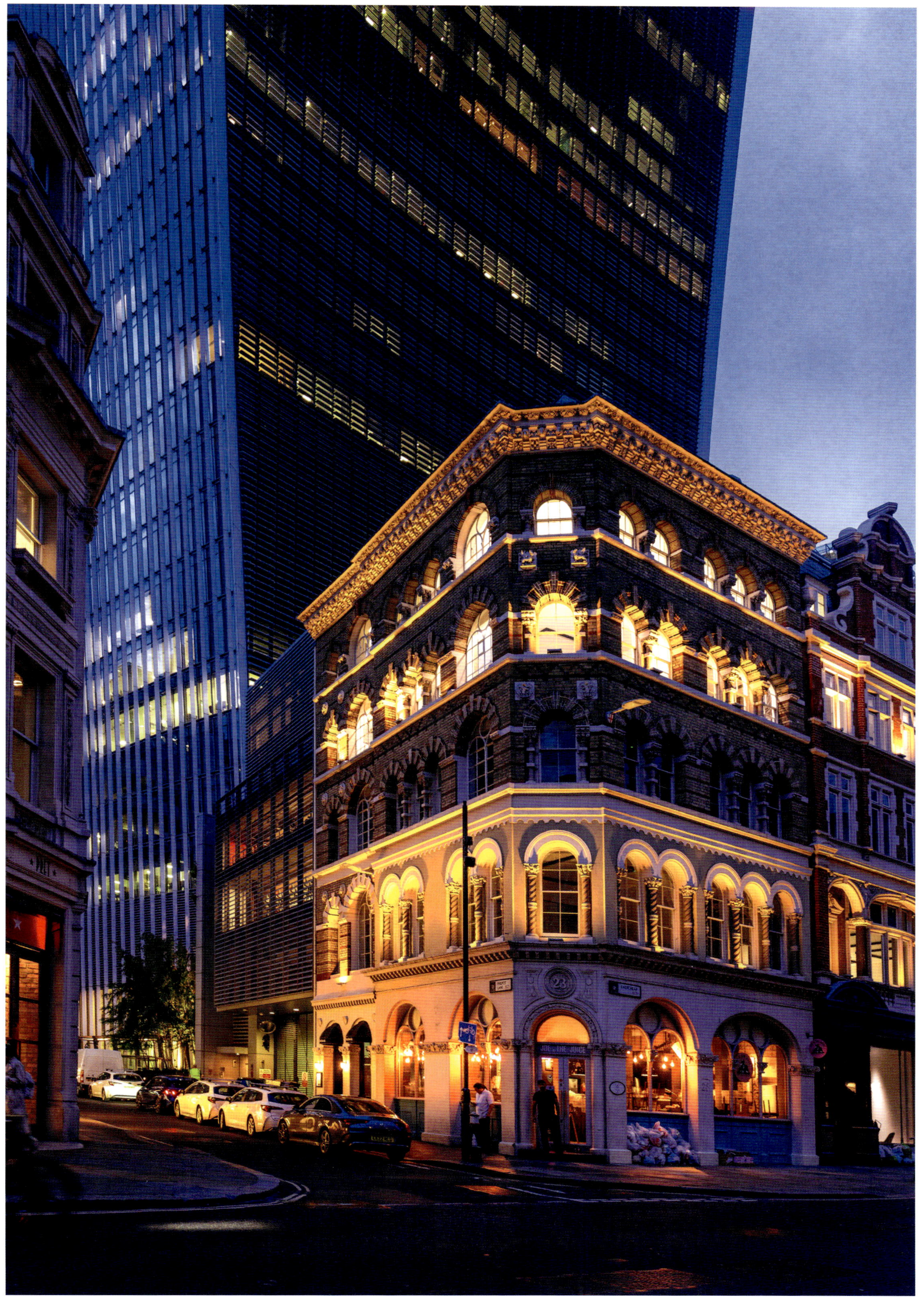

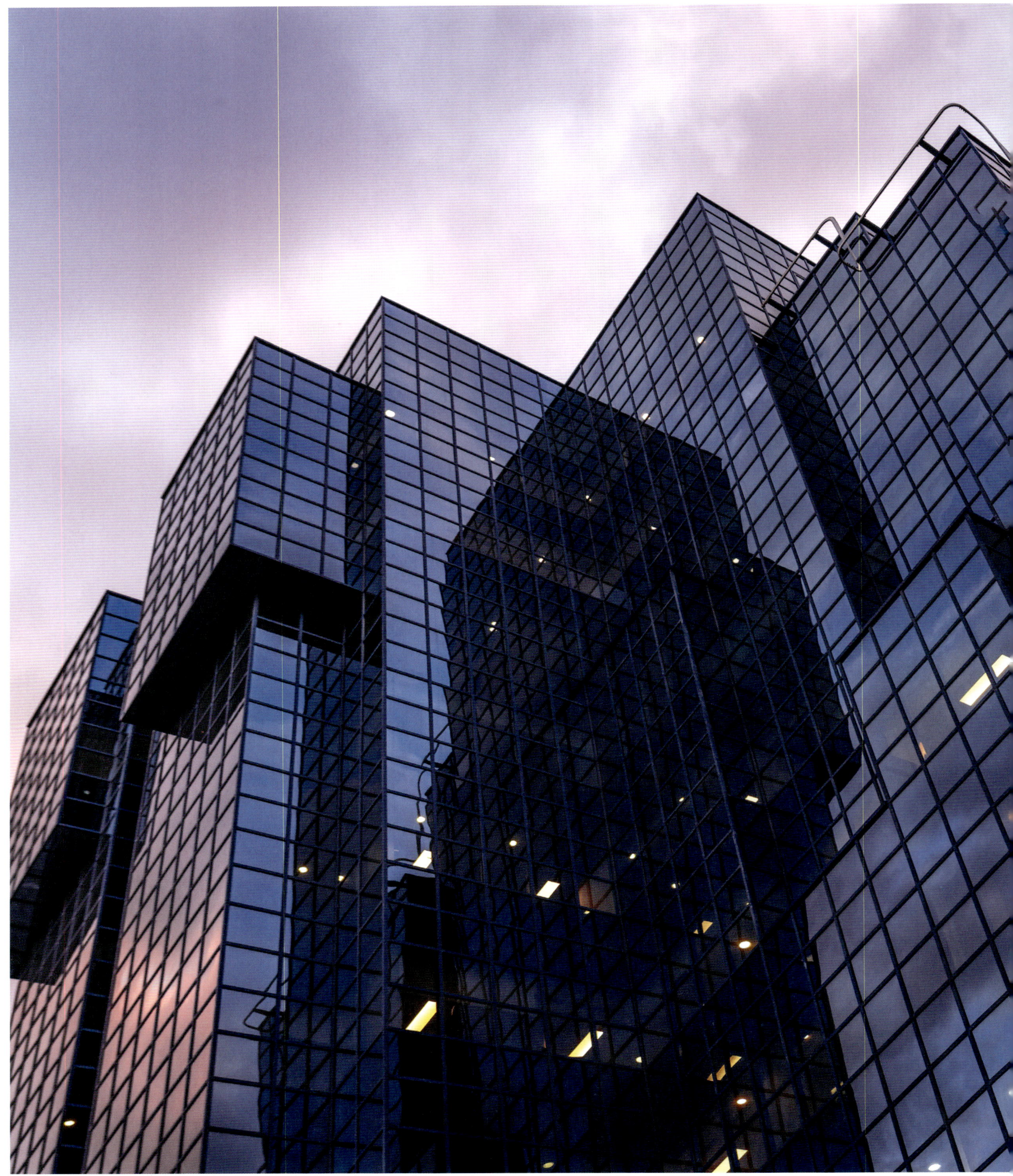

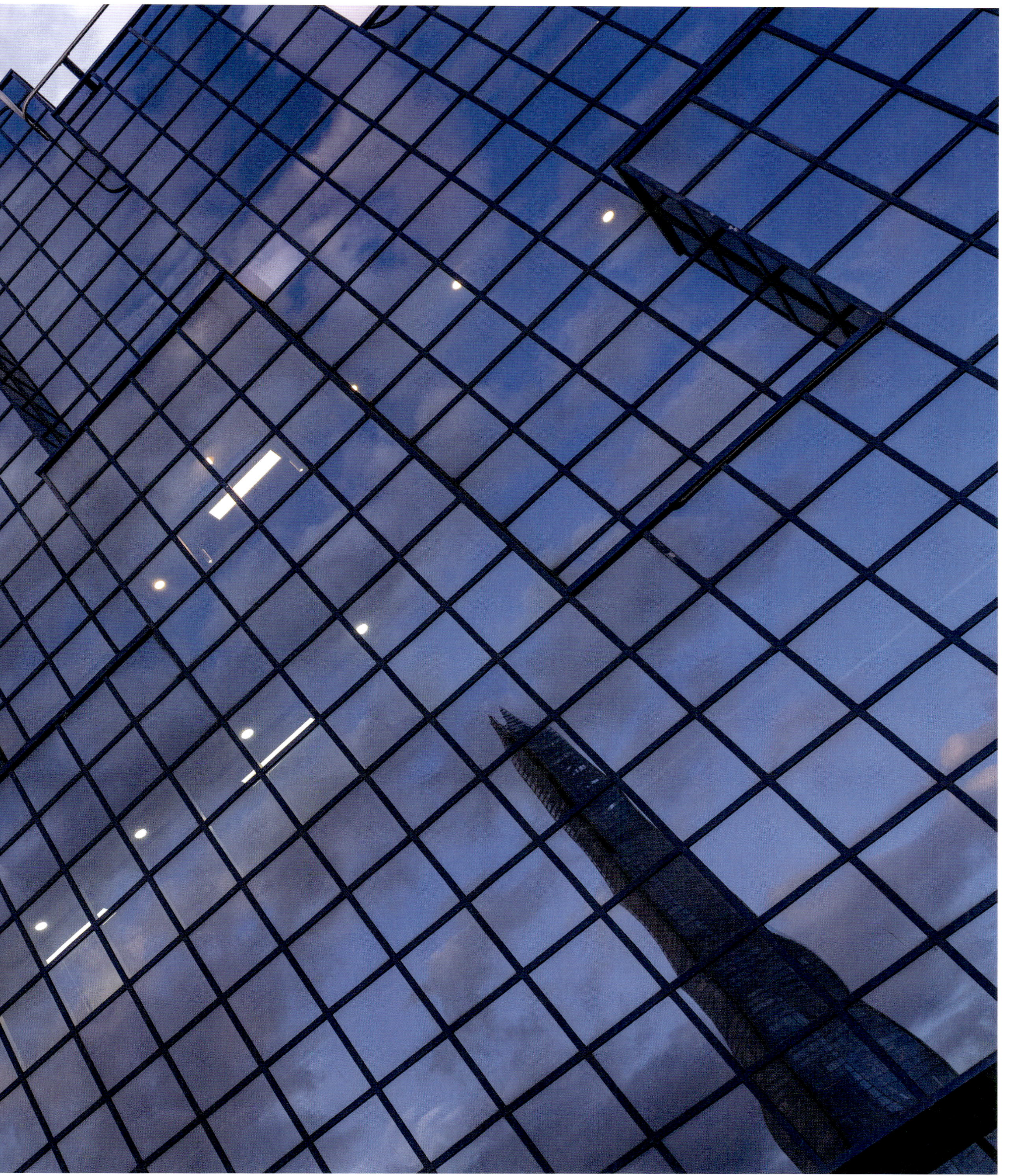

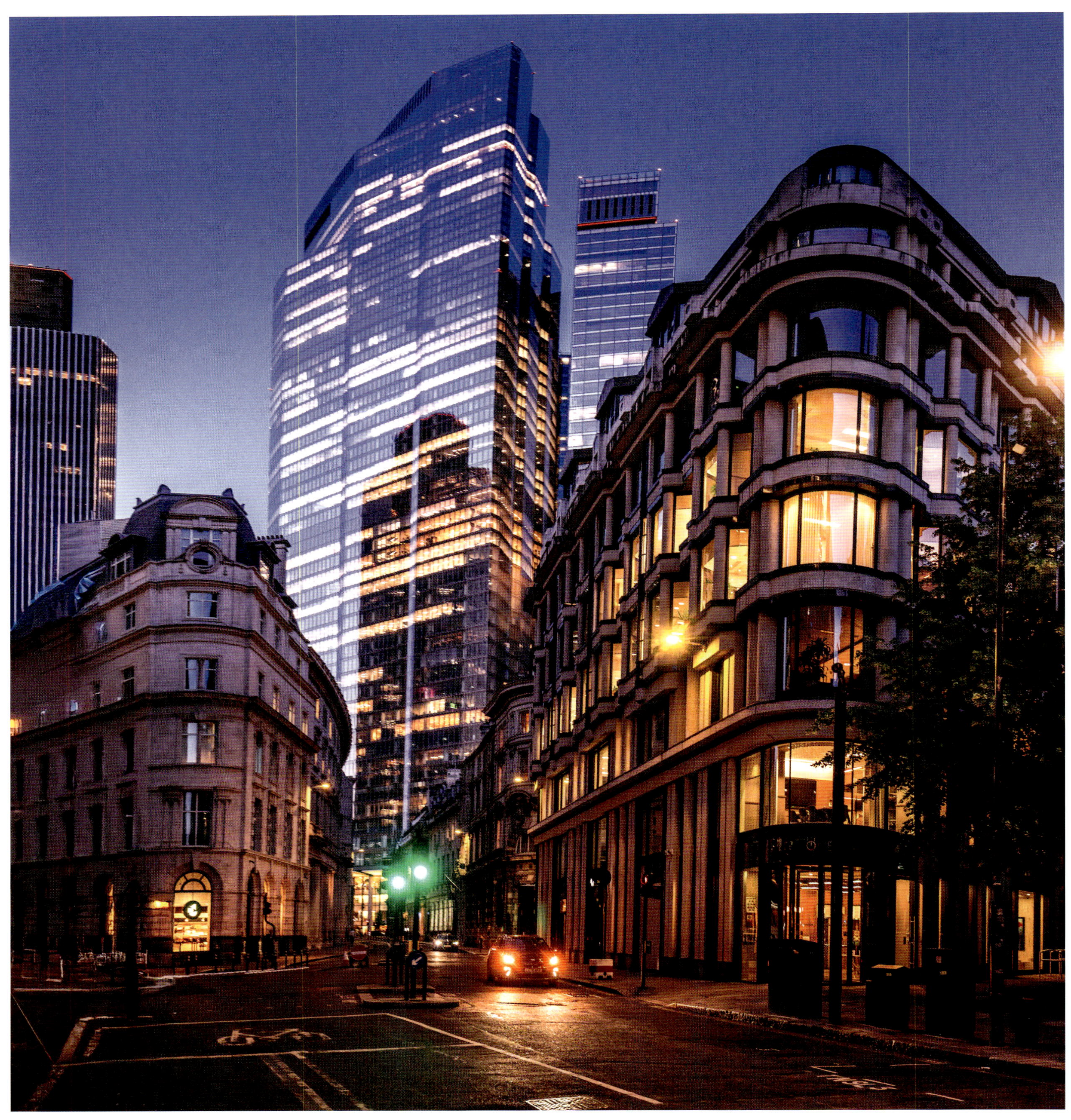

A testament to its long history, London's architectural landscape ranges from medieval structures to Victorian buildings and contemporary skyscrapers.

Following pages: A street lined with historic buildings leads to the modern 20 Fenchurch Street—also known as the Walkie Talkie—which houses the Sky Garden, London's highest public garden.

Pages 36–37: The Royal Exchange, the city's first stock exchange, is now home to luxury brand shops.

Zeugnis einer langen Historie: Londons architektonische Landschaft reicht von mittelalterlichen Strukturen über viktorianische Bauwerke bis hin zu zeitgenössischen Wolkenkratzern.

Nächste Seite: Eine von historischen Gebäuden gesäumte Straße führt zum modernen Bauwerk 20 Fenchurch Street (auch als „Walkie Talkie" bekannt), in dem sich der Sky Garden, Londons höchstgelegener öffentlicher Garten, befindet.

Seiten 36–37: Die Royal Exchange war die erste Börse der Stadt und beherbergt heute Geschäfte mit Luxusmarken.

Témoins de la longue histoire de la ville, constructions médiévales, édifices victoriens et gratte-ciel contemporains forment le paysage architectural de Londres.

Page suivante : Une rue bordée de bâtiments anciens conduit au gratte-ciel futuriste situé au 20 Fenchurch Street – surnommé le « Walkie Talkie » (le talkie walkie) – qui abrite le Sky Garden, le jardin public le plus en hauteur de la ville.

Pages 36–37 : Le Royal Exchange, la bourse historique de Londres, réunit désormais sous son toit des boutiques de luxe.

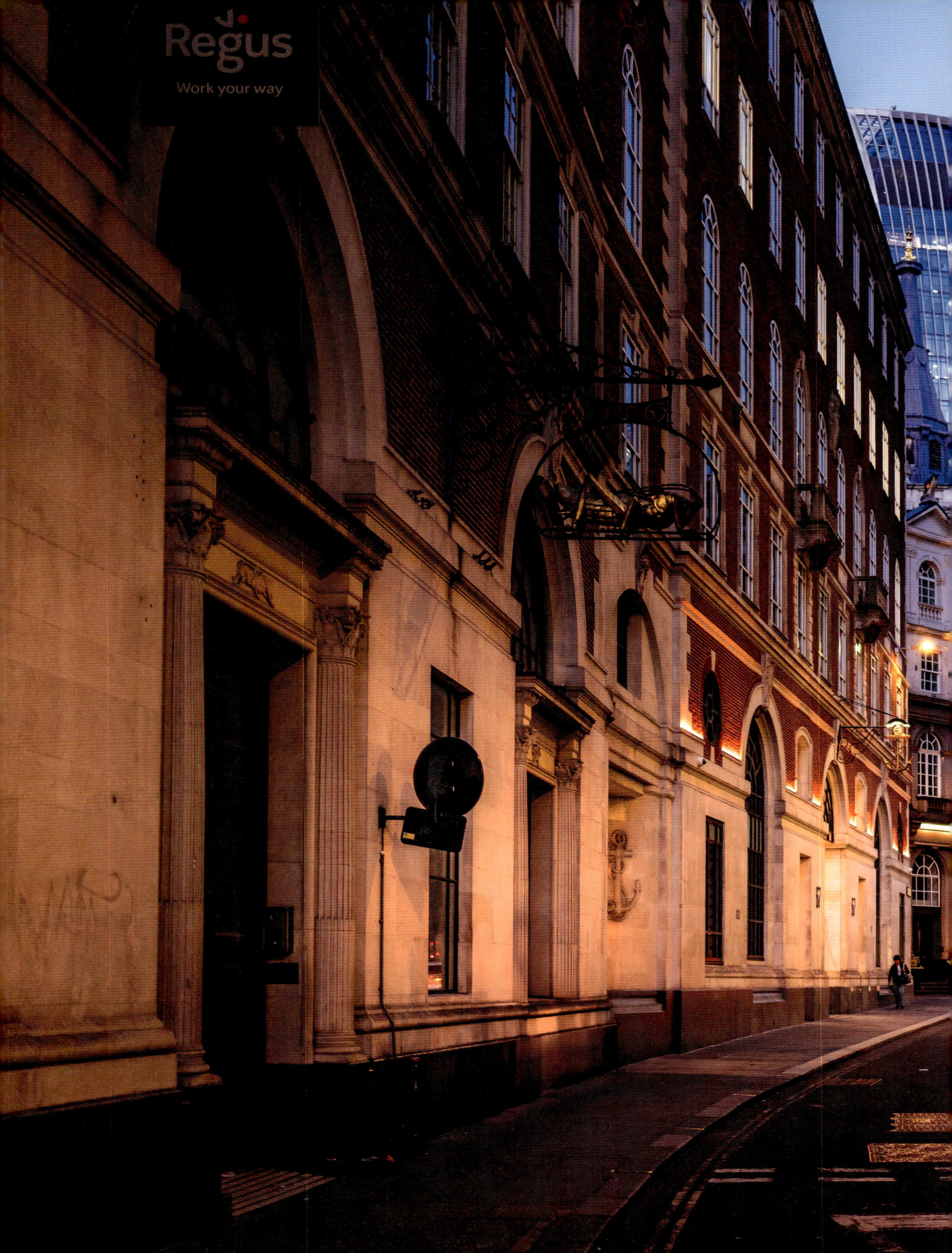
Regus
Work your way

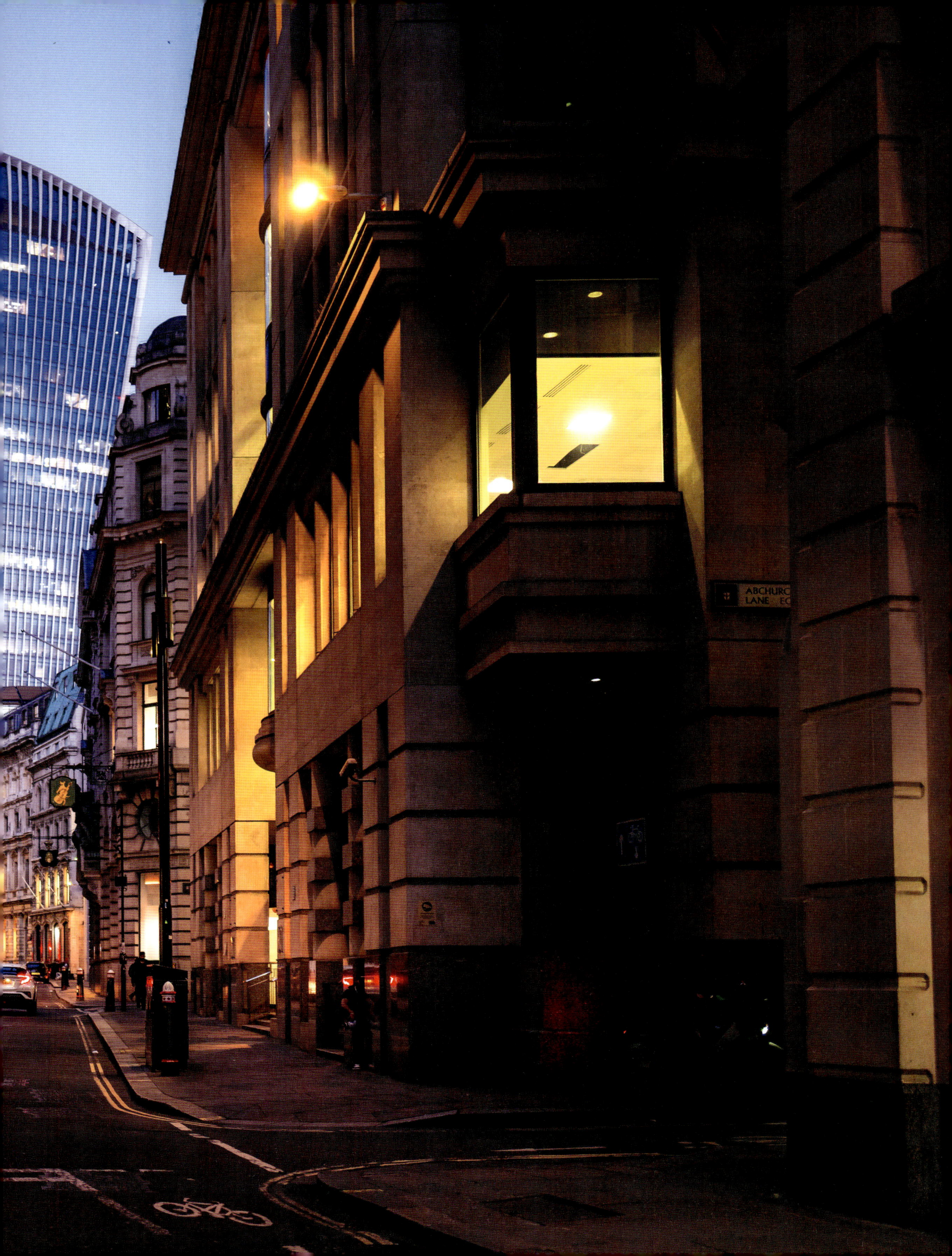
ABCHURC
LANE EC

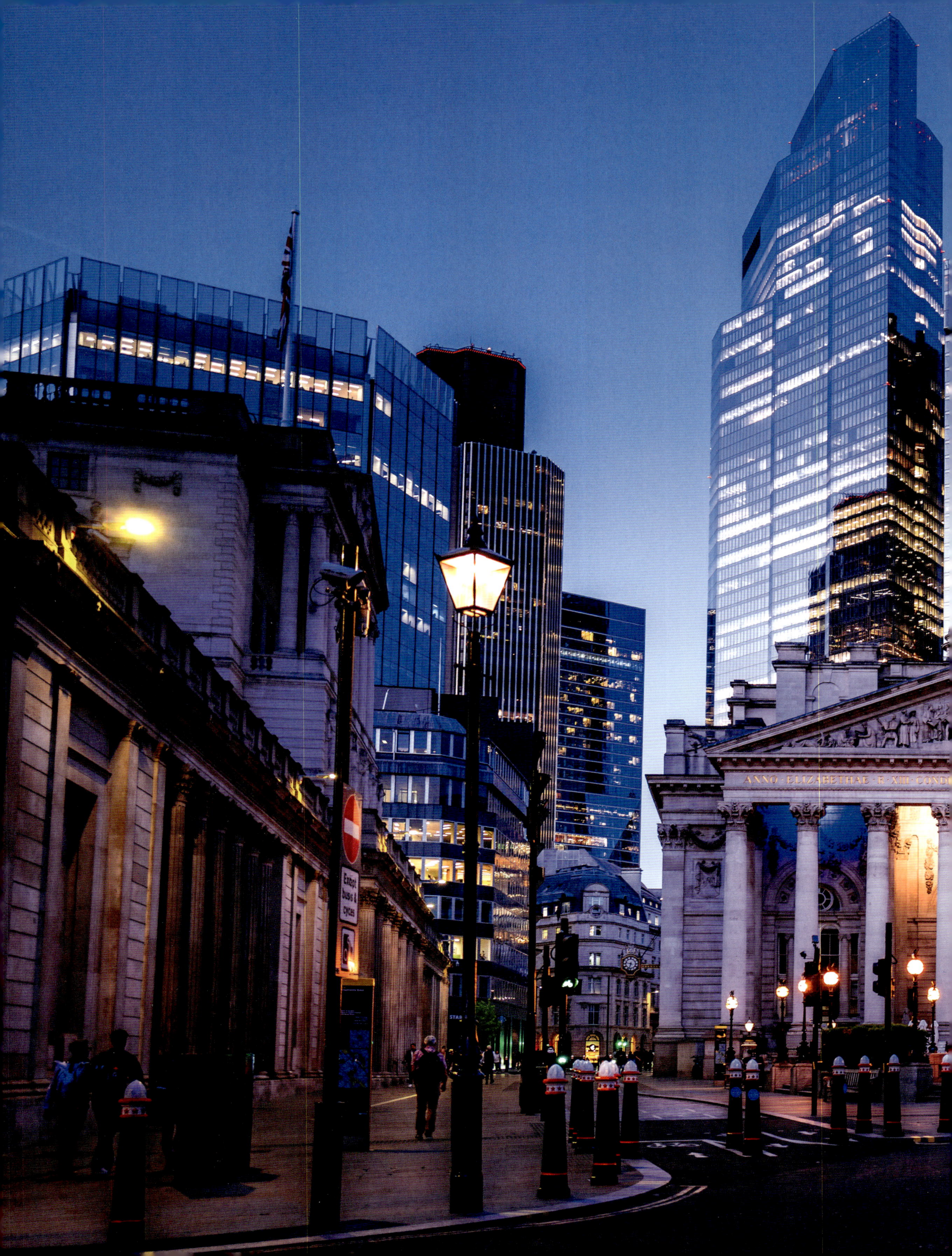
ANNO · ELIZABETHAE · R · XIII · COND
Except buses & cycles

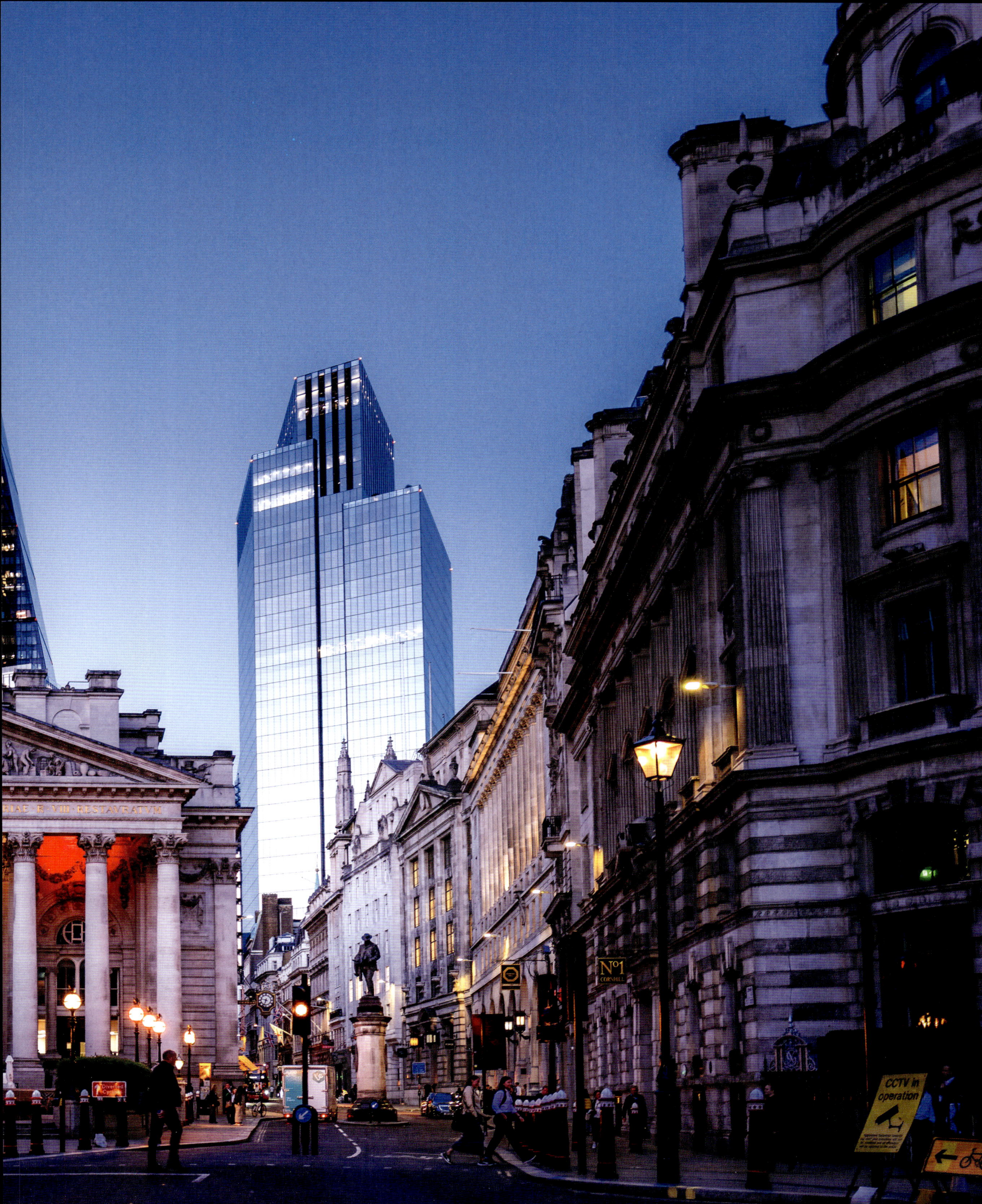
Nº1
CORNHILL
CCTV in operation

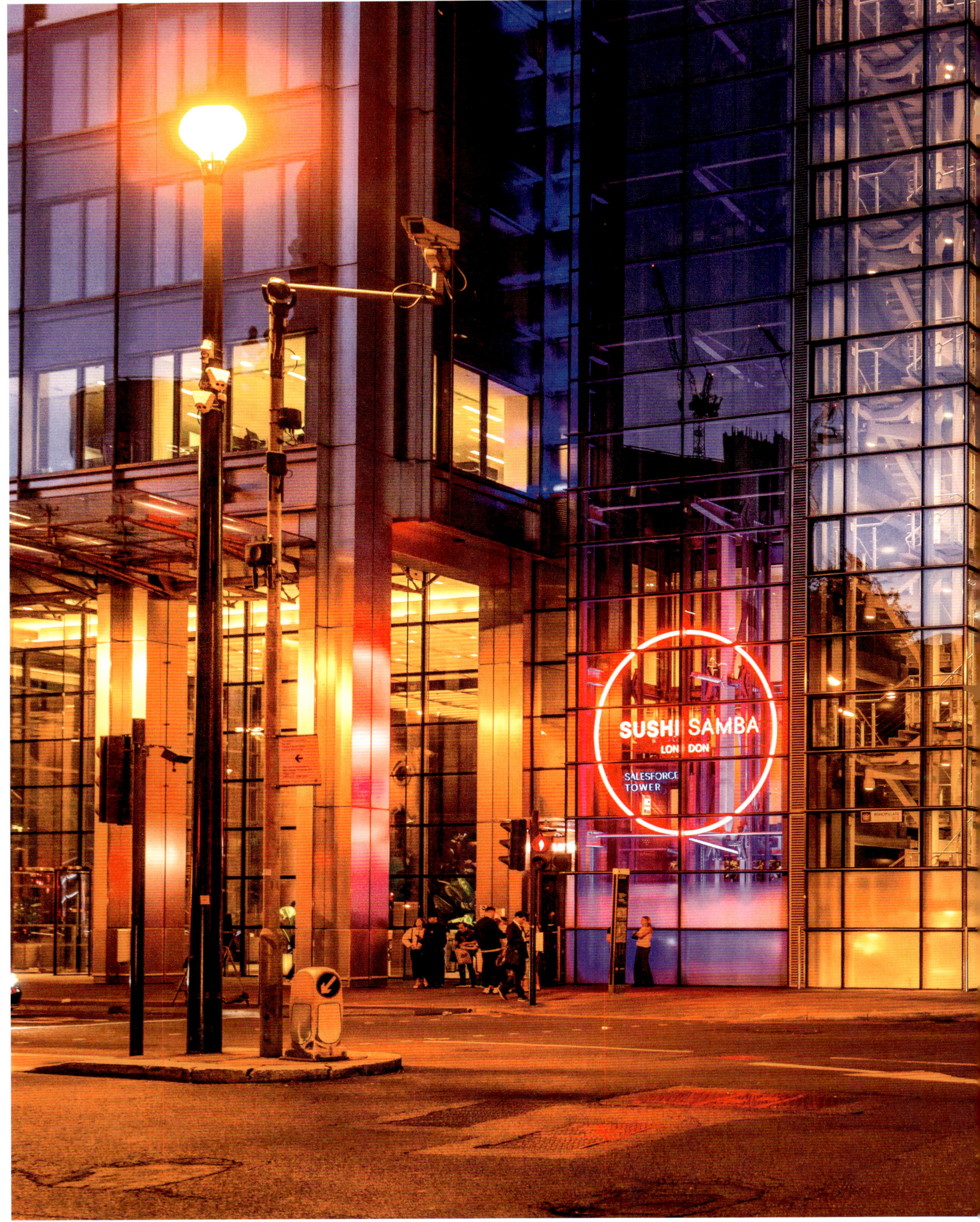
SUSHI SAMBA
LON DON
SALESFORCE
TOWER

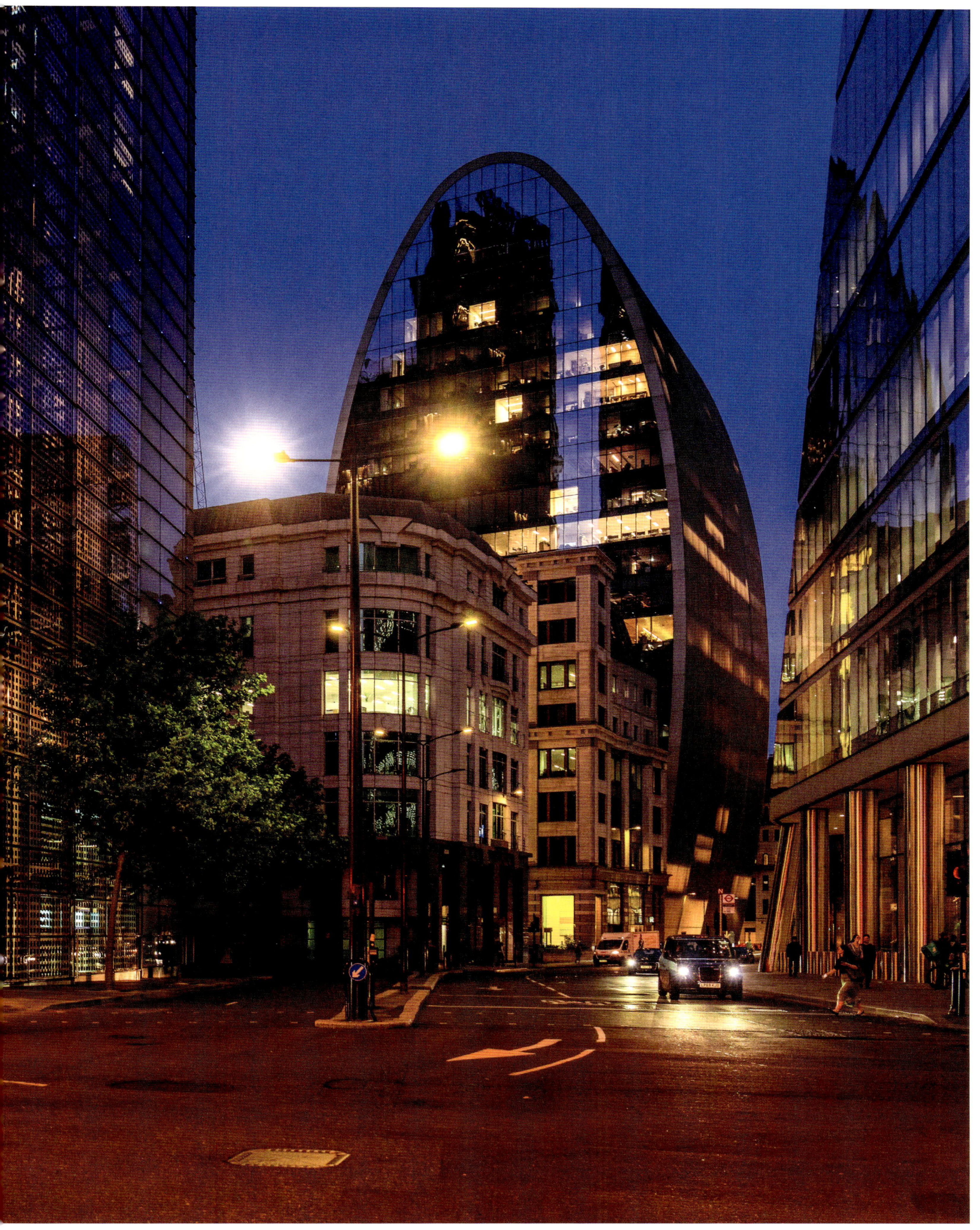

Londoners are famously creative when it comes to naming architectural landmarks—many are better known by their nicknames than their official names. One example is the Can of Ham, an office building located at 70 St. Mary Axe.

Londoner sind ziemlich kreativ im Benennen ihrer architektonischen Wahrzeichen – viele Bauwerke sind eher unter ihren Spitznamen als unter ihren offiziellen Bezeichnungen bekannt. Ein Beispiel ist der „Can of Ham“ (Frühstücksfleischdose), das Bürogebäude 70 St Mary Axe.

Les Londoniens font preuve de beaucoup d'imagination pour nommer les emblèmes architecturaux de leur ville. D'ailleurs, un grand nombre d'entre eux sont davantage connus par leur surnom que par leur appellation officielle, comme par exemple la « Can of Ham » (conserve de jambon), un immeuble de bureaux situé au 70 St Mary Axe.

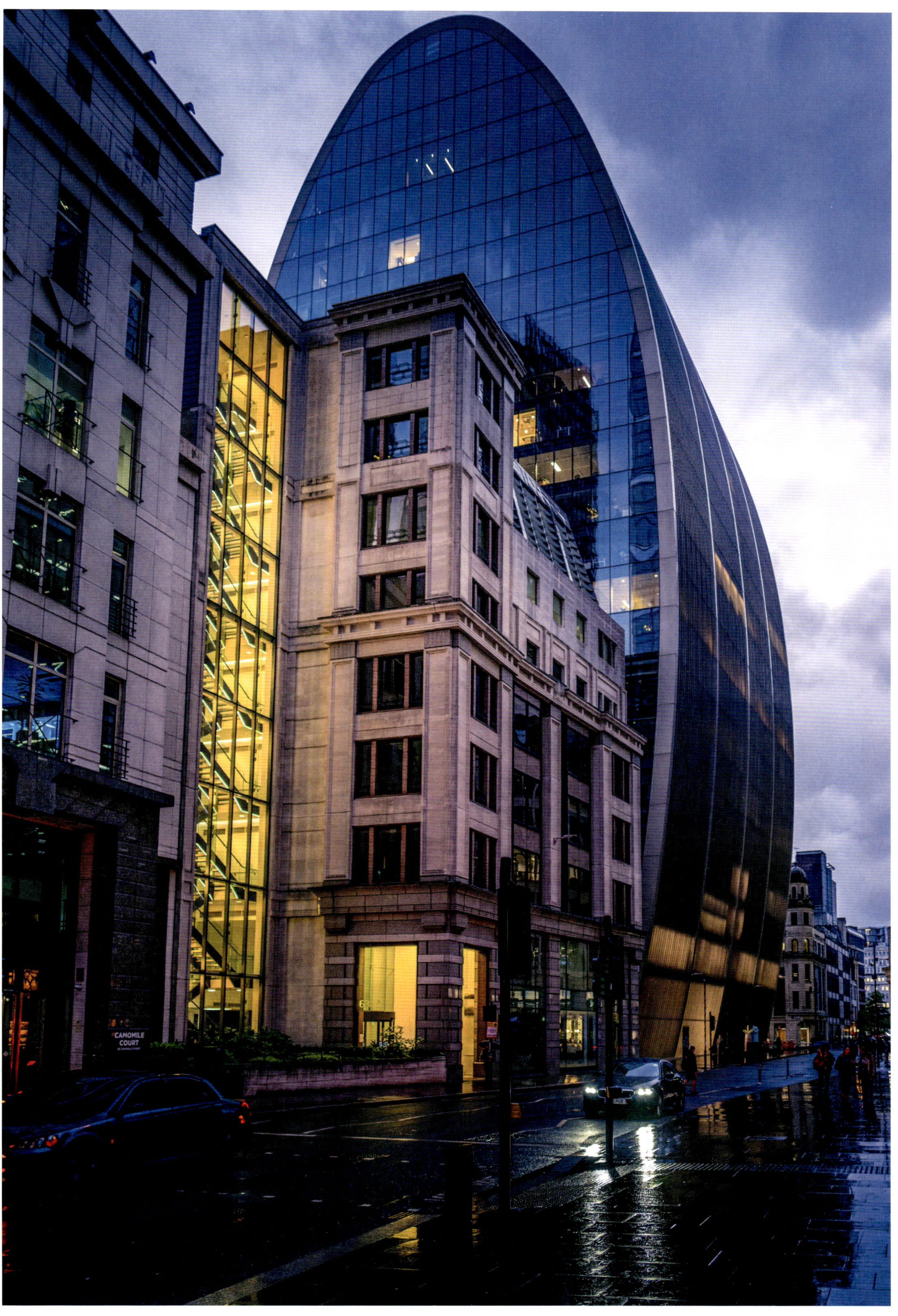
CAMOMILE
COURT

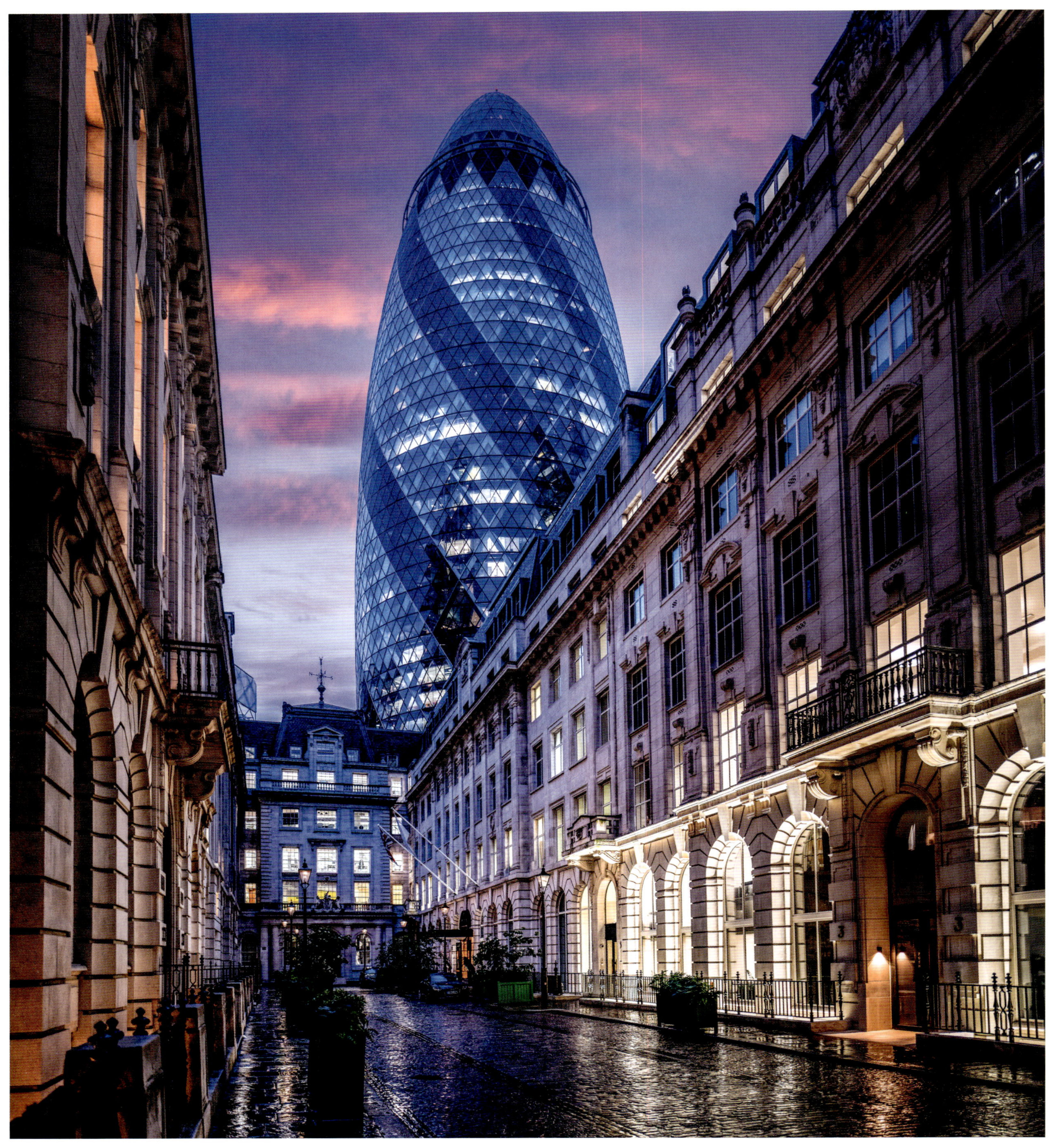

The Gherkin—officially 30 St. Mary Axe—is one of the best-known examples of contemporary architecture. Designed by Norman Foster and Ken Shuttleworth, it was completed in 2003 after two years of construction.

Der „Gherkin“ (Gewürzgurke) – offiziell 30 St Mary Axe – ist eines der bekanntesten Beispiele zeitgenössischer Architektur. Das von Norman Foster und Ken Shuttleworth entworfene Hochhaus wurde 2003 nach zweijähriger Bauzeit vollendet.

Le « Gherkin » (cornichon) – officiellement le 30 St Mary Axe – est un représentant de l’architecture contemporaine parmi les plus connus. Conçu par Norman Foster et Ken Shuttleworth, il a été achevé en 2003, sa construction ayant duré deux ans.

The view northward from the Walkie Talkie offers glimpses of the Cheesegrater, the Gherkin, and the Scalpel.

Following pages: The Sky Garden at 20 Fenchurch Street, with a view of the River Thames.

Blick vom „Walkie Talkie“ Richtung Norden. Zu sehen sind der „Cheesegrater“ (Käsereibe), der „Gherkin“ und der „Scalpel“.

Nächste Seite: Vom Sky Garden in 20 Fenchurch Street hat man einen wunderschönen Blick auf die Themse.

Du « Walkie Talkie », on a vue au nord sur le « Cheesegrater » (râpe à fromage), le « Gherkin » (cornichon) et le « Scalpel » (bistouri).

Page suivante : Vue imprenable sur la Tamise depuis le Sky Garden du 20 Fenchurch Street.

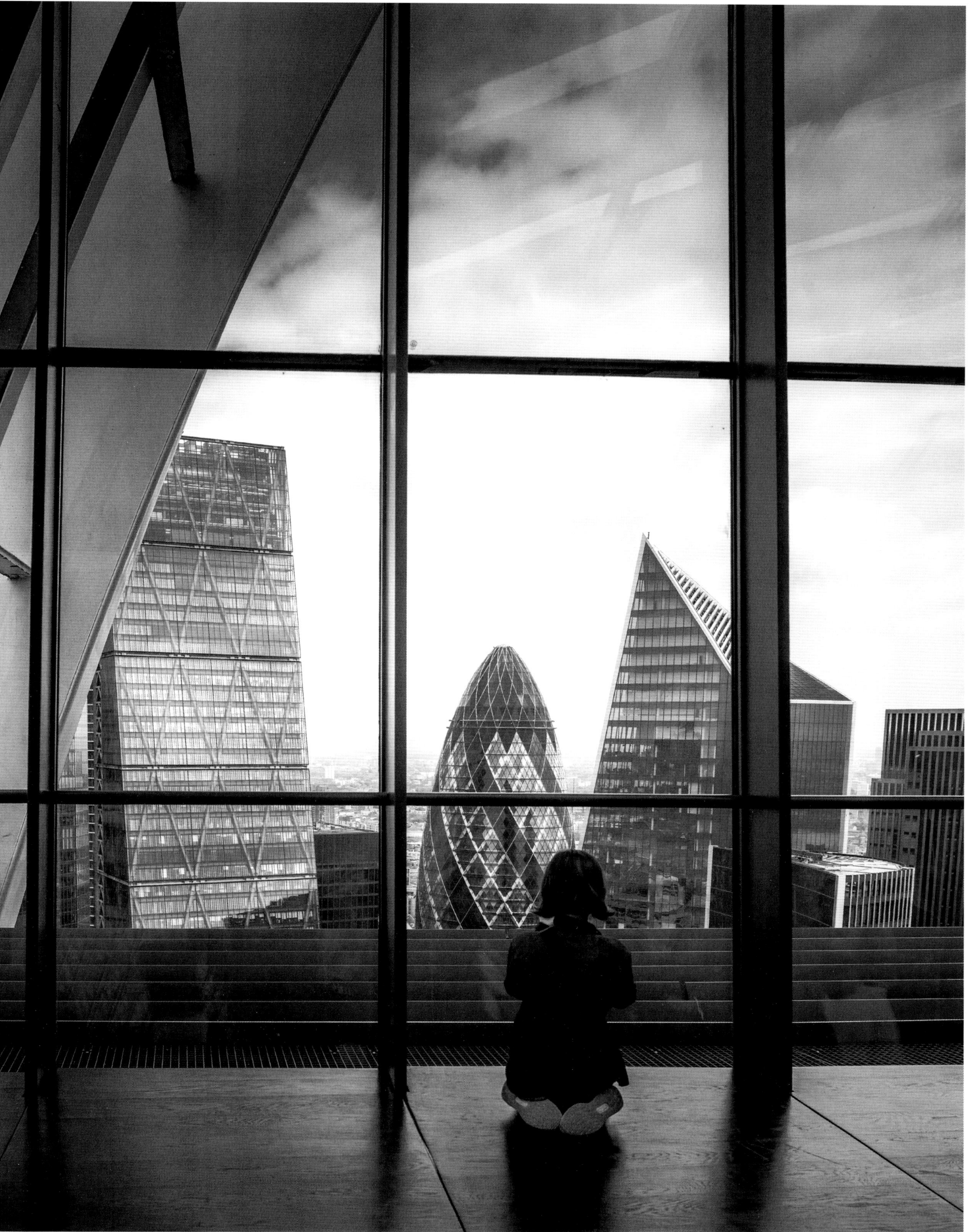

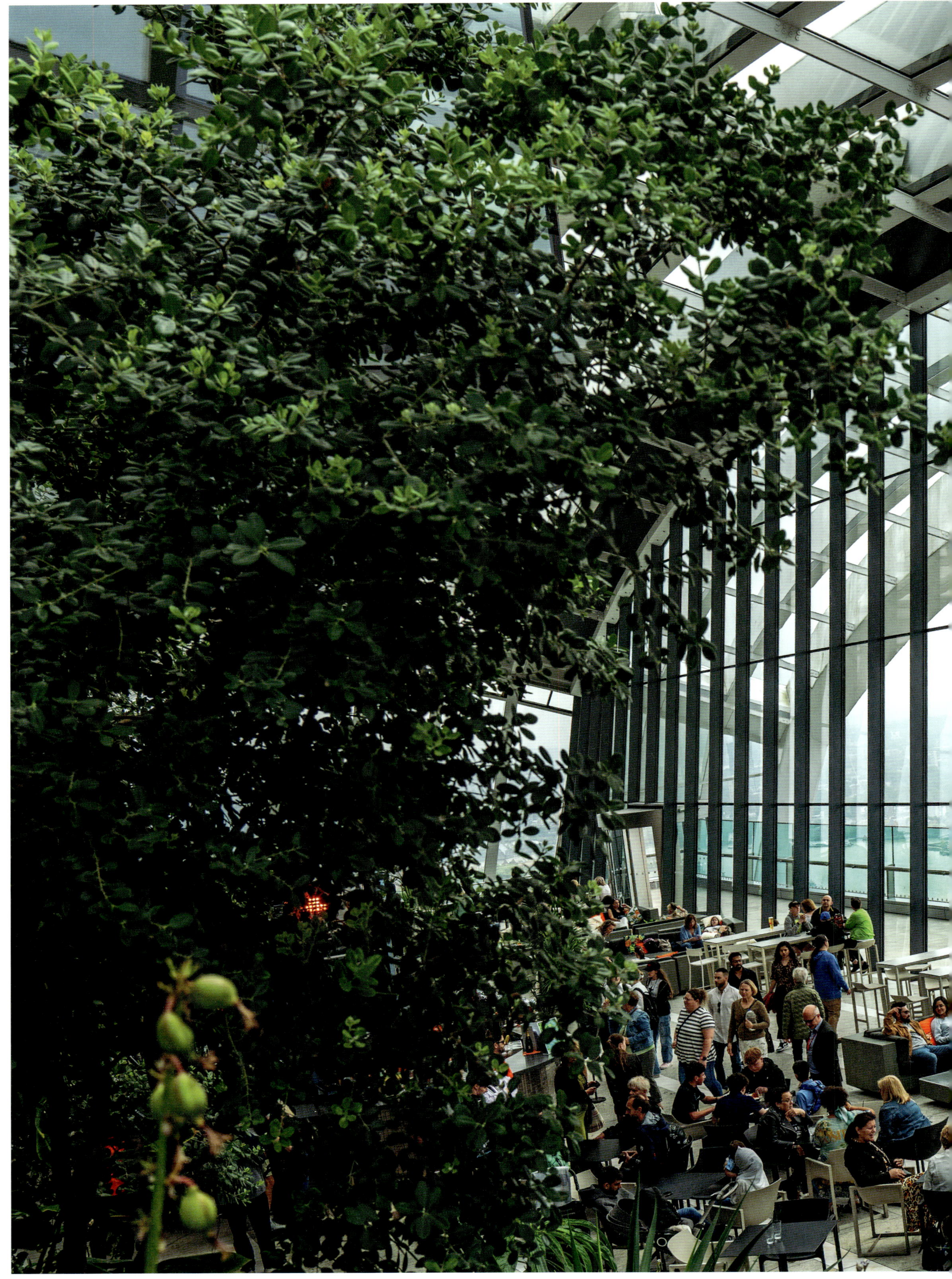

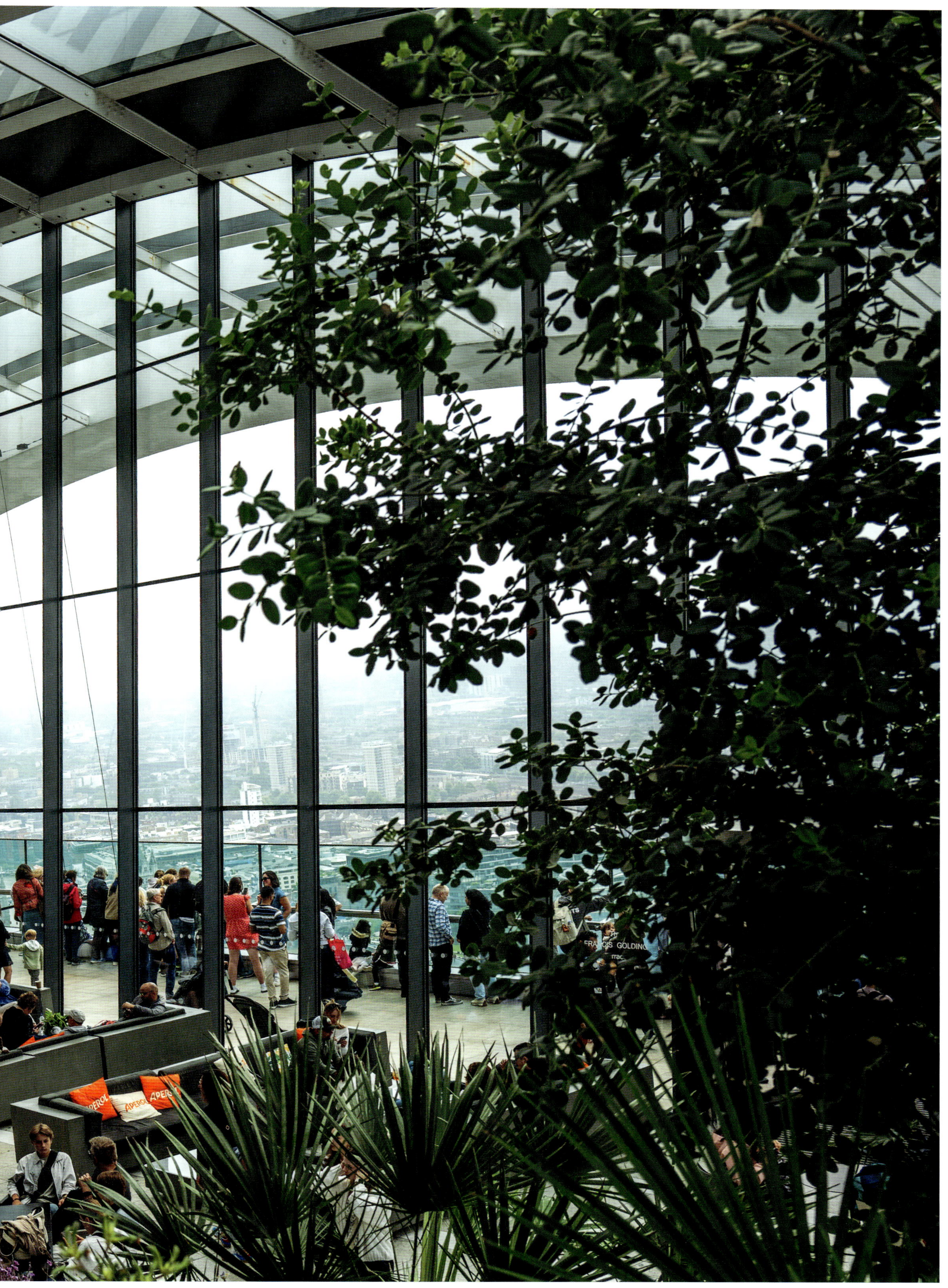
APEROL

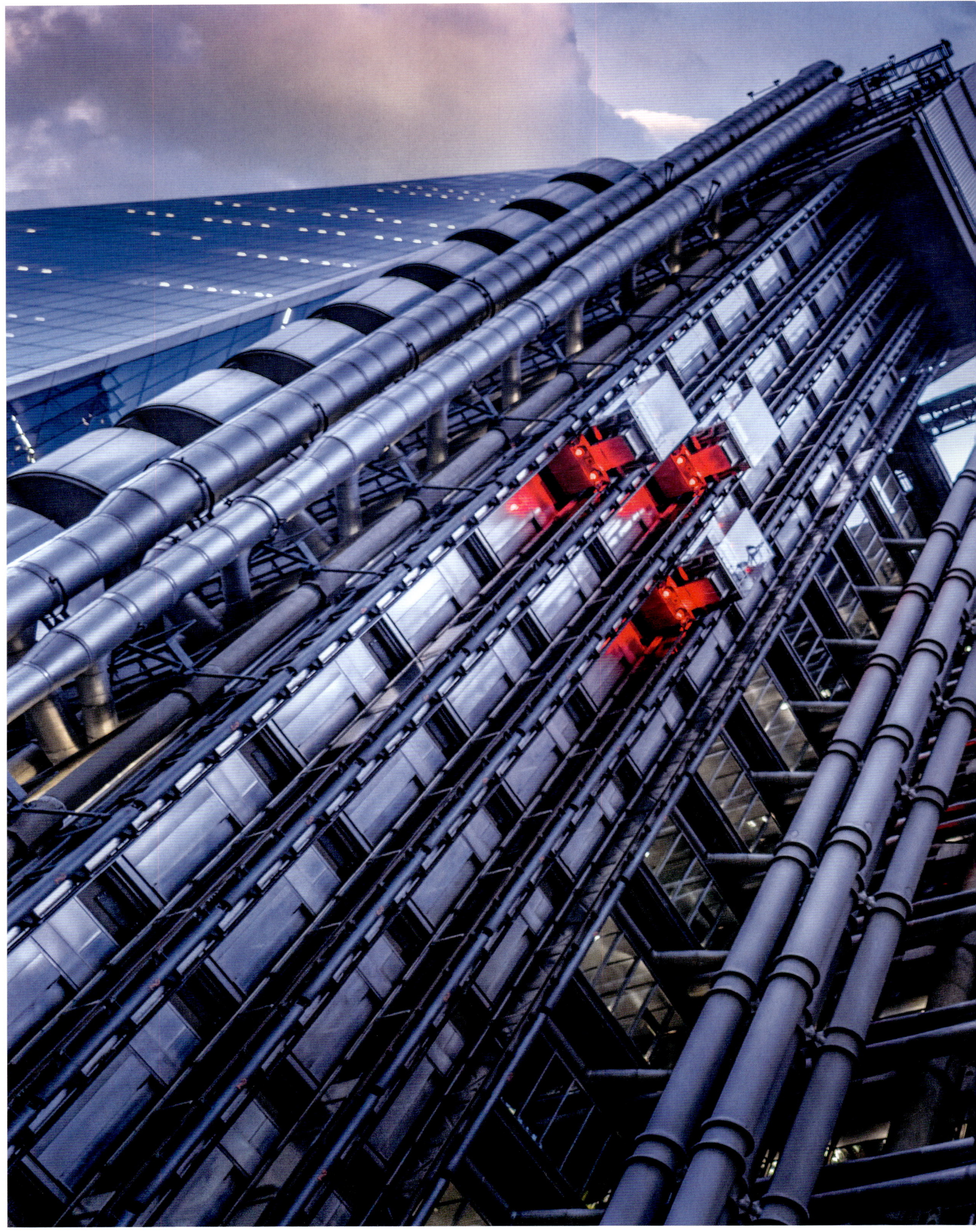

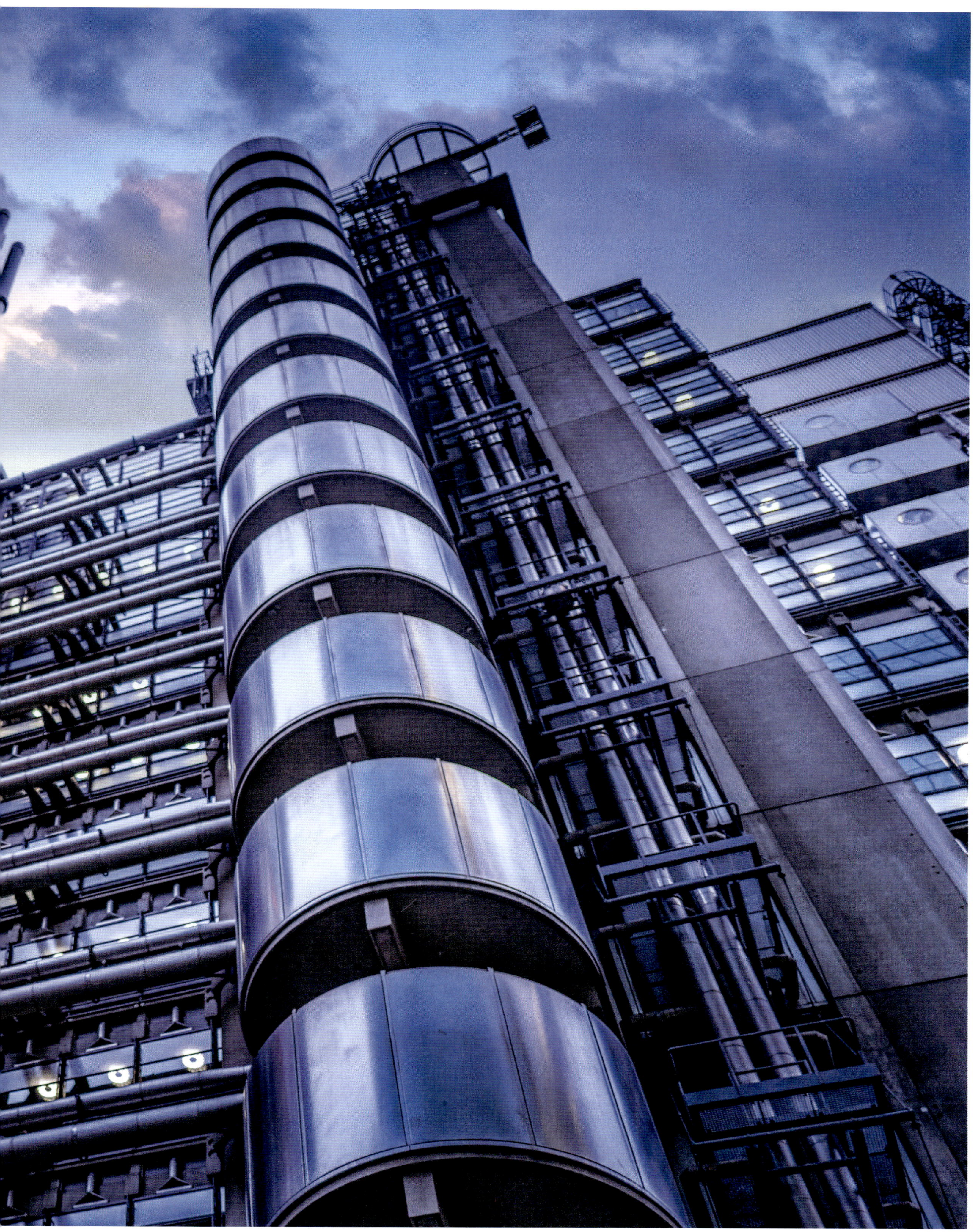

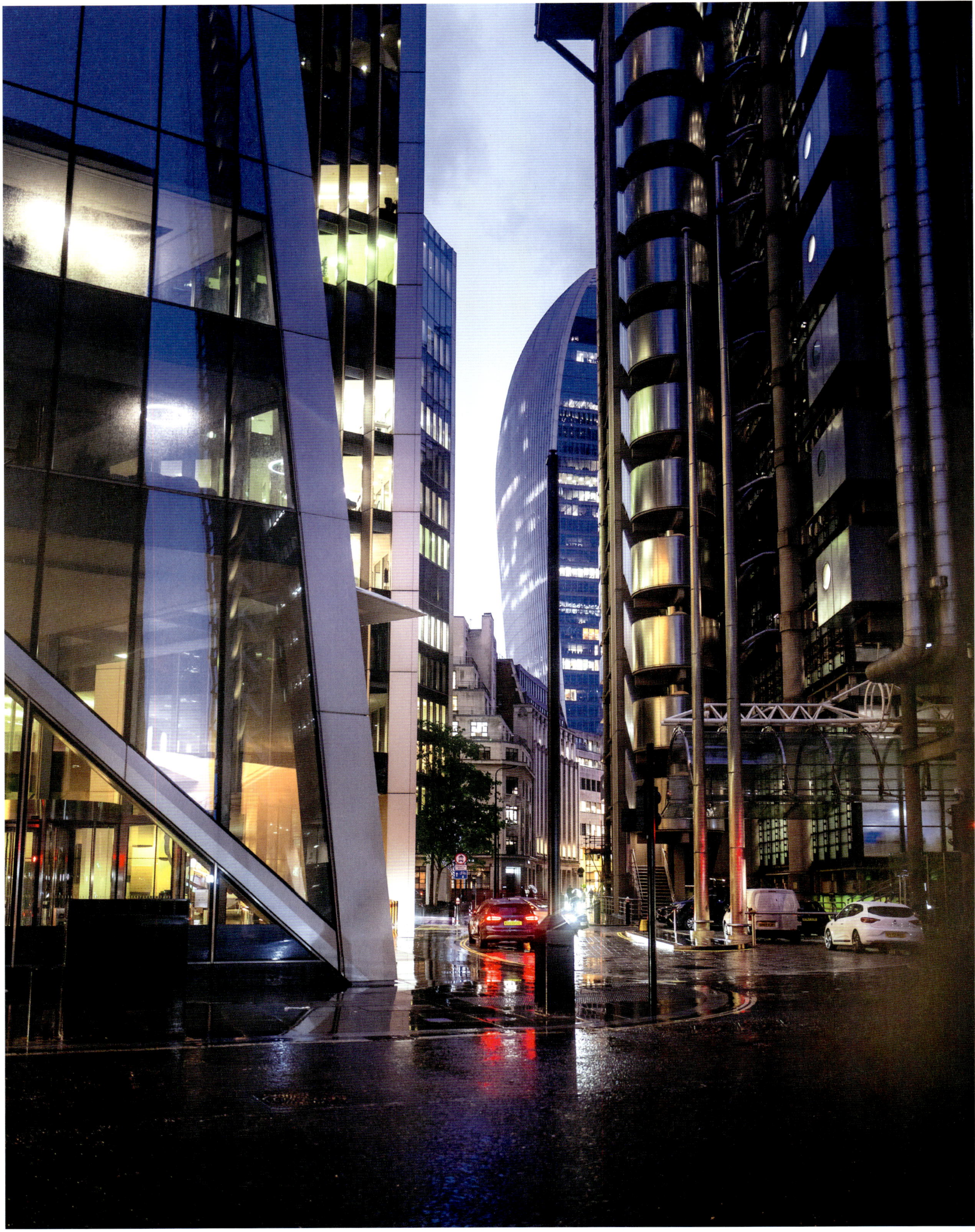

Previous pages and opposite: The striking modern architecture of the Lloyd's building at dusk. Designed by Richard Rogers and opened in 1986, this structure is instantly recognizable for its exposed pipes and innovative design.

Vorherige und diese Seite: Die imposante moderne Architektur des Lloyd's-Gebäudes in der Dämmerung. Das von Richard Rogers entworfene, 1986 eröffnete Bauwerk ist durch die außen verlaufenden Röhren und das innovative Design sofort erkennbar.

Cette page et la précédente : Le building de la Lloyd's au crépuscule. Cet édifice signé Richard Rogers et inauguré en 1986 se reconnaît immédiatement à ses circulations apparentes et à son design novateur.

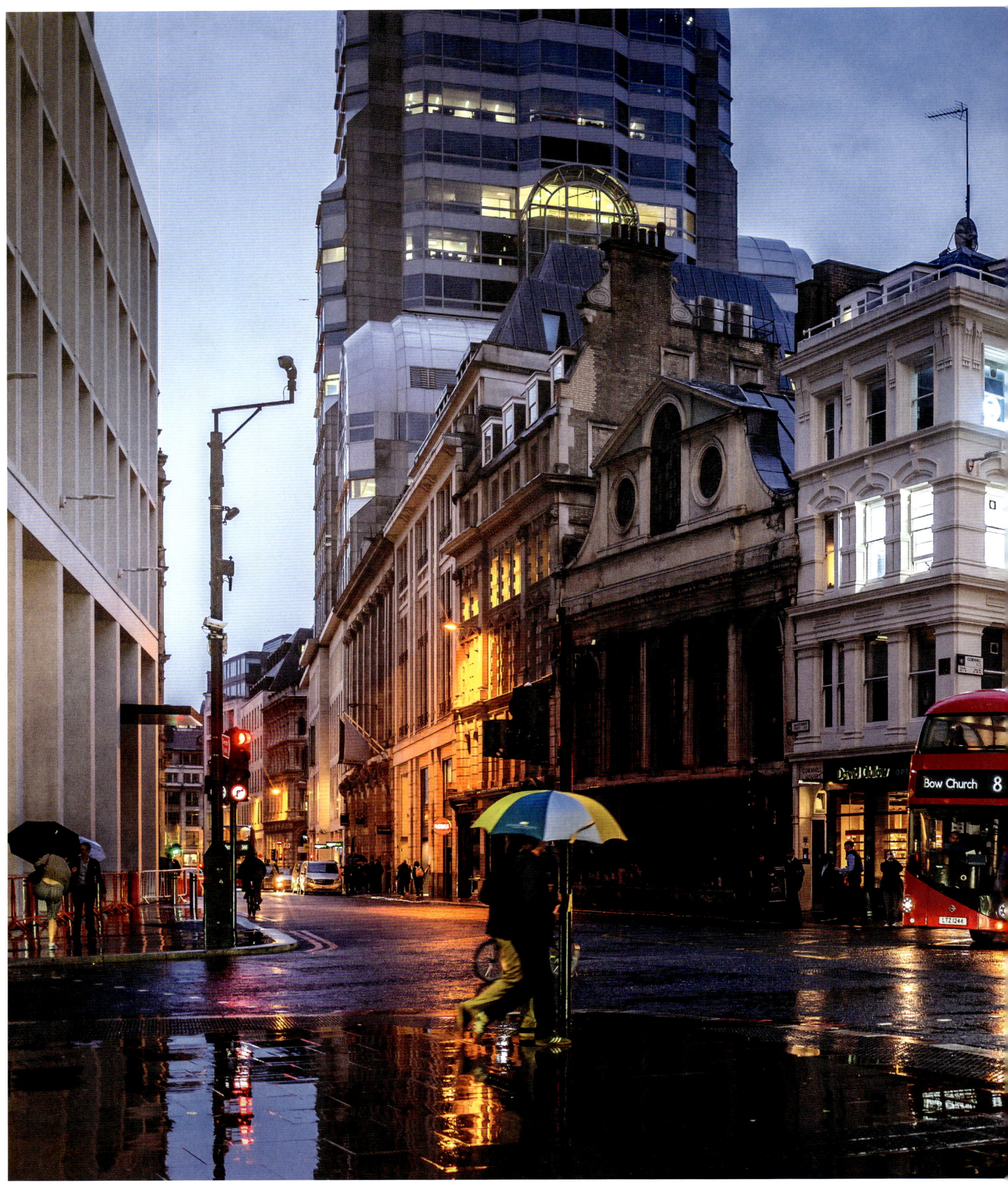
Bow Church 8

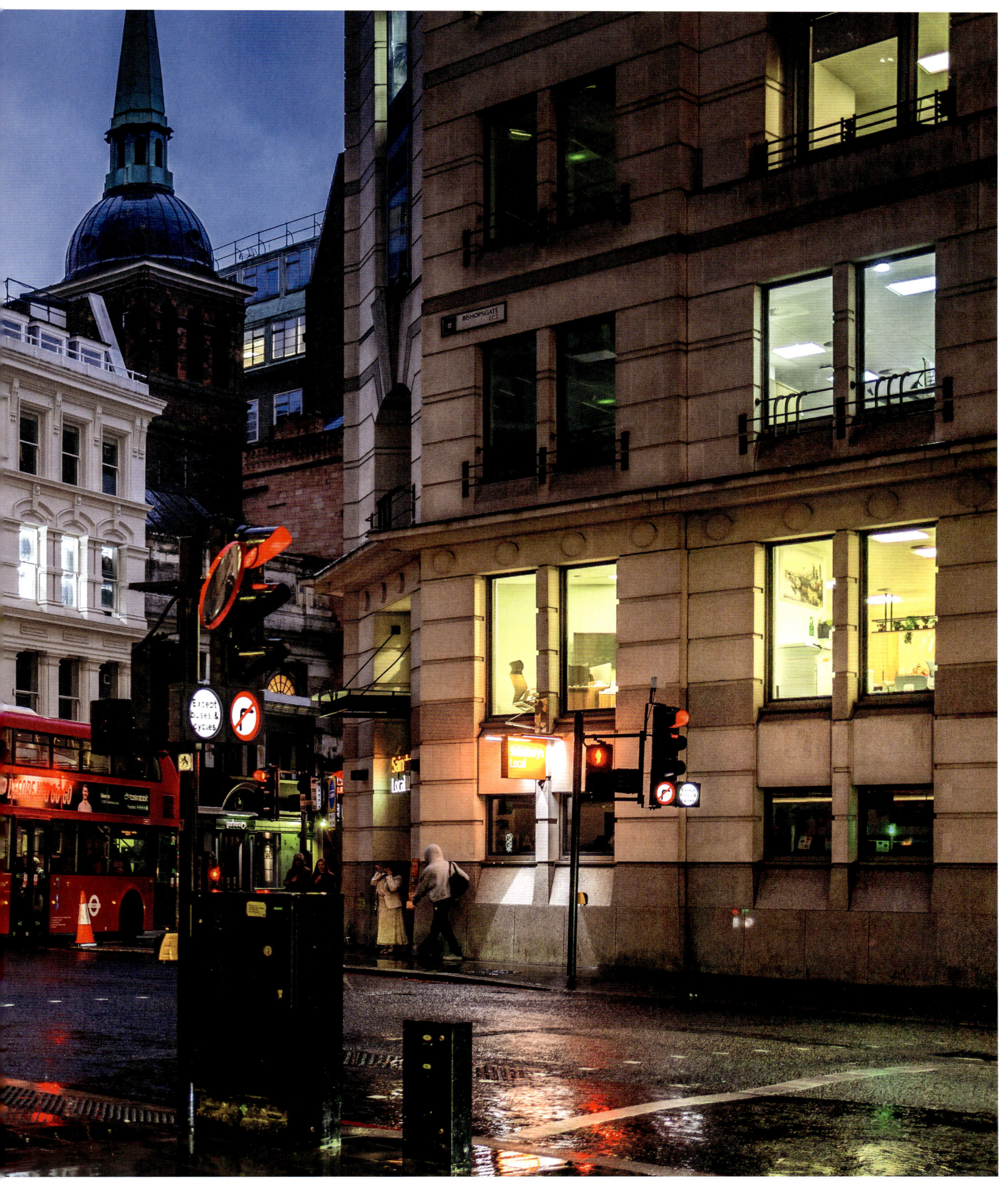

BISHOPSGATE
EC2
Except buses & cycles

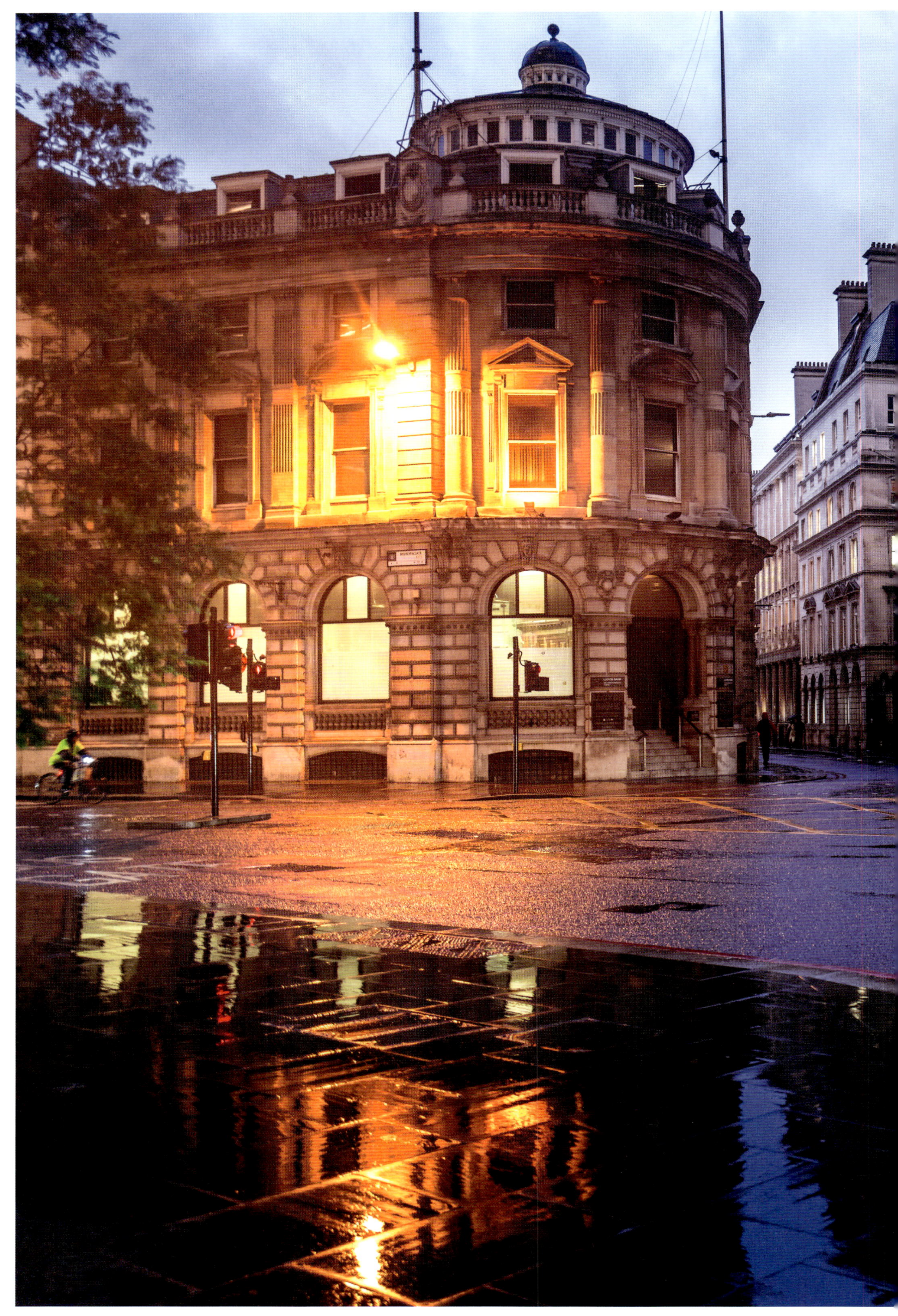

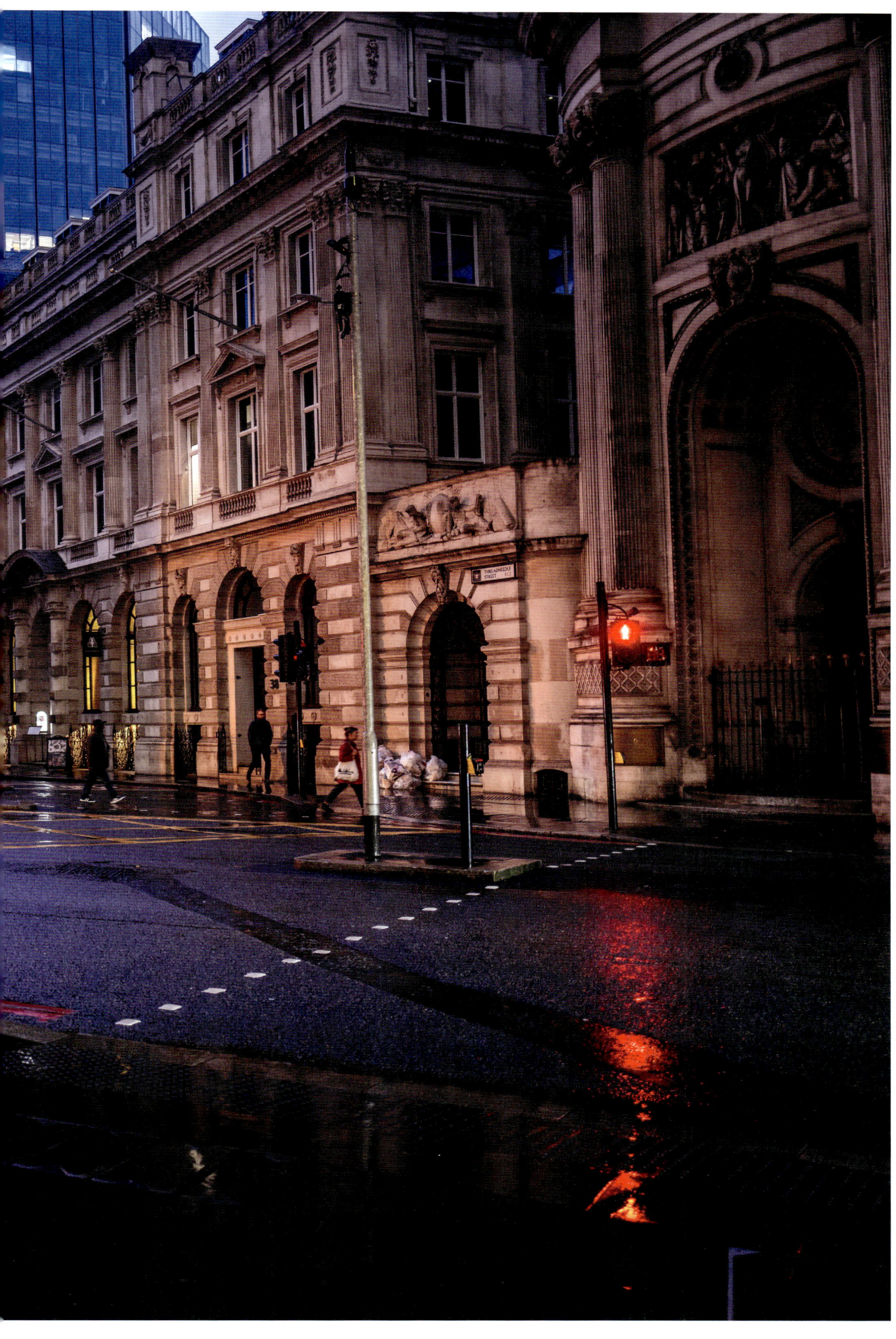
THREADNEEDLE
STREET

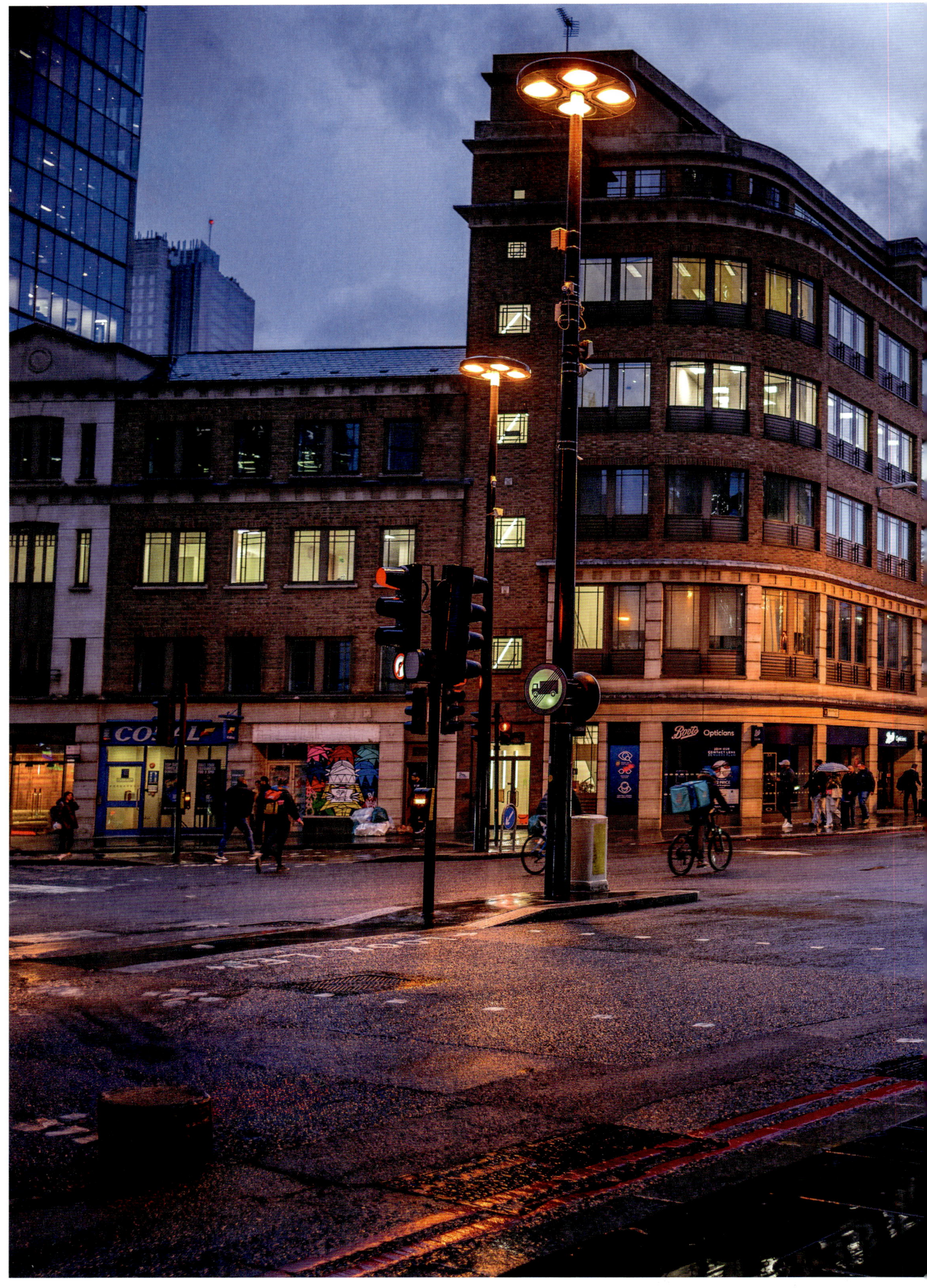
Boots Opticians

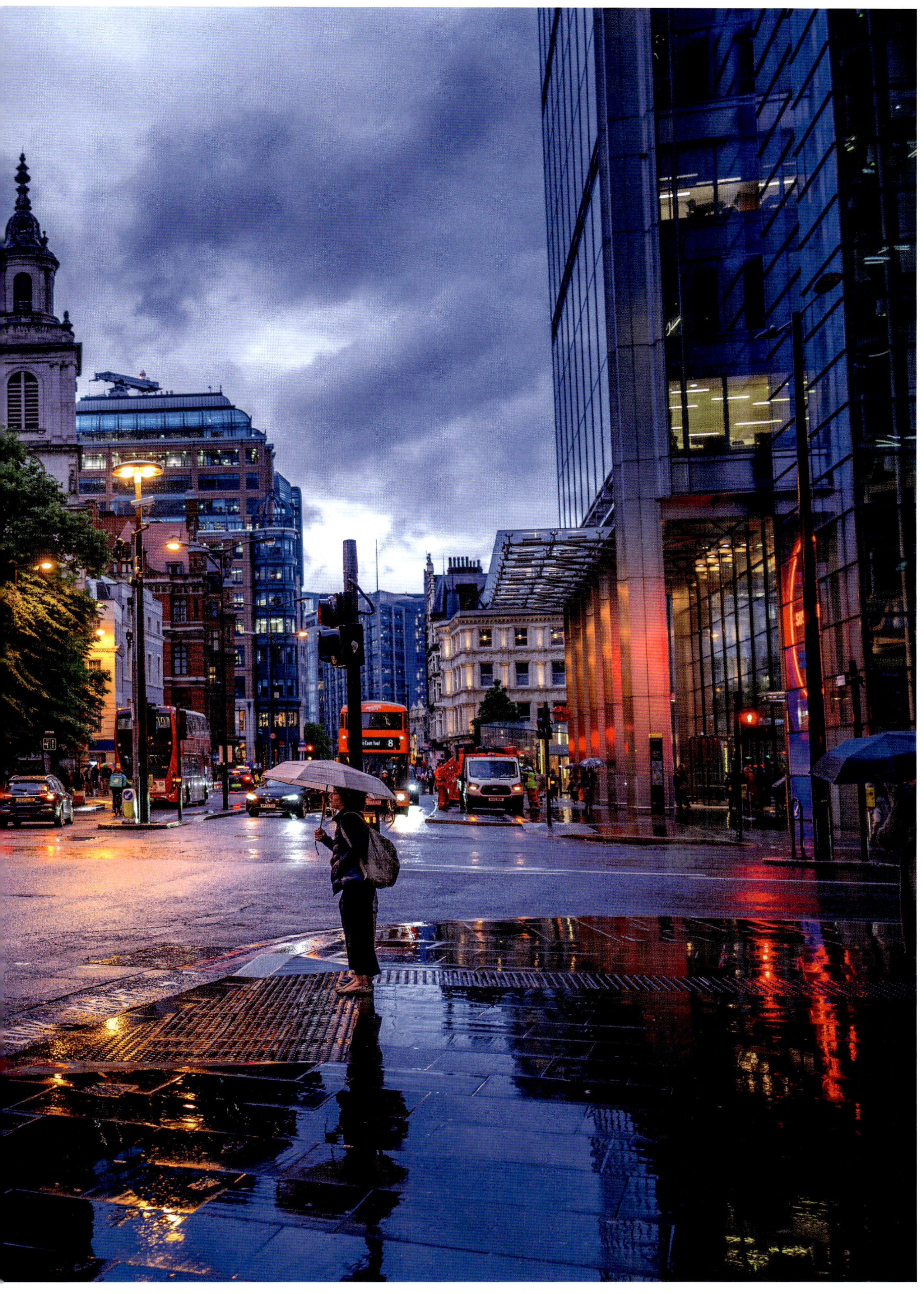

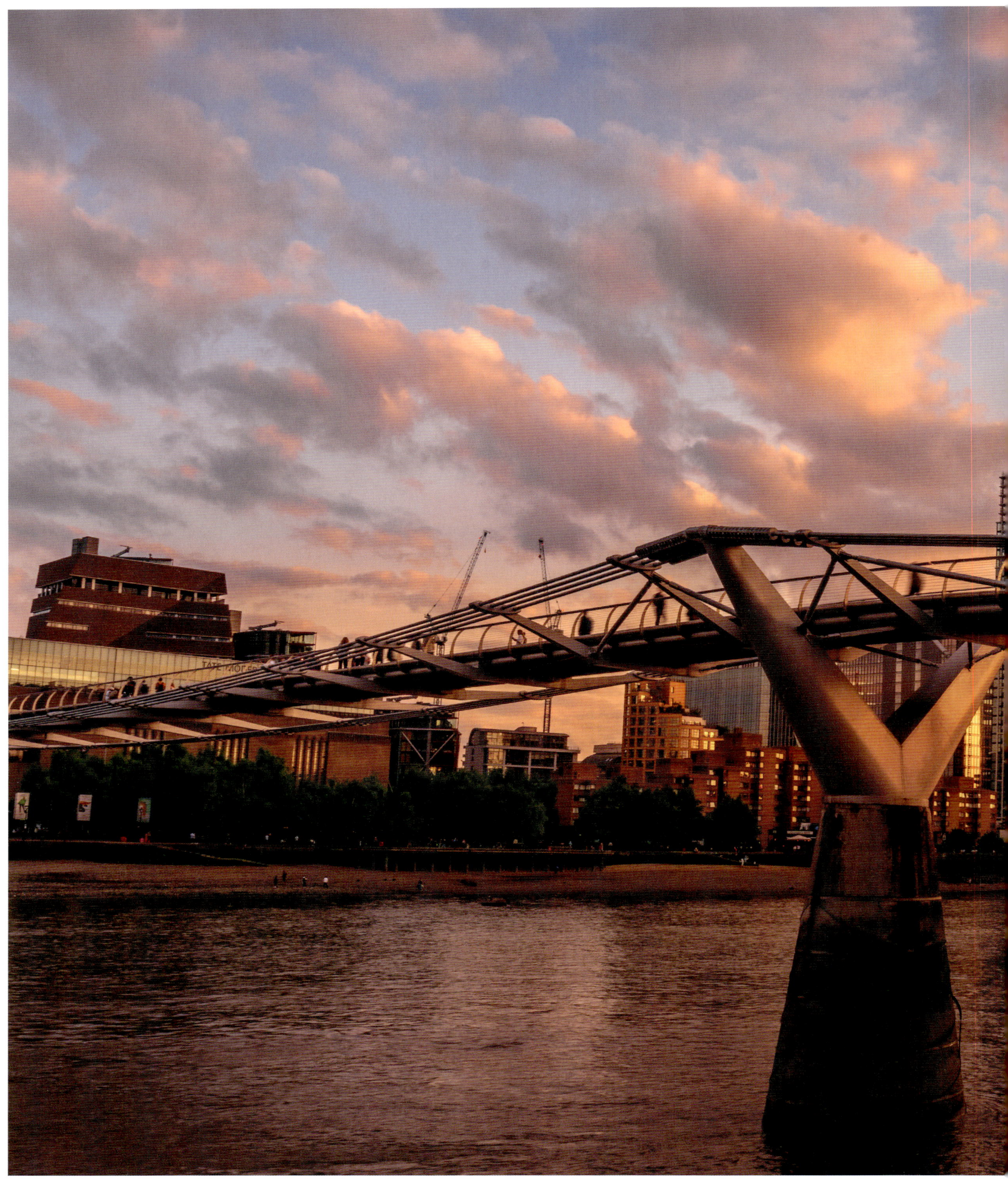

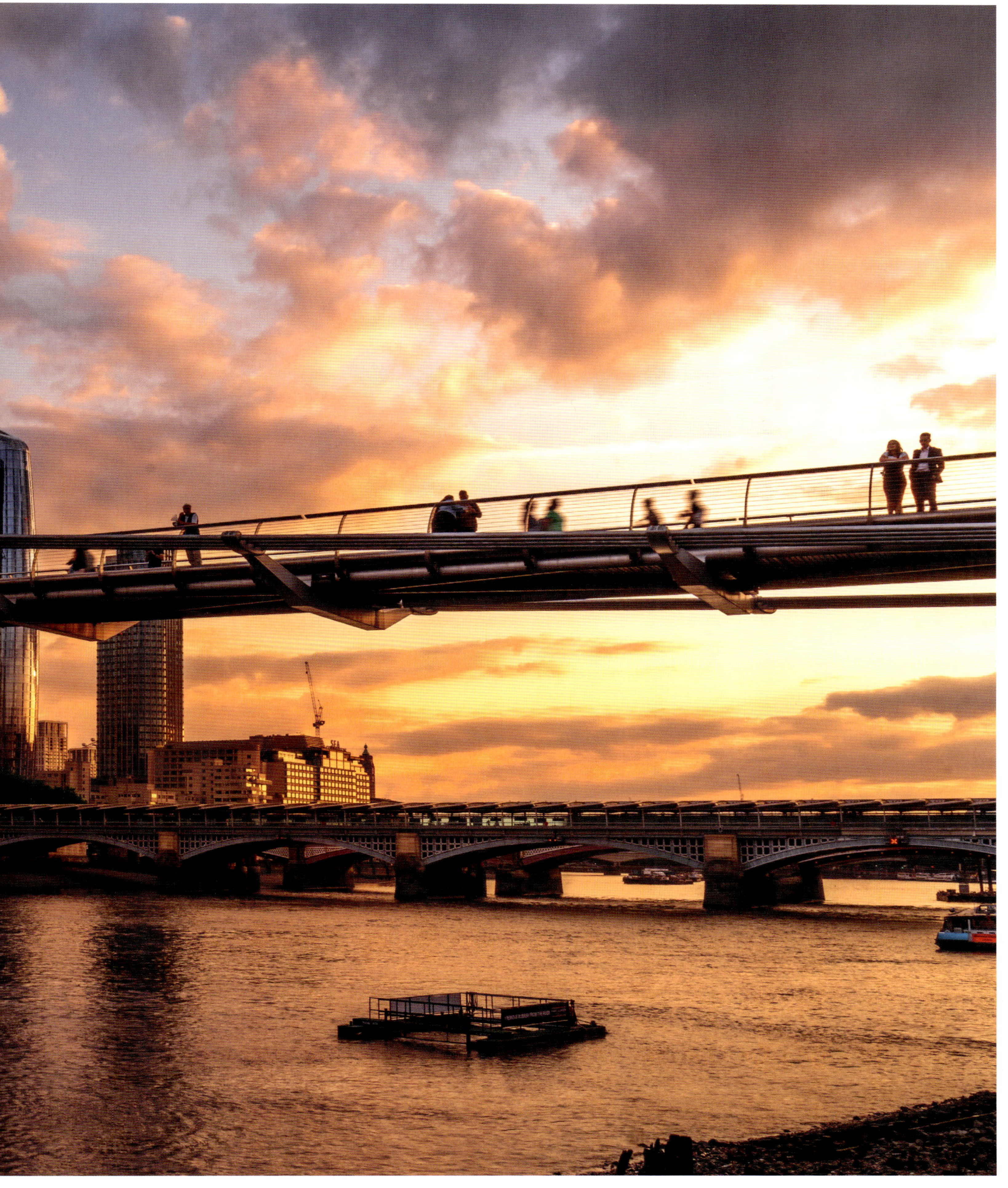

The Millennium Bridge with St. Paul's Cathedral in the distance at sunset.
This sleek pedestrian bridge, opened in 2000, connects the City of London with the vibrant Southwark, offering stunning views of the River Thames and the city skyline.

Auf der Millennium Bridge bei Sonnenuntergang. Im Hintergrund zu sehen: St Paul's Cathedral.
Die 2000 eingeweihte elegant geschwungene Fußgängerbrücke verbindet die City of London mit dem lebendigen Southwark und bietet atemberaubende Ausblicke auf die Themse und die City-Skyline.

Le Millennium Bridge, avec la cathédrale Saint-Paul dans le soleil couchant à l'arrière-plan.
Reliant la City au trépidant quartier de Southwark, cette élégante passerelle inaugurée en 2000 offre une vue époustouflante sur la Tamise et la silhouette de la ville.

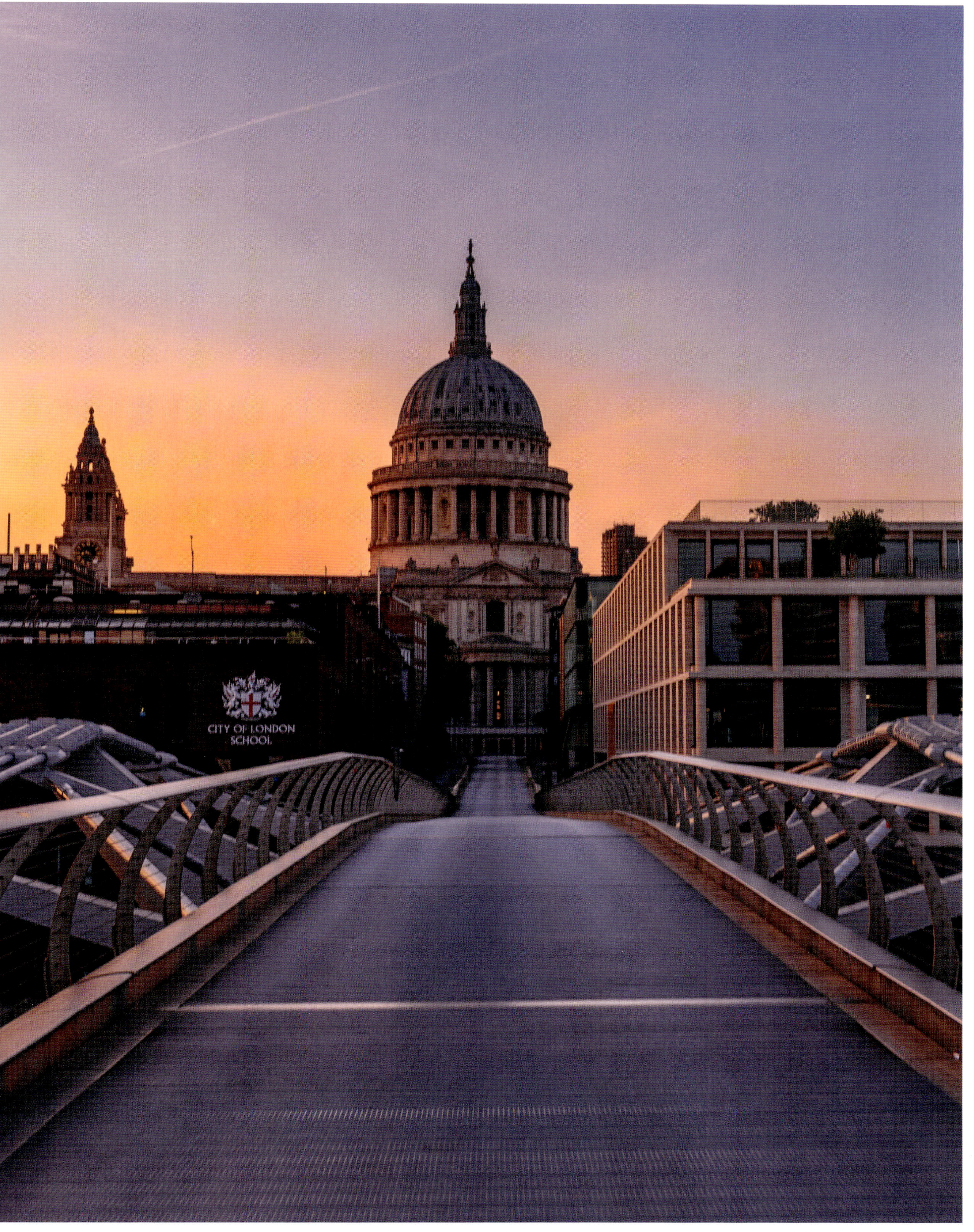
CITY OF LONDON
SCHOOL

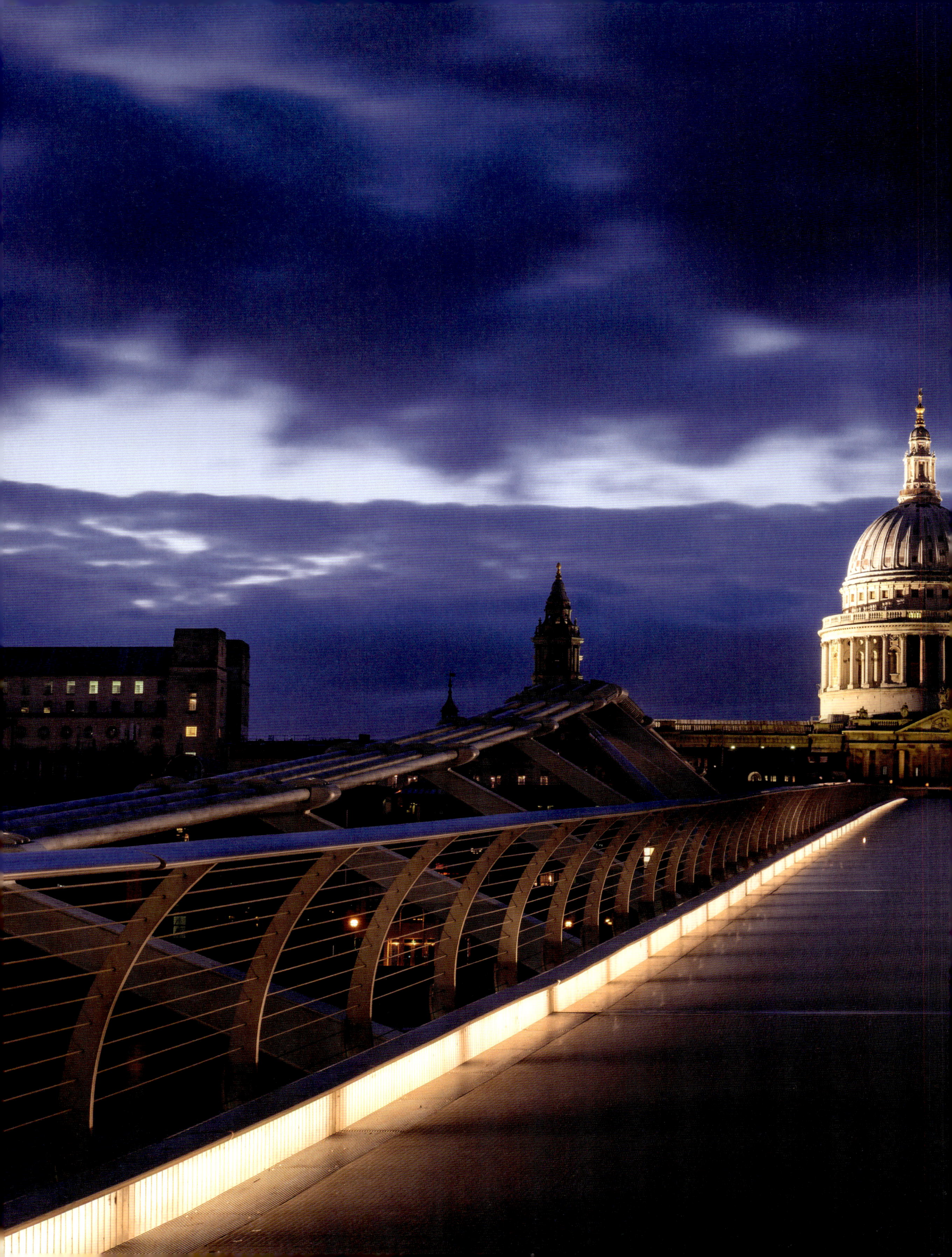

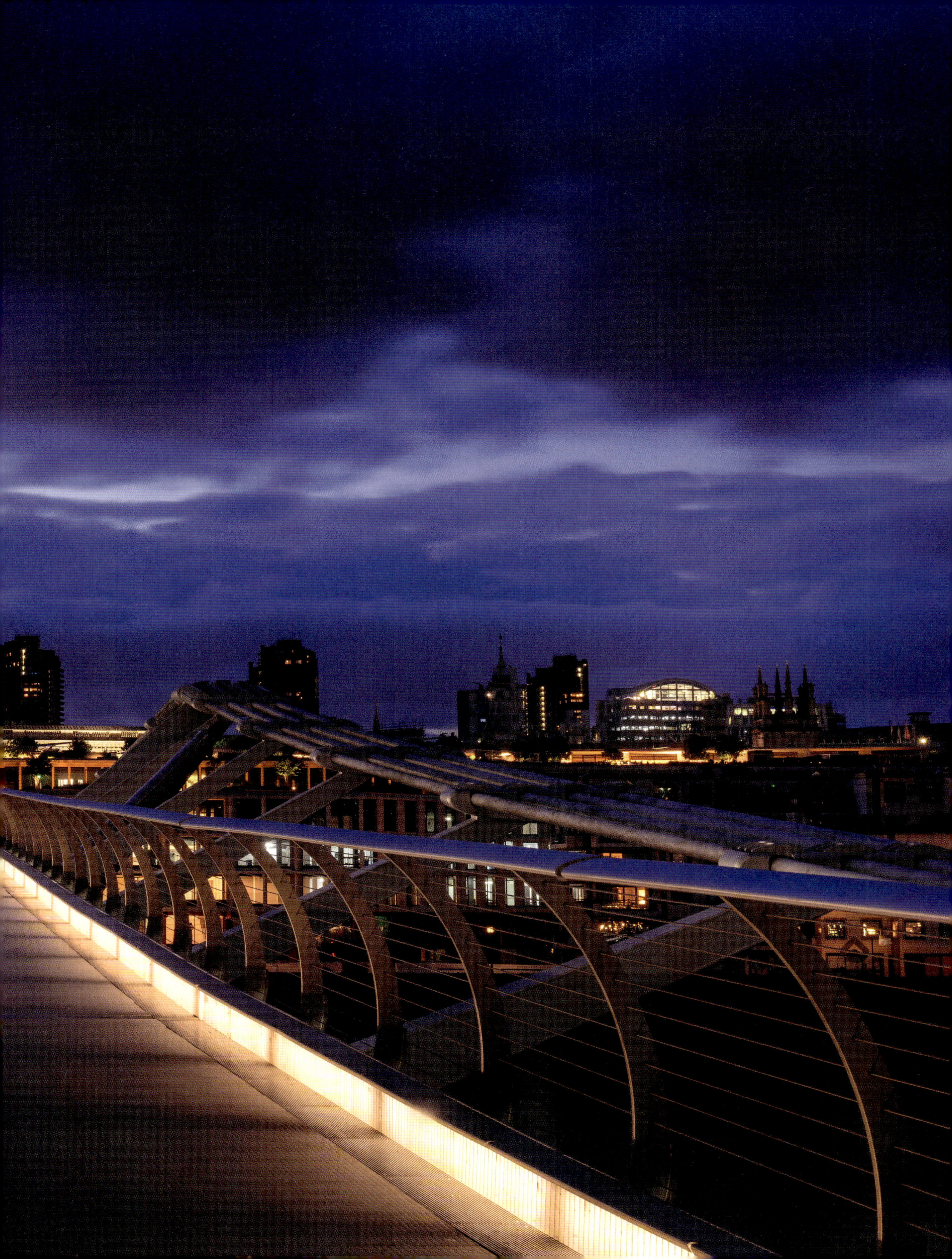

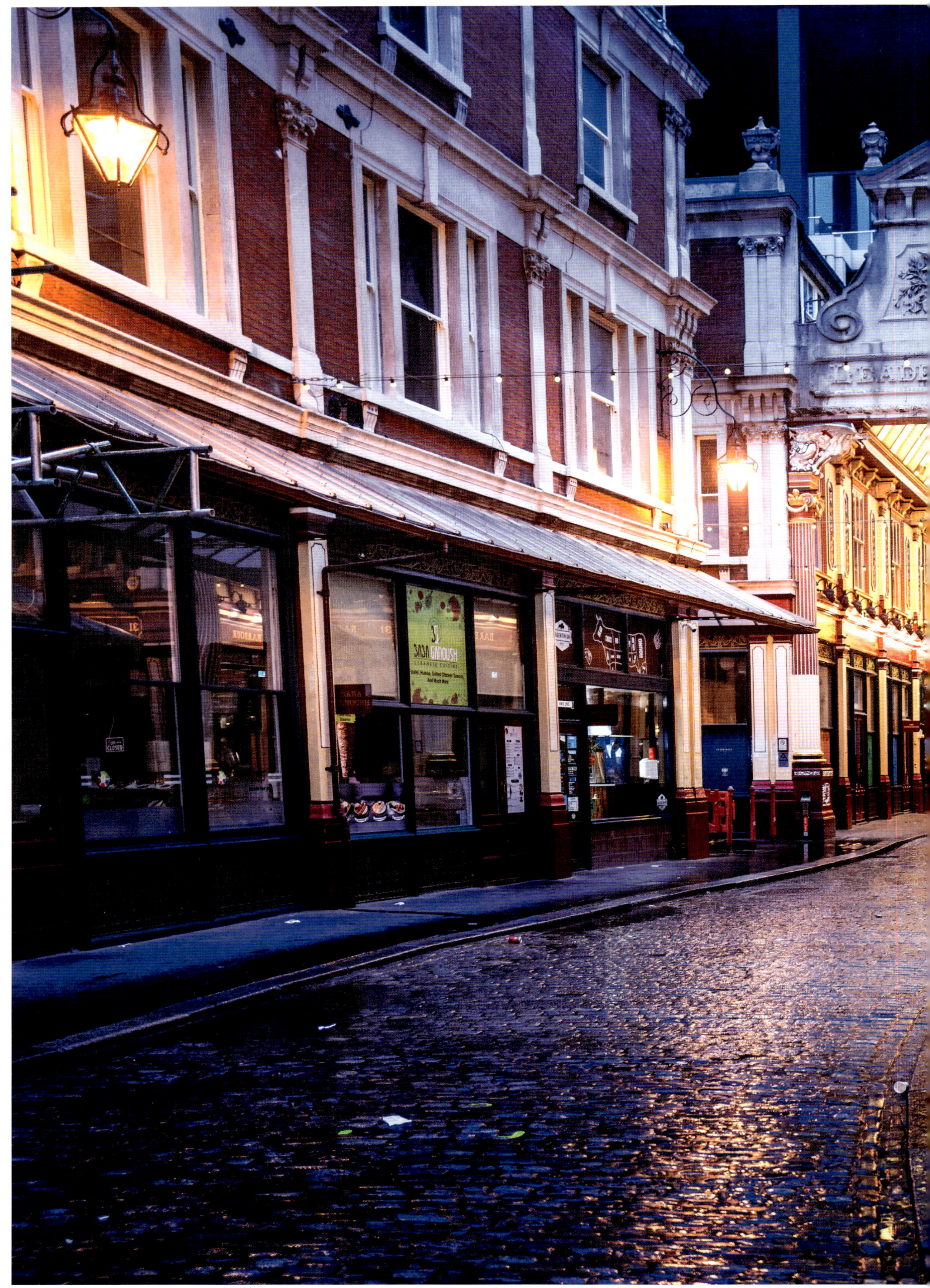
GANOUSH
CLOSED

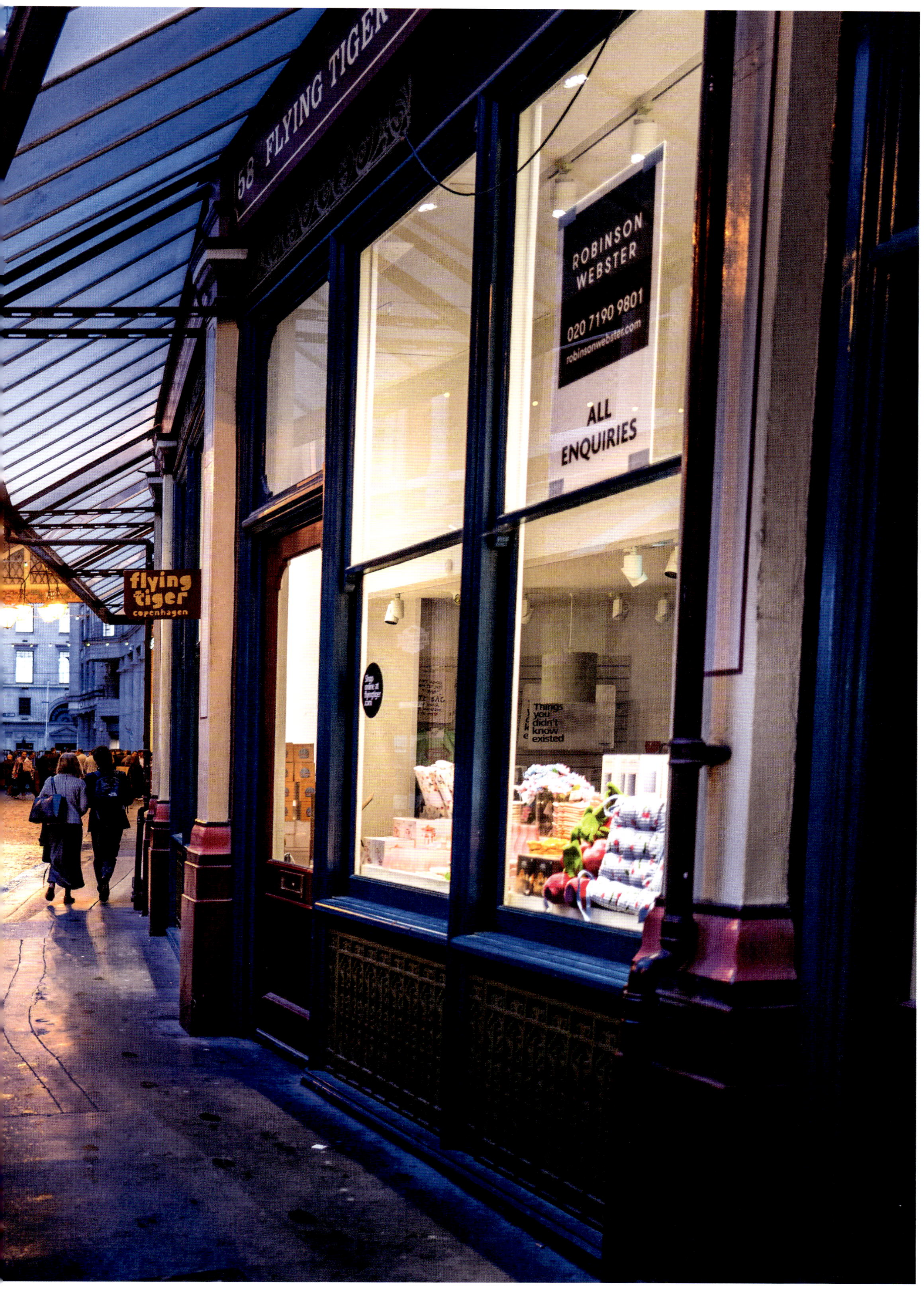
58 FLYING TIGER
ROBINSON WEBSTER
020 7190 9801
robinsonwebster.com
ALL ENQUIRIES
flying tiger copenhagen
Things you didn't know existed

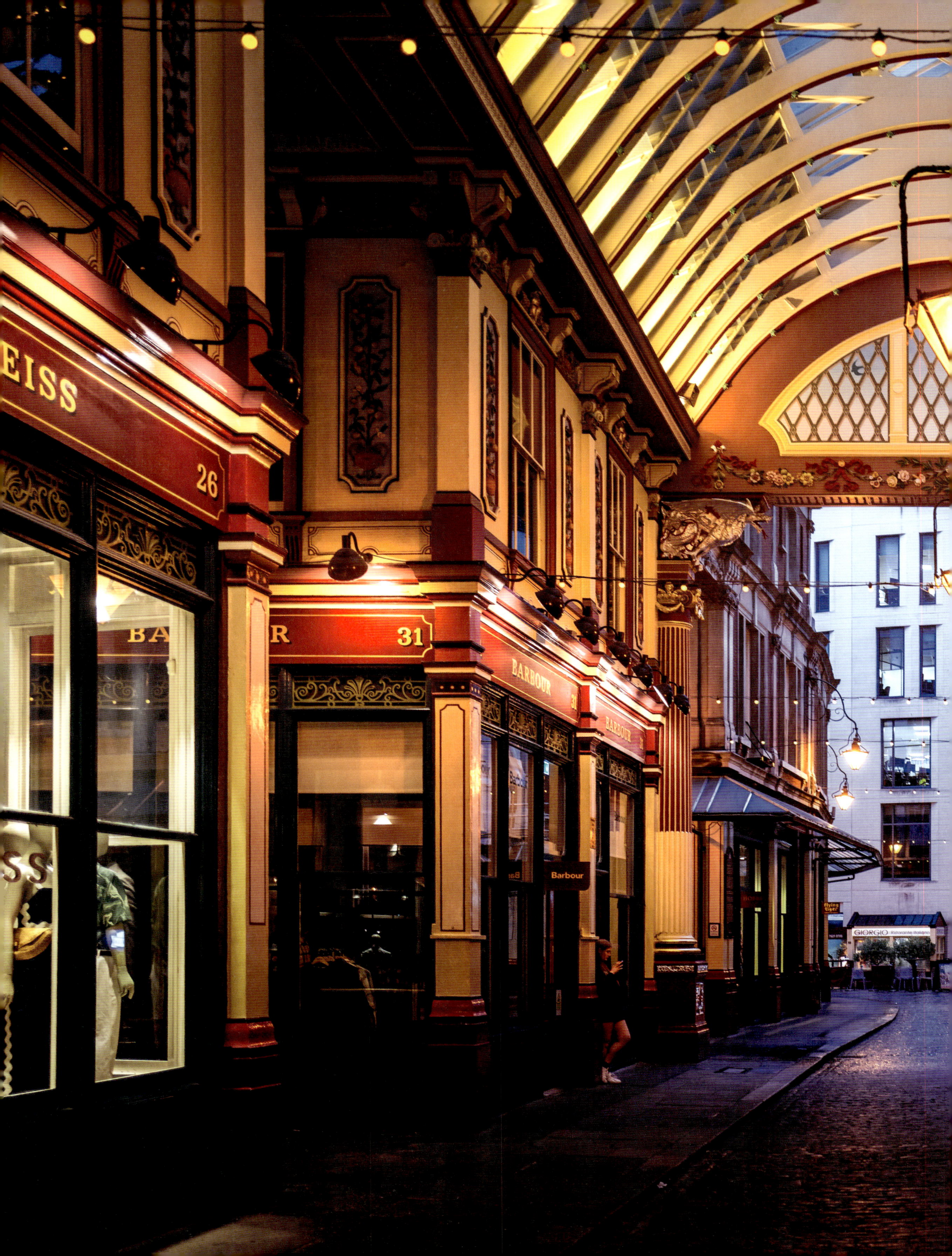
EISS
26
31
BARBOUR
BARBOUR
Barbour
GIORGIO

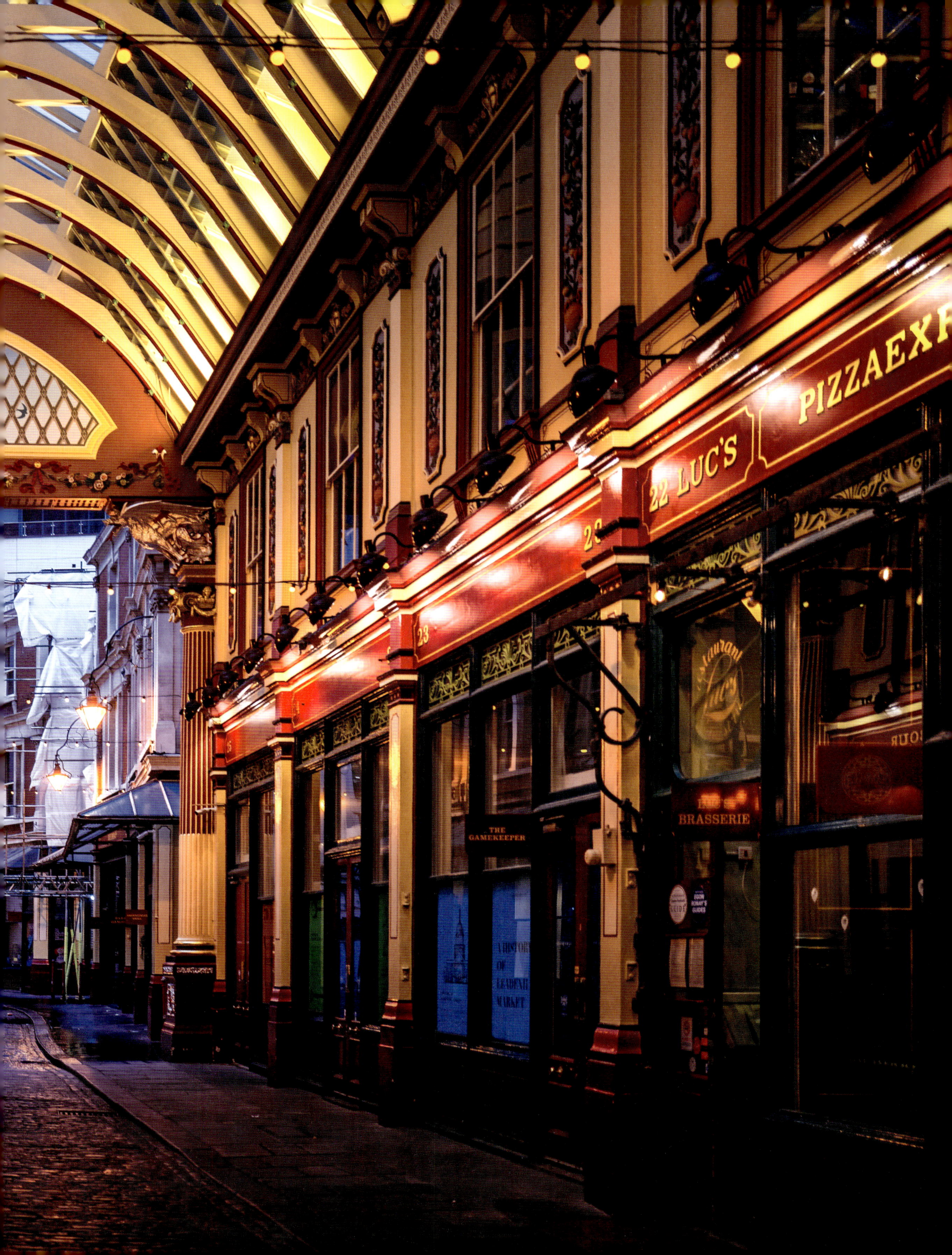
22 LUC'S
23
THE GAMEKEEPER
BRASSERIE

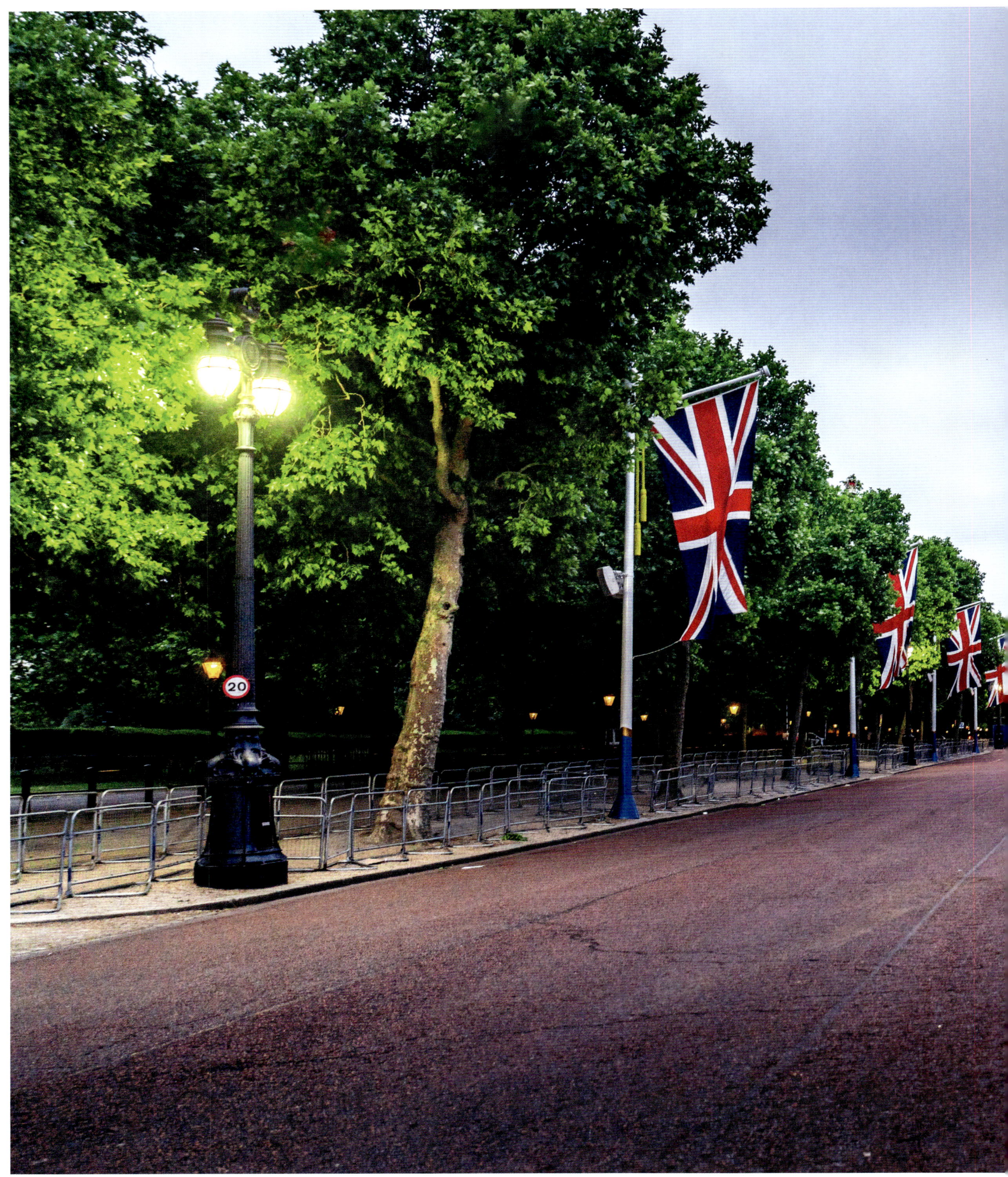
20

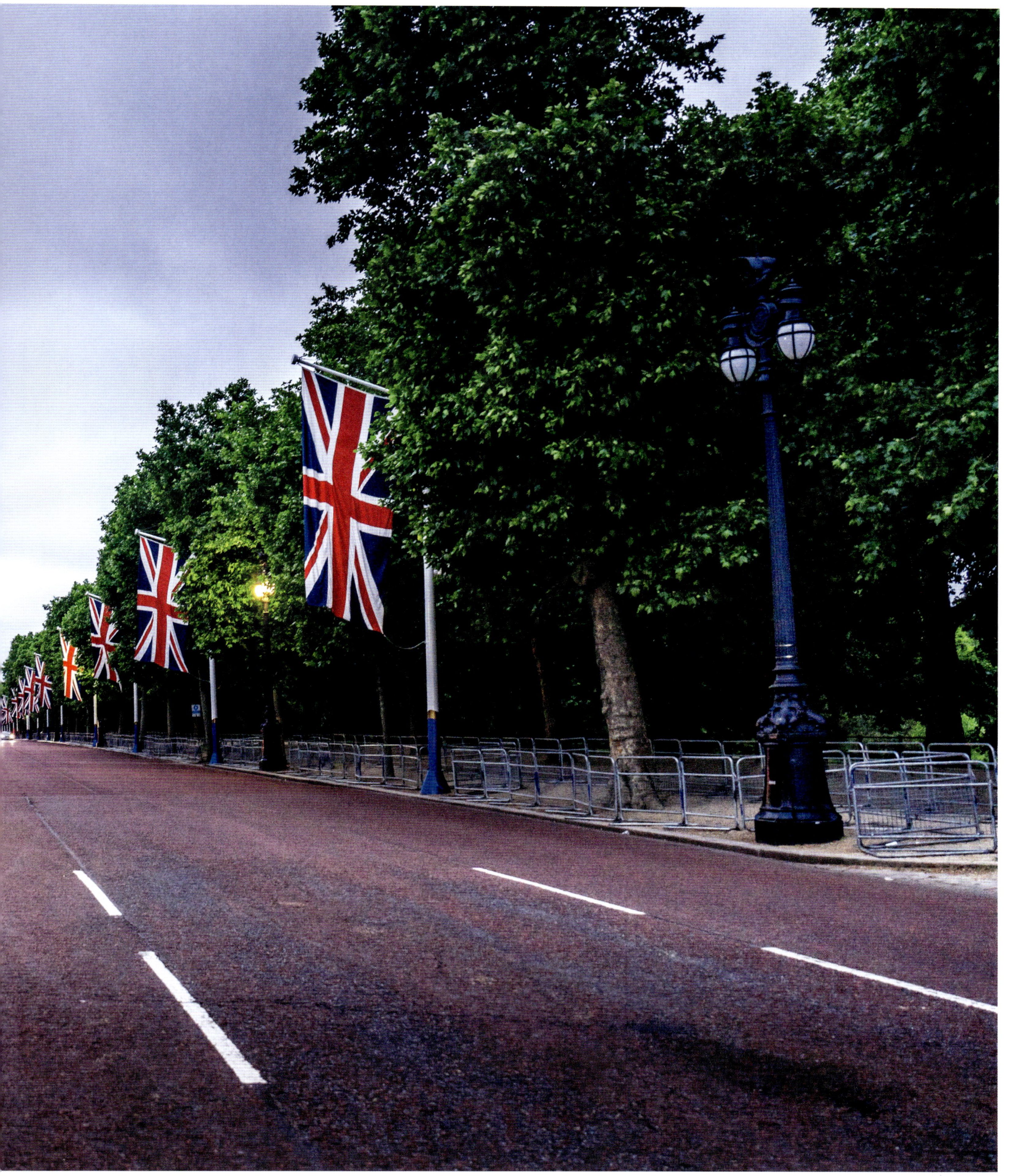

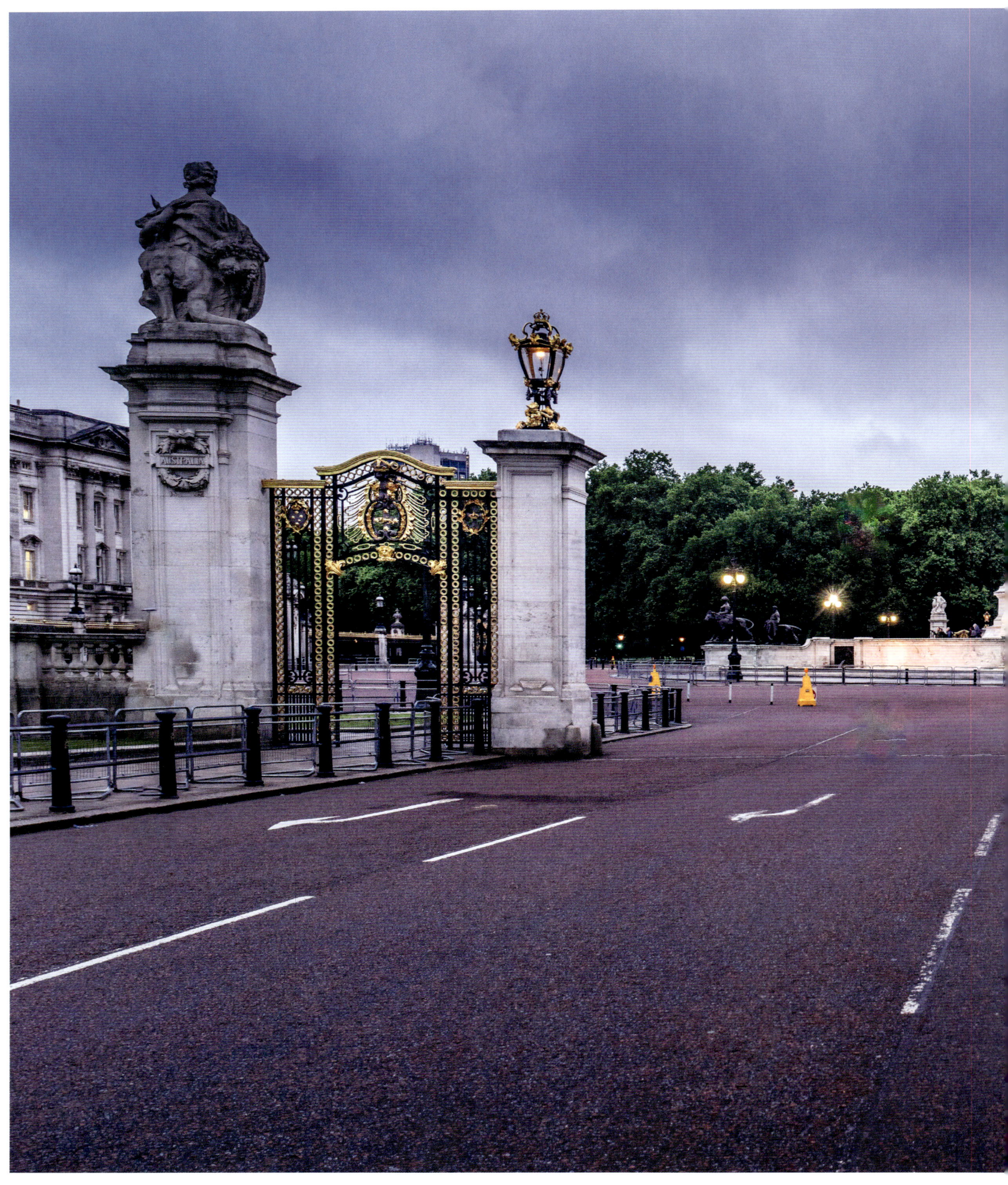

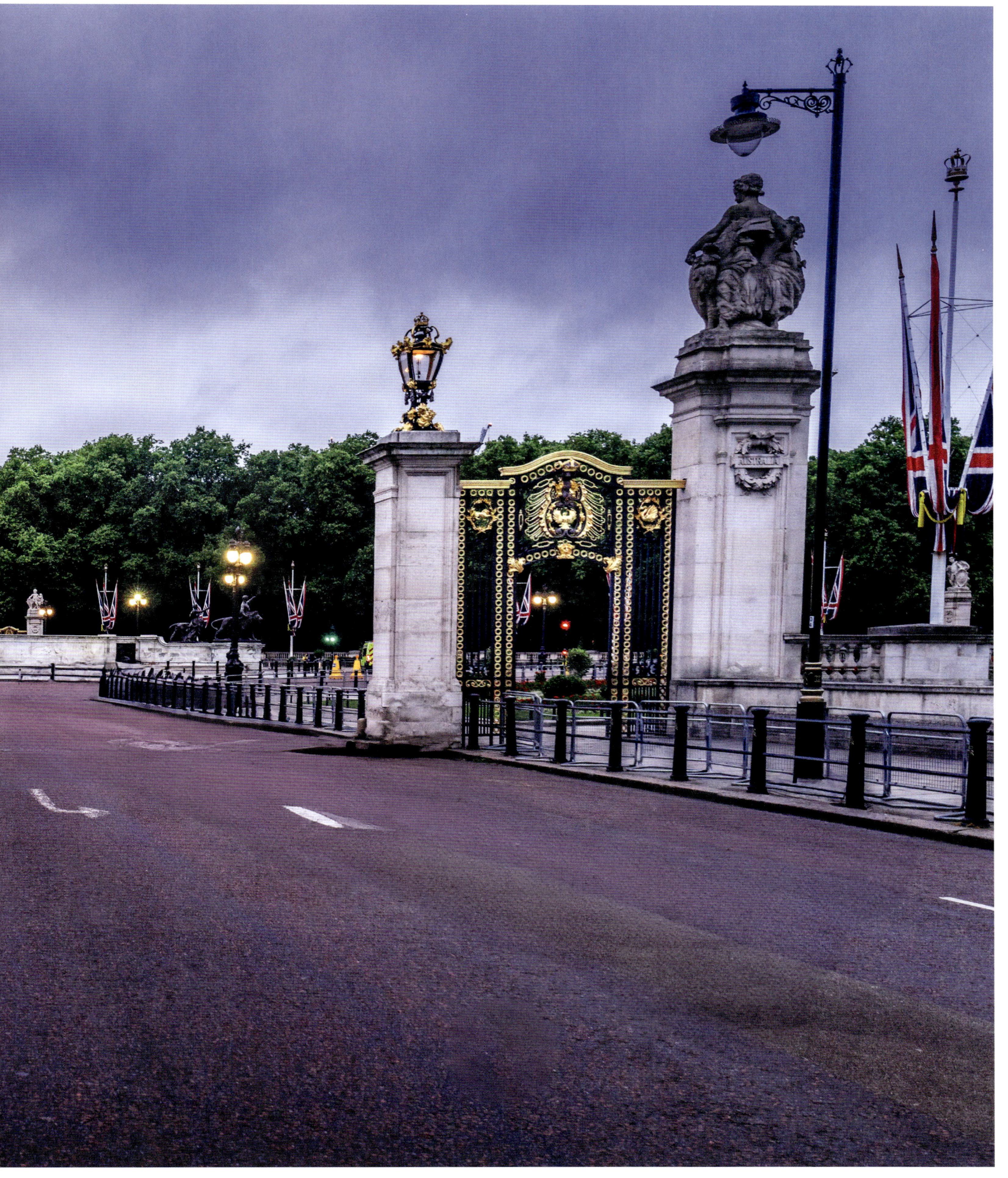

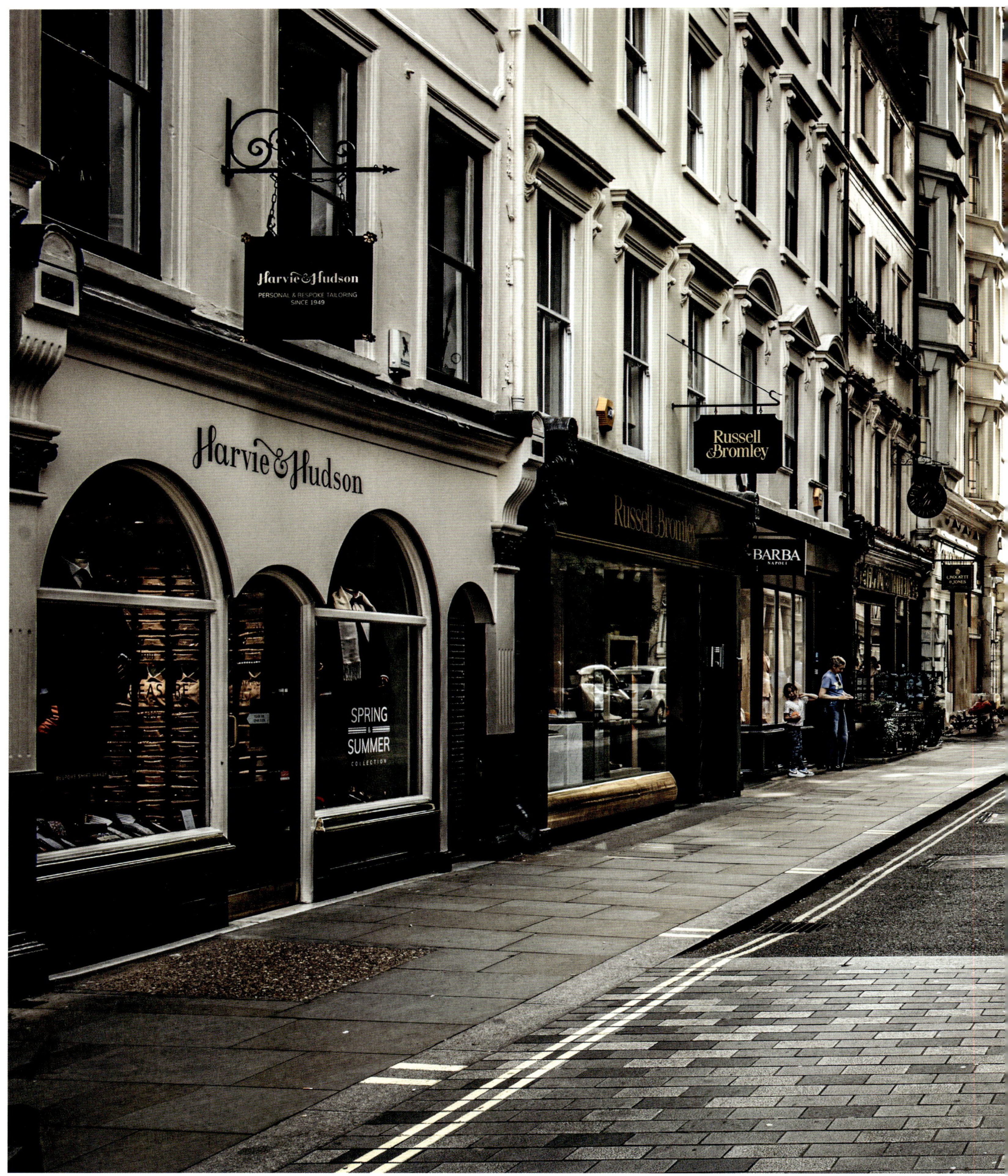
Harvie & Hudson
PERSONAL & RESPOKE TAILORING
SINCE 1949
Harvie & Hudson
Russell & Bromley
Russell Bromley
BARBA
SPRING & SUMMER
COLLECTION

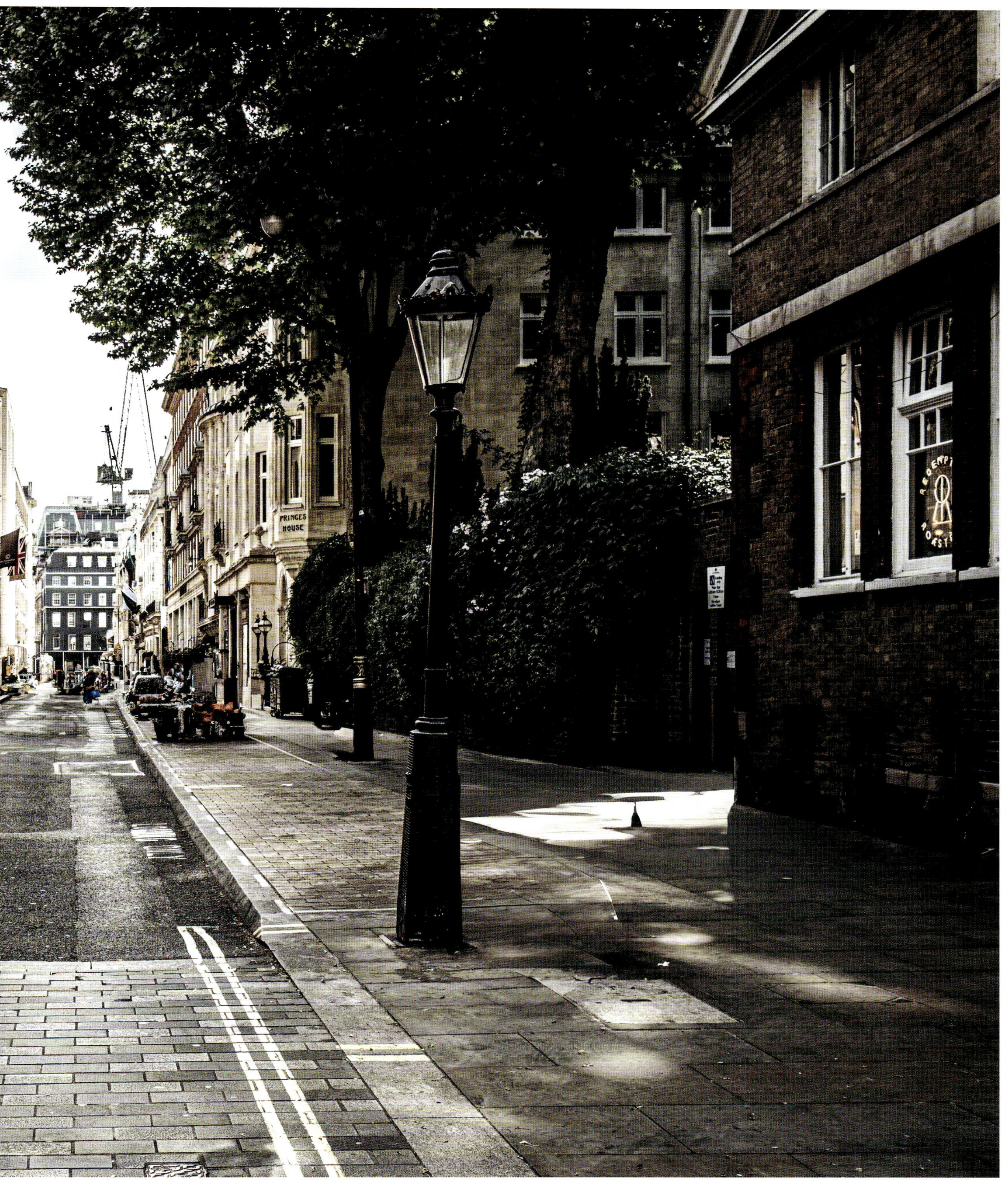
PRINCES
HOUSE

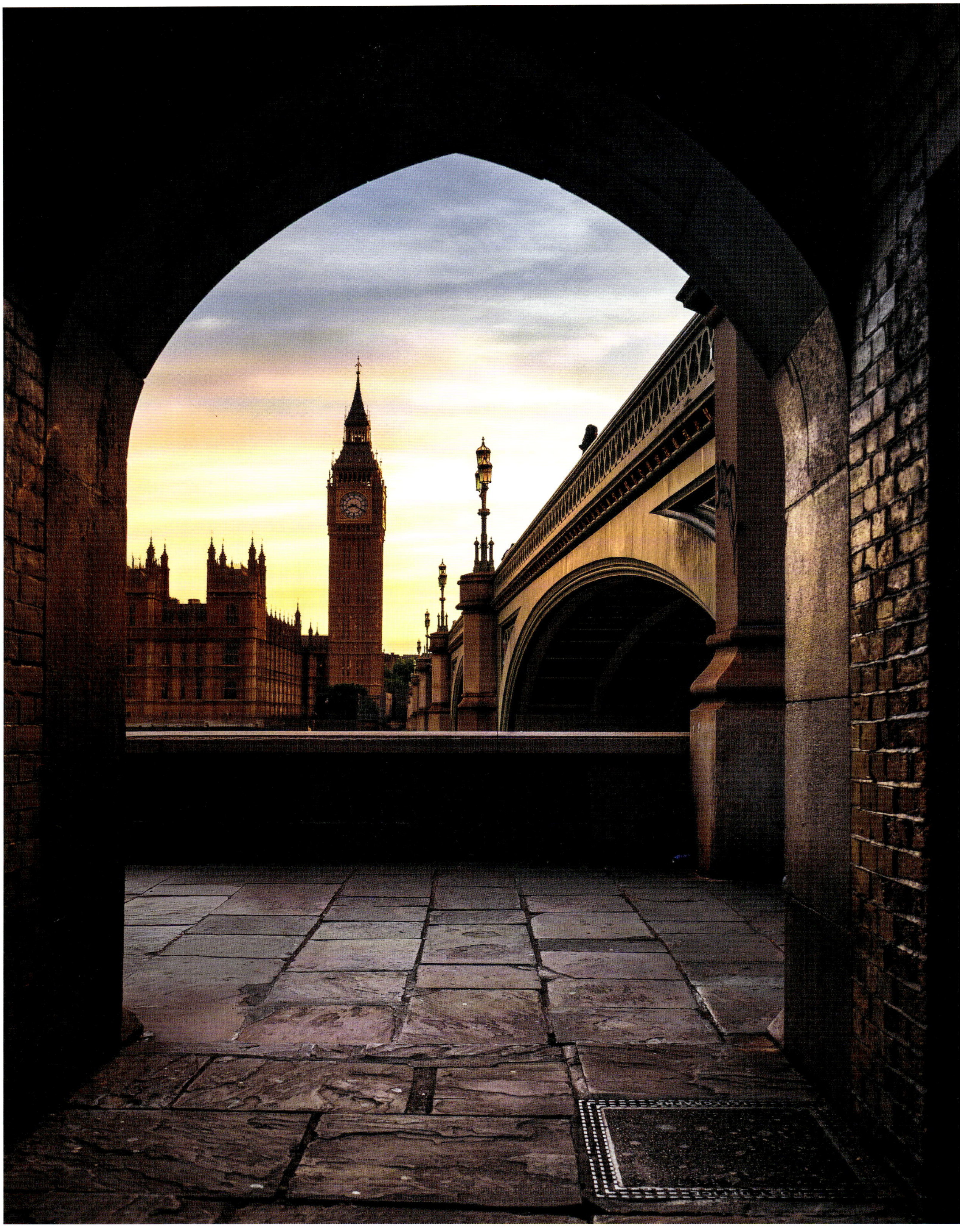

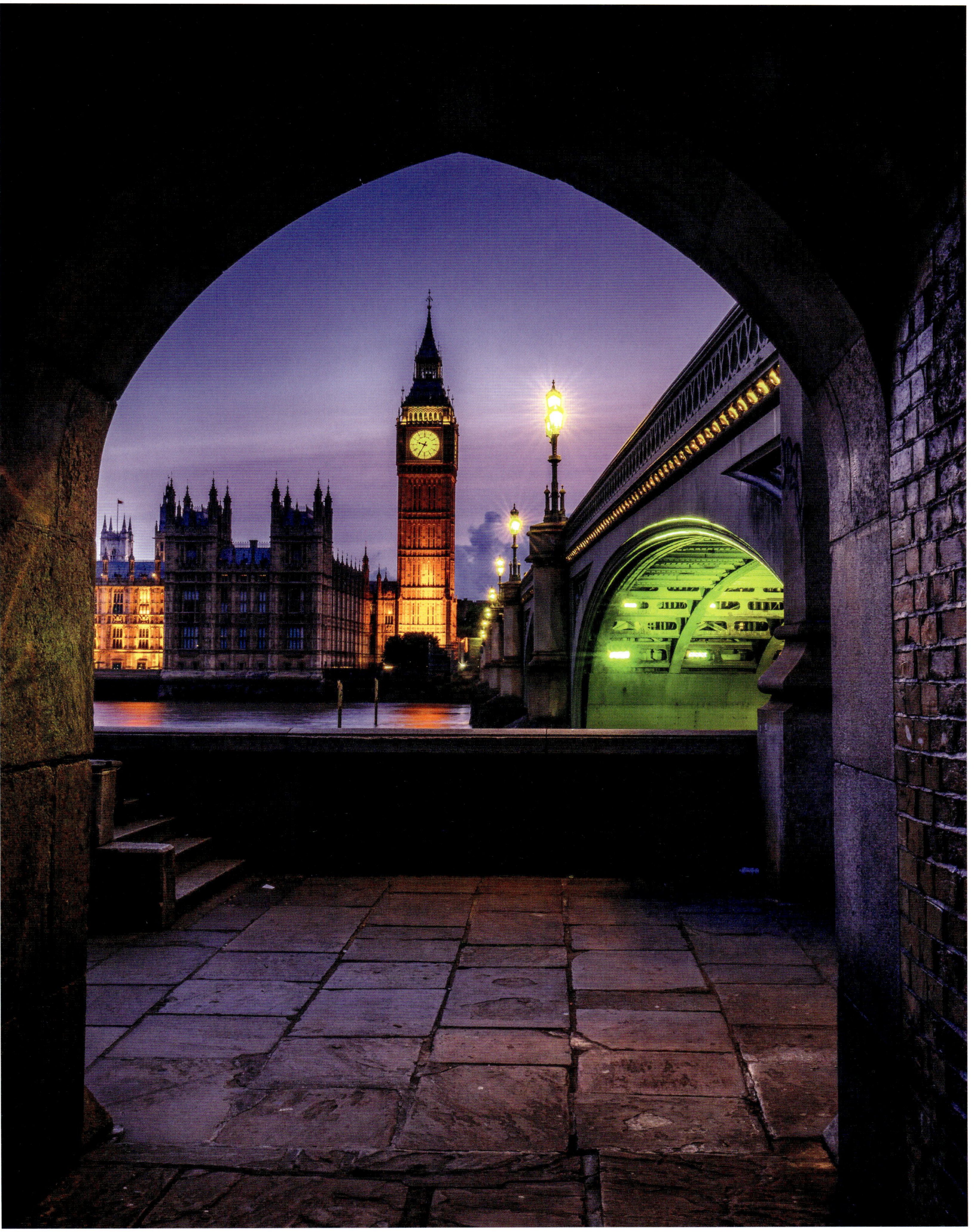

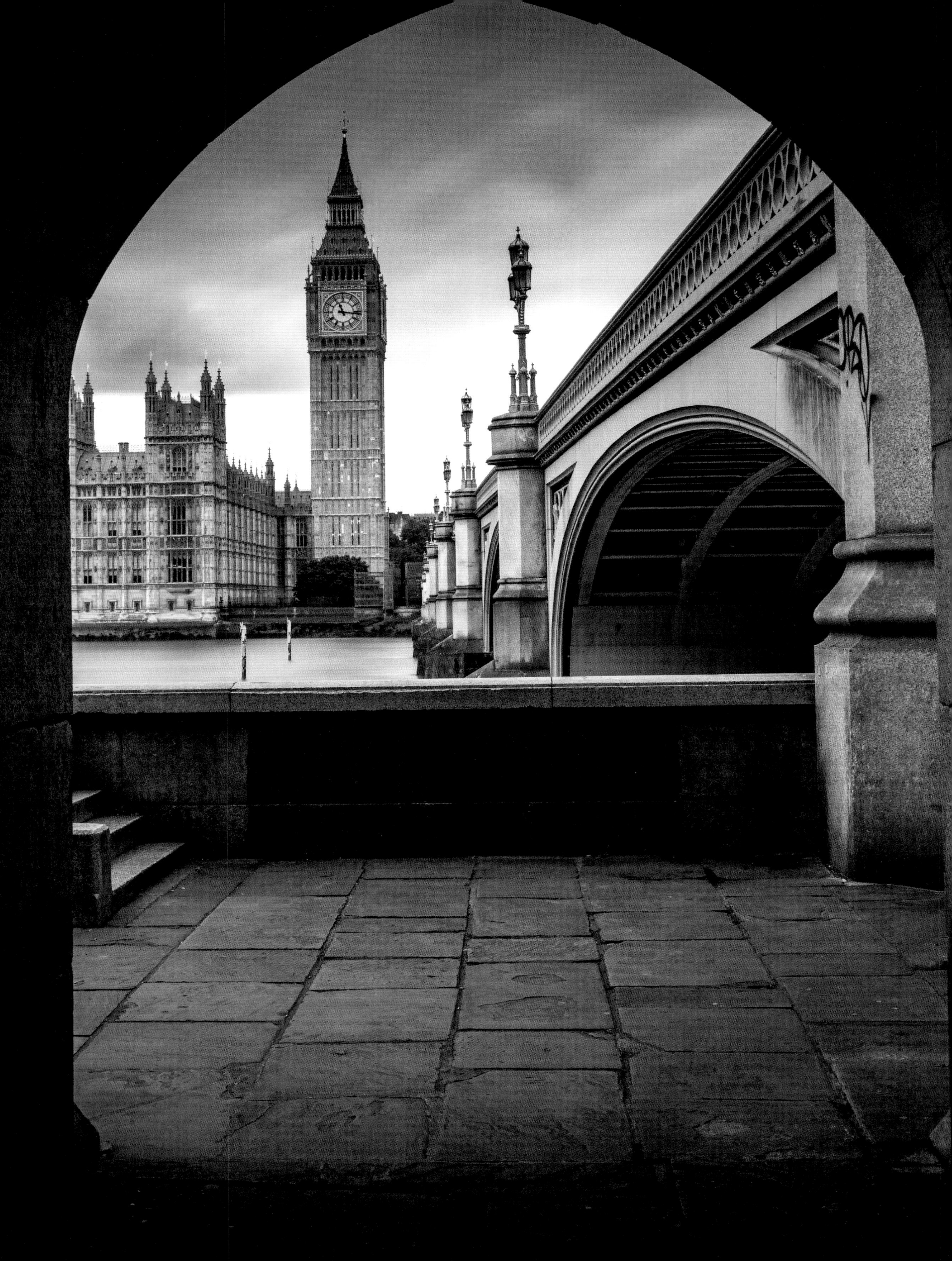

Pages 68–69: The Mall, lined with Union Jack flags and trees, serves as a grand ceremonial route toward Buckingham Palace for national celebrations and royal events. Its red asphalt symbolizes a red carpet.

Previous pages and opposite: The Elizabeth Tower (with its famous bell, Big Ben), Parliament, and Westminster Bridge, captured through an archway at different times of day.

Seiten 68–69: The Mall, gesäumt von Union-Jack-Flaggen und Bäumen, fungiert bei nationalen Feierlichkeiten und royalen Ereignissen als Paradestrecke zum Buckingham Palace. Der rote Asphalt symbolisiert einen roten Teppich.

Vorherige und diese Seite: Der Elizabeth Tower (mit seiner berühmten Glocke „Big Ben"), das Parlament und Westminster Bridge fotografiert durch einen Torbogen zu unterschiedlichen Tageszeiten.

Pages 68–69 : Bordé d'arbres et de drapeaux britanniques, le « Mall » est une longue allée d'apparat empruntée par les cortèges officiels et royaux se rendant au palais de Buckingham. Son revêtement en asphalte de couleur tient lieu de tapis rouge.

Cette page et la précédente : Elizabeth Tower et sa célèbre cloche « Big Ben », le Parlement et le pont de Westminster capturés à travers une arcade à différentes heures de la journée.

A classic red telephone booth stands on a London street at dusk, with the iconic Big Ben visible in the distance. Today, traditional phone booths are rarely used to make calls; most have been repurposed as tiny libraries, defibrillator stations, or for other creative uses.

Eine traditionelle rote Telefonzelle im Dämmerlicht, im Hintergrund ist „Big Ben" zu sehen. Diese ikonischen Kästen werden heutzutage kaum noch zum Telefonieren benutzt, sondern wurden u. a. zu Mini-Bibliotheken und Defibrillator-Stationen umfunktioniert.

La fameuse cabine téléphonique rouge dans la lumière du crépuscule, avec l'emblématique « Big Ben » visible dans le lointain. De nos jours, on ne passe plus guère d'appels de ces cabines, la plupart ayant été transformées en boîtes à lire, dépôts de défibrillateur ou pour d'autres usages encore.

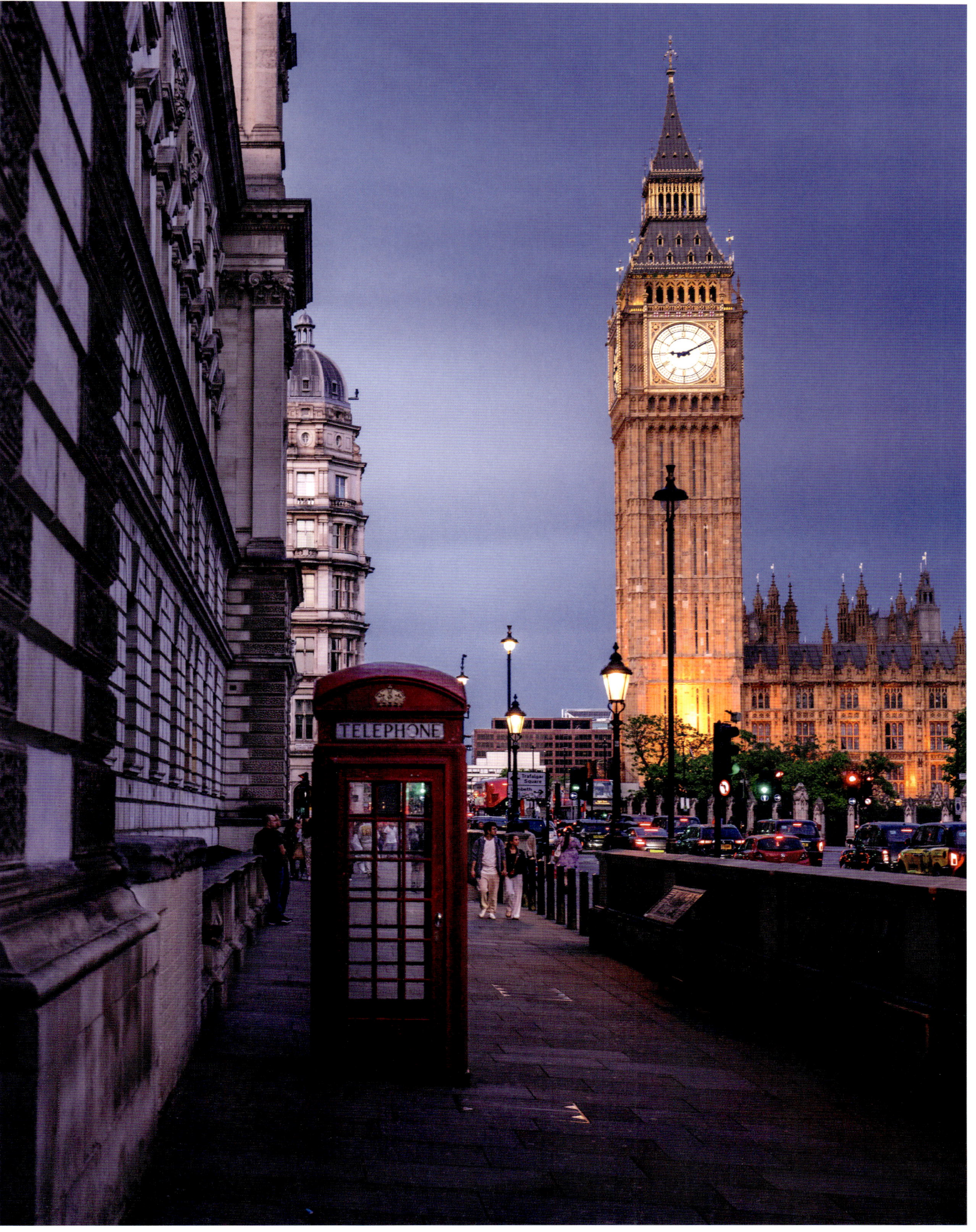
TELEPHONE

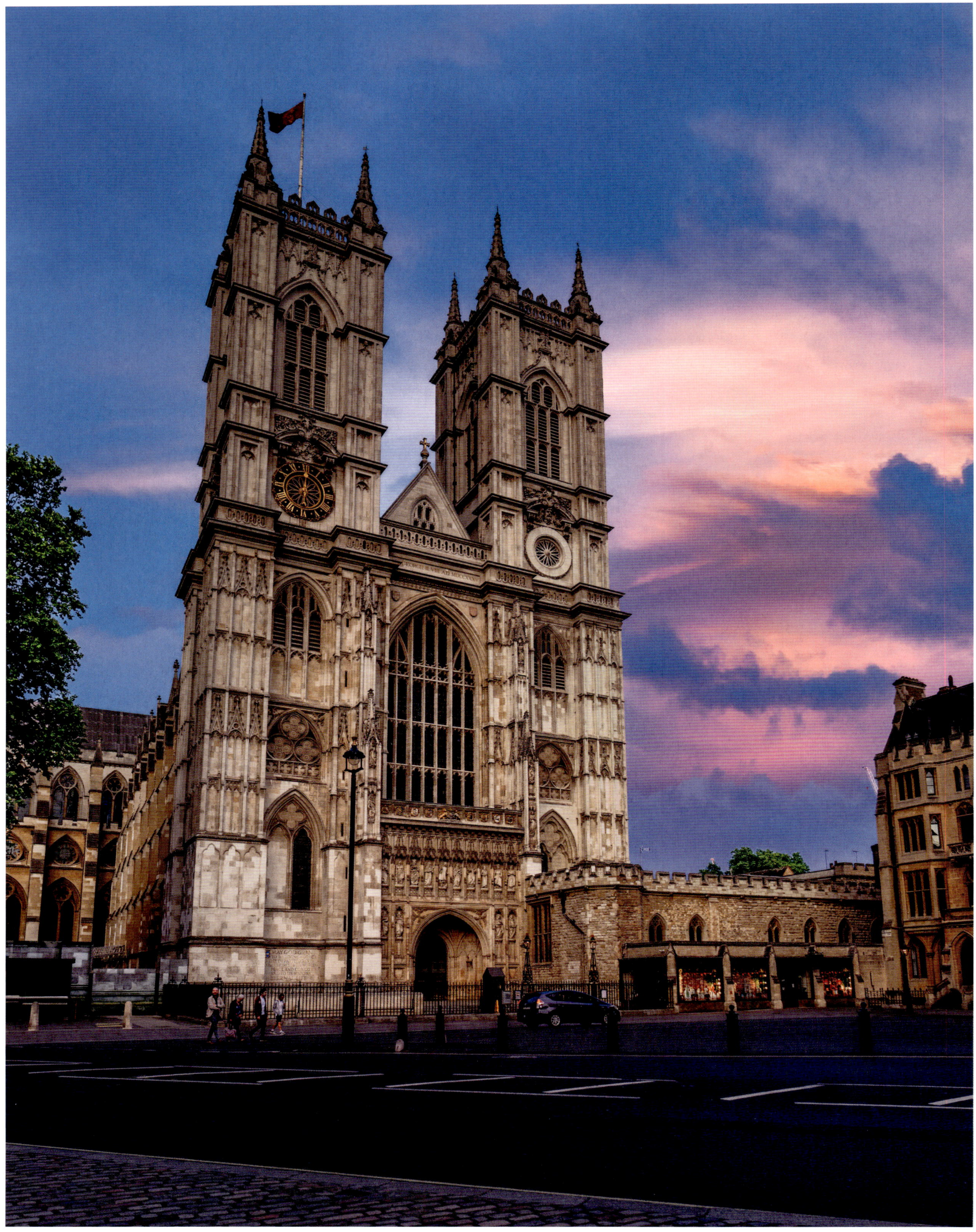

The grand Westminster Abbey under a colorful evening sky. The Anglican church, a UNESCO World Heritage Site, has been the setting of coronations, royal weddings, and burials for nearly a thousand years.

Die imposante Westminster Abbey vor einem farbenprächtigen Abendhimmel. Die anglikanische Kirche ist ein UNESCO-Weltkulturerbe, an deren Standort seit fast 1000 Jahren Krönungen, royale Hochzeiten und Begräbnisse stattfinden.

La majestueuse abbaye de Westminster se détachant sur les couleurs du crépuscule. Cette église anglicane est classée patrimoine culturel mondial de l'Unesco. Depuis bientôt mille ans, couronnements, mariages et obsèques de membres de la famille royale y sont célébrés.

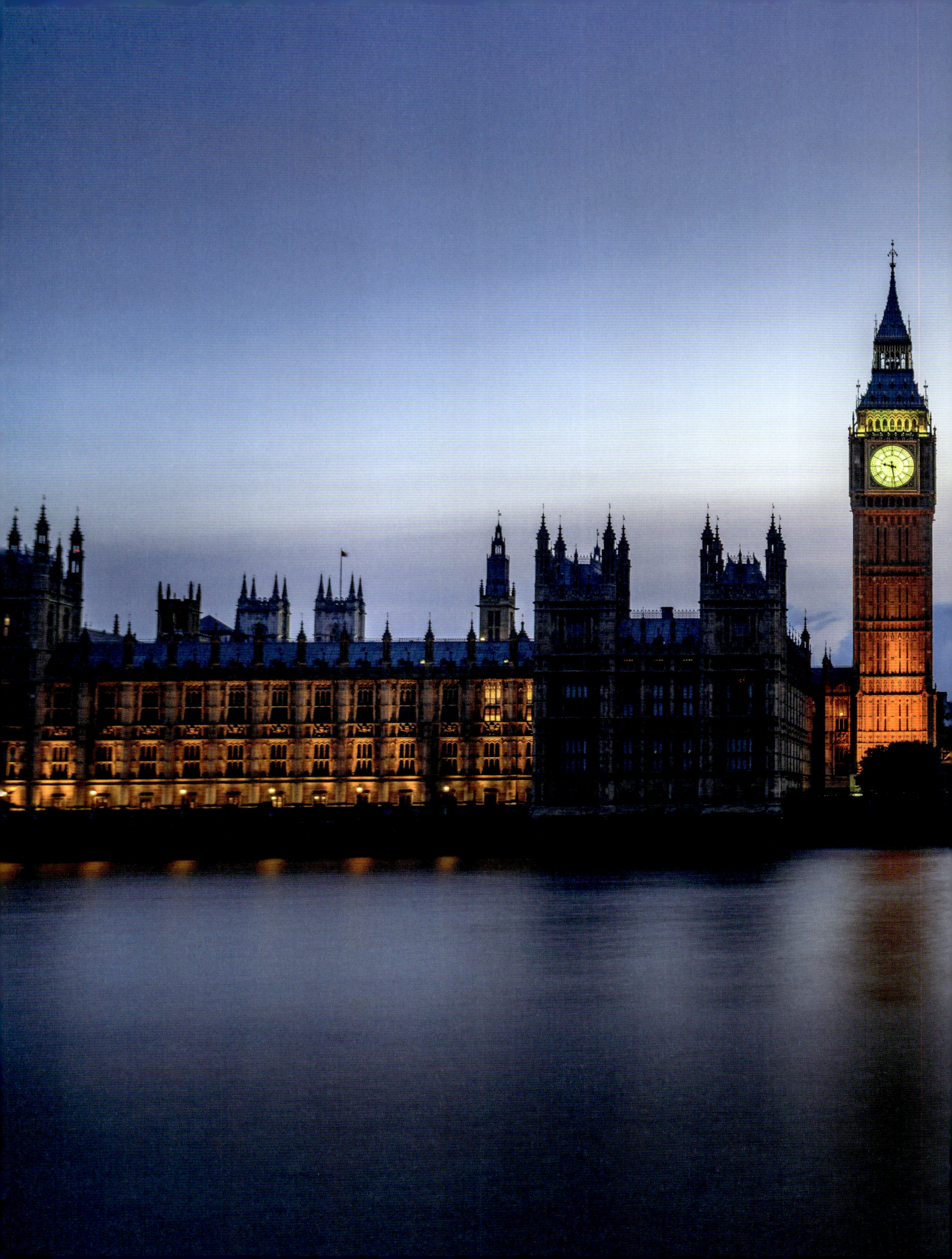

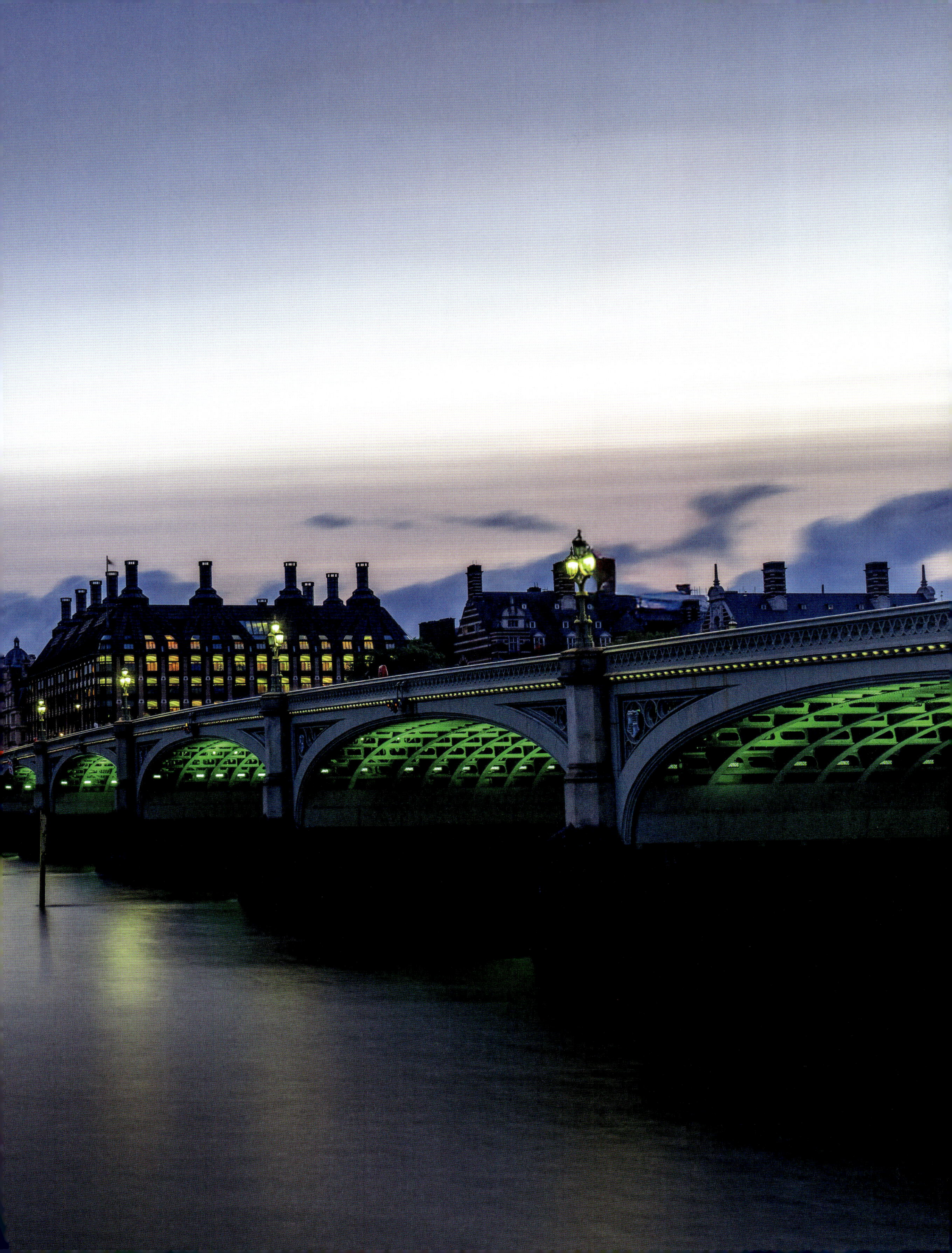

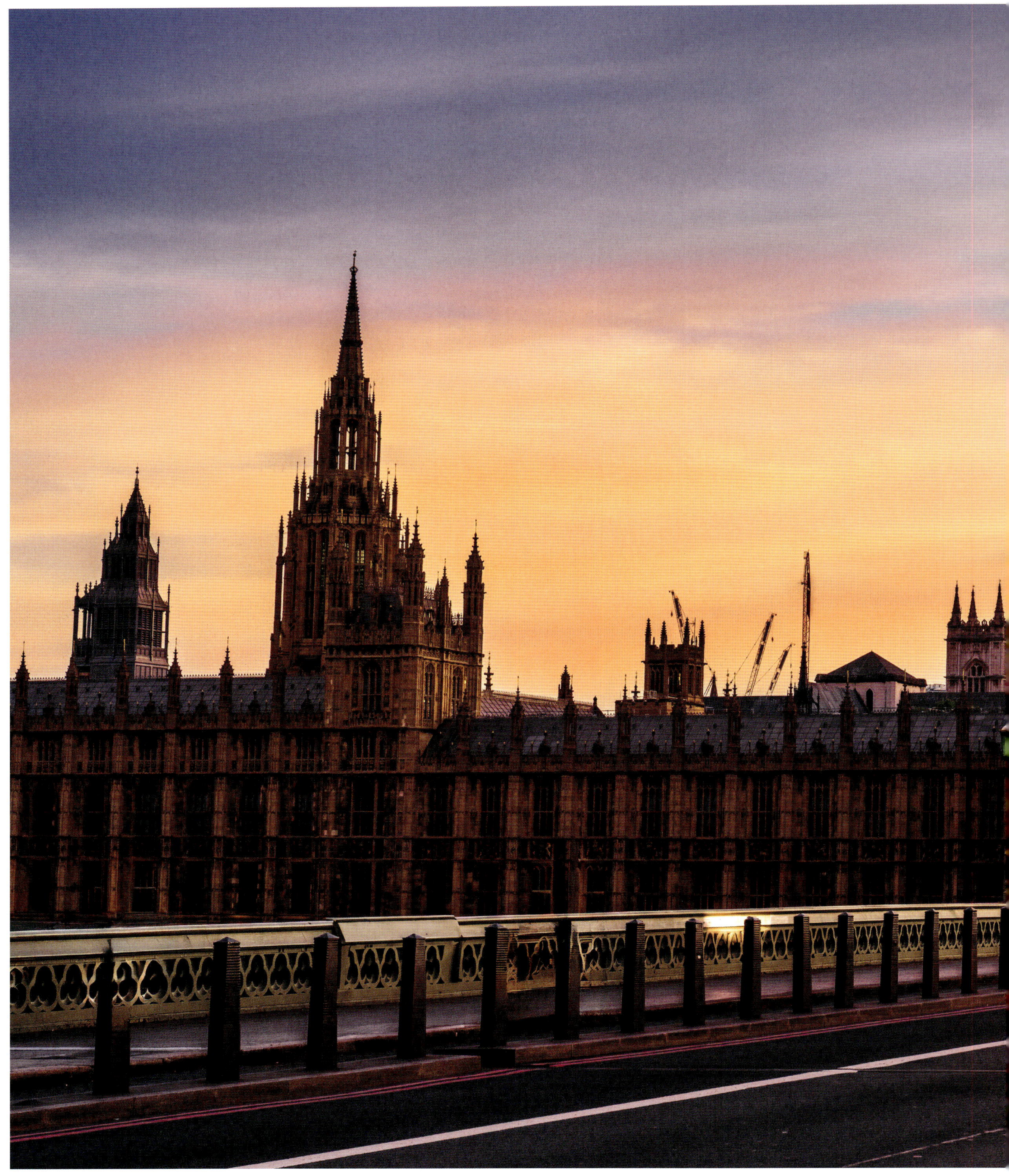

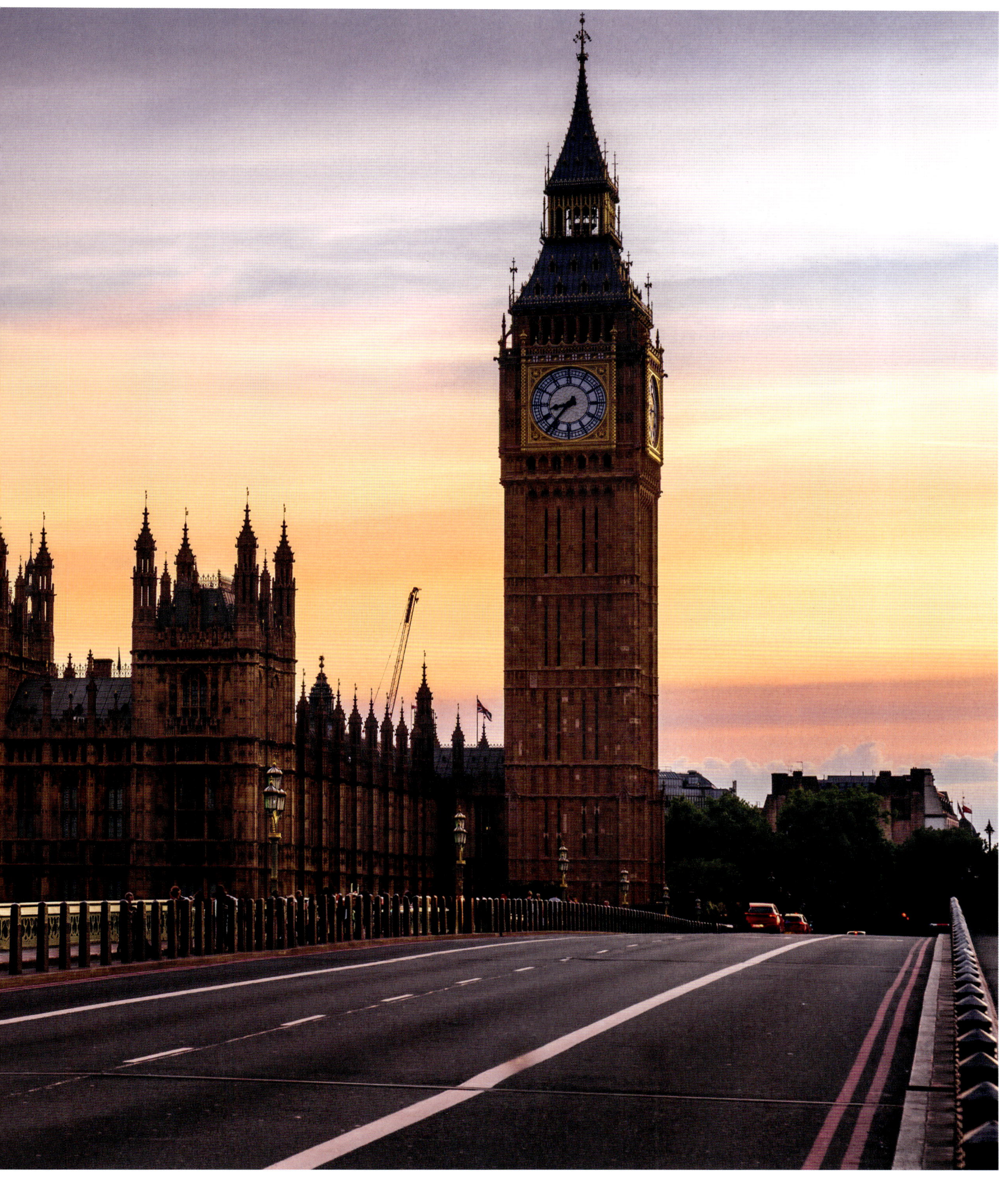

The bronze statue of former British prime minister Winston Churchill in Parliament Square at sunset, with the Elizabeth Tower—formerly known as the *Clock Tower*—in the background.

Die Bronzestatue des ehemaligen britischen Premierministers Winston Churchill am Parliament Square bei Sonnenuntergang. Im Hintergrund zu sehen: der Elizabeth Tower (der ursprünglich *Clock Tower* hieß).

La statue en bronze de l'ancien Premier ministre britannique Winston Churchill dans Parliament Square au crépuscule, avec l'Elizabeth Tower, connue autrefois sous l'appellation « tour de l'horloge », à l'arrière-plan.

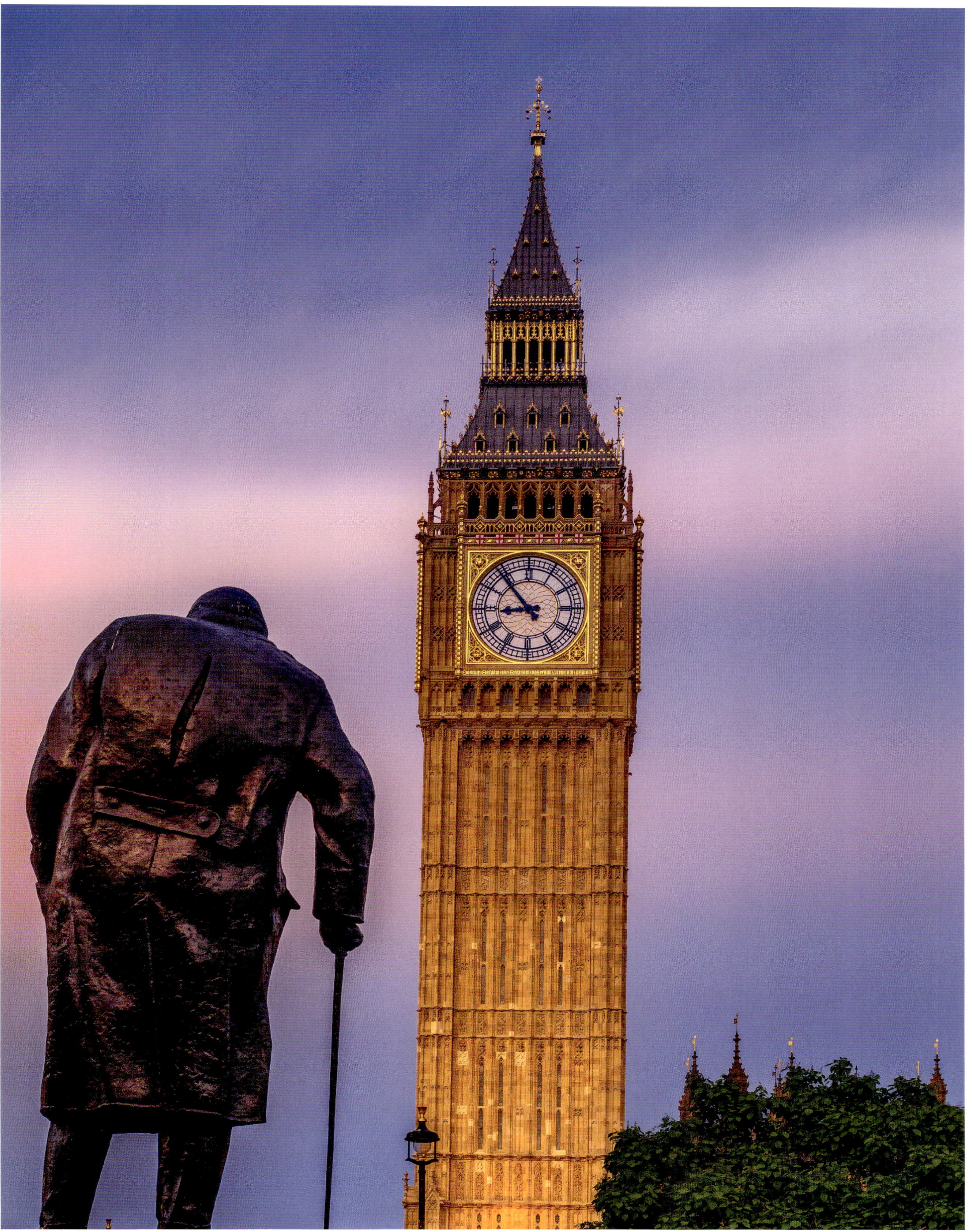

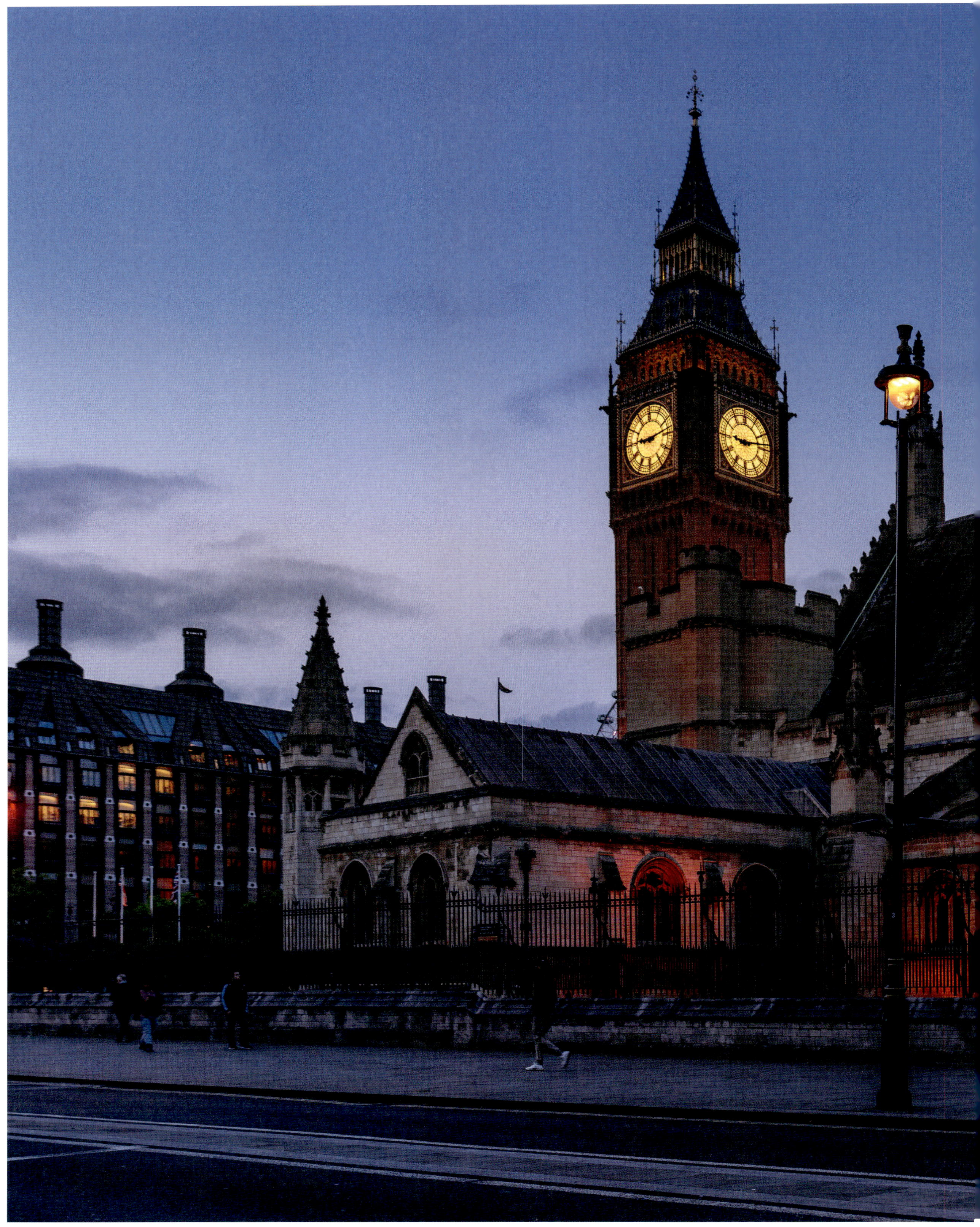

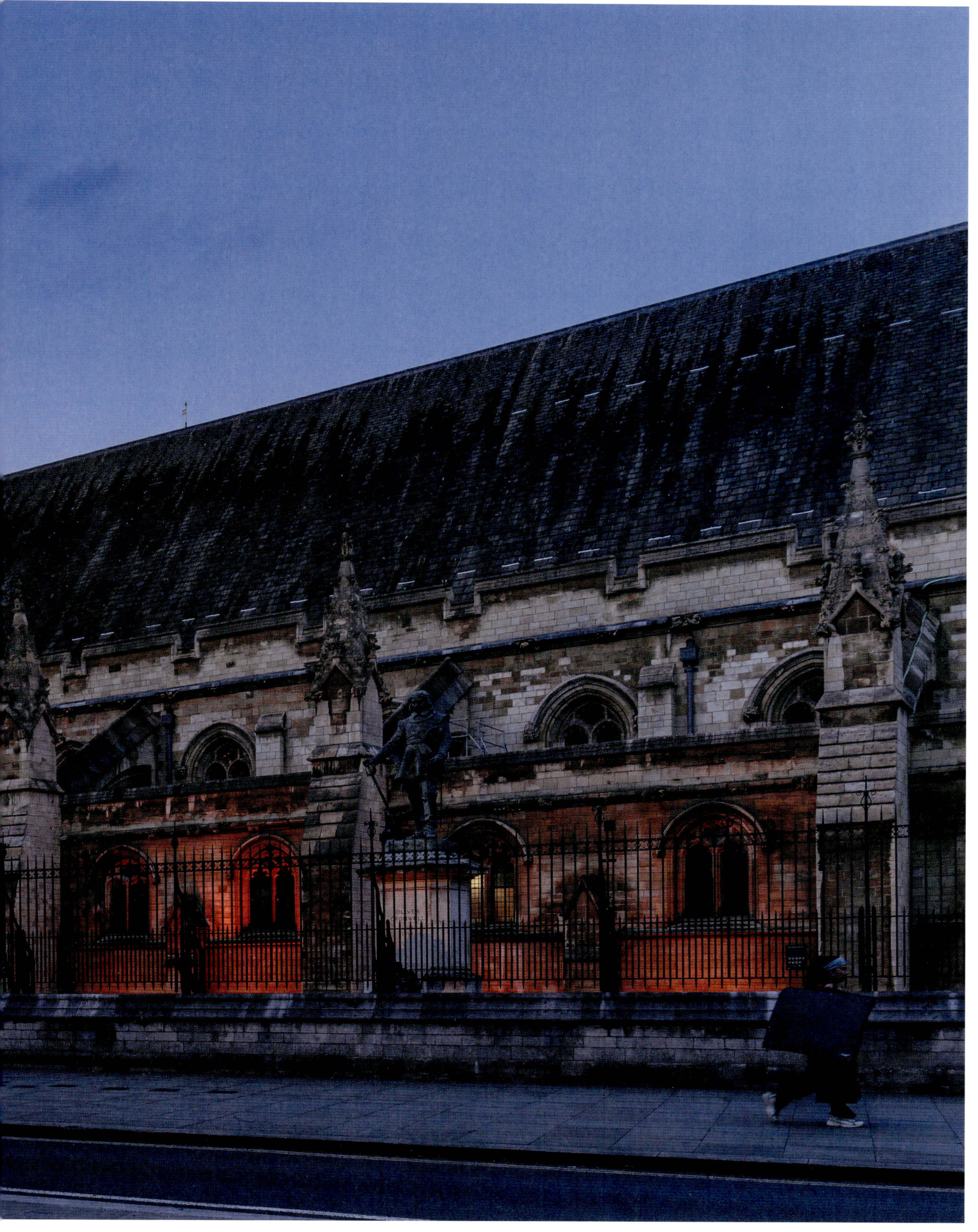

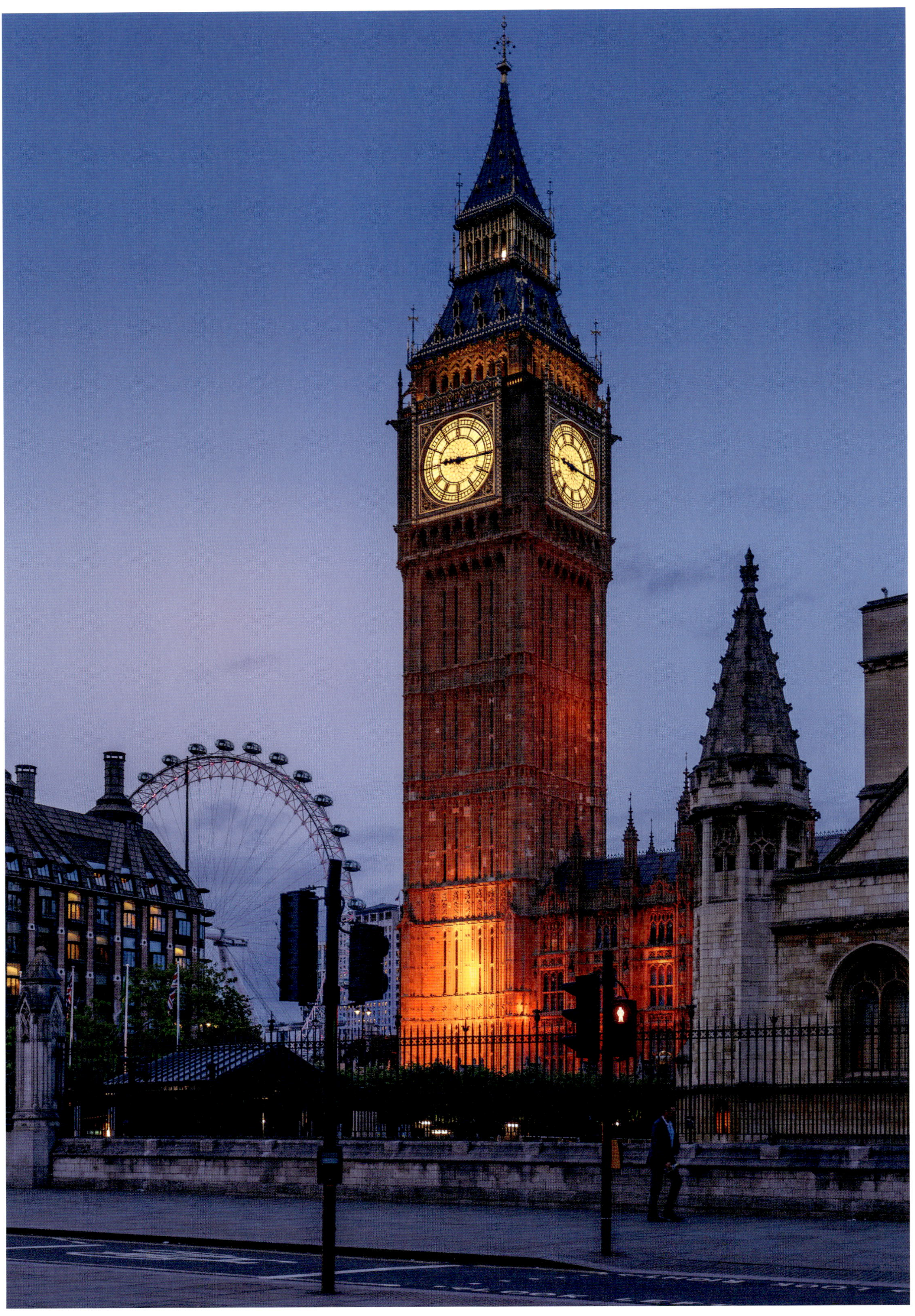

The Elizabeth Tower with the London Eye in the background. Completed in 1859 and designed by Sir Charles Barry and Augustus Pugin, it stands 316 feet (96 meters) tall at the north end of the Palace of Westminster.

Der Elizabeth Tower mit dem London Eye im Hintergrund. Der von Sir Charles Barry und Augustus Pugin entworfene Uhrenturm wurde 1859 vollendet. Er ist 96 Meter hoch und steht am Nordende des Palace of Westminster.

La tour Élizabeth et le London Eye dans le lointain. Œuvre de sir Charles Barry et Augustus Pugin, la tour de l'horloge a été achevée en 1859. Elle culmine à une hauteur de 96 mètres, à l'extrémité nord du Palais de Westminster.

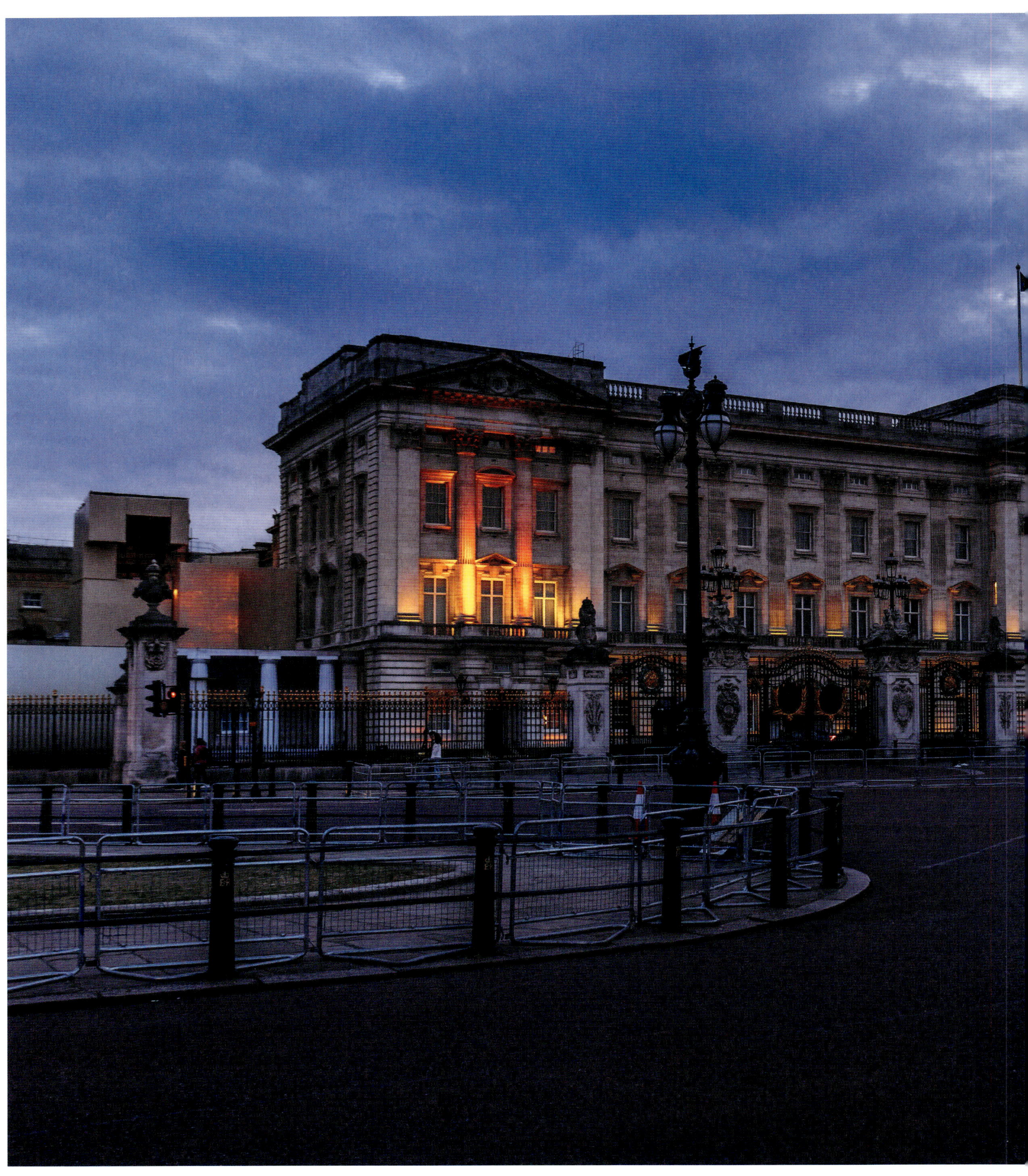

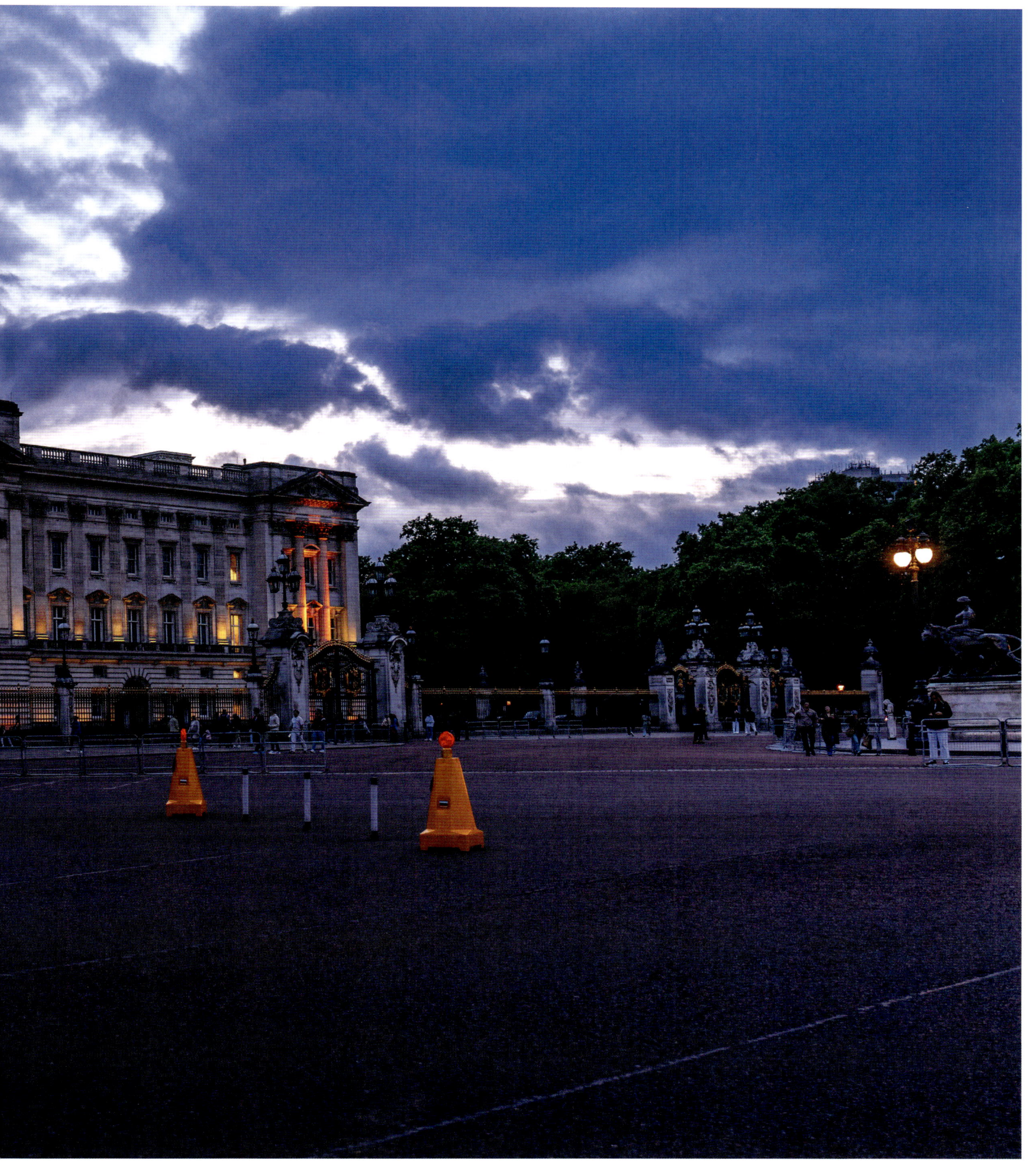

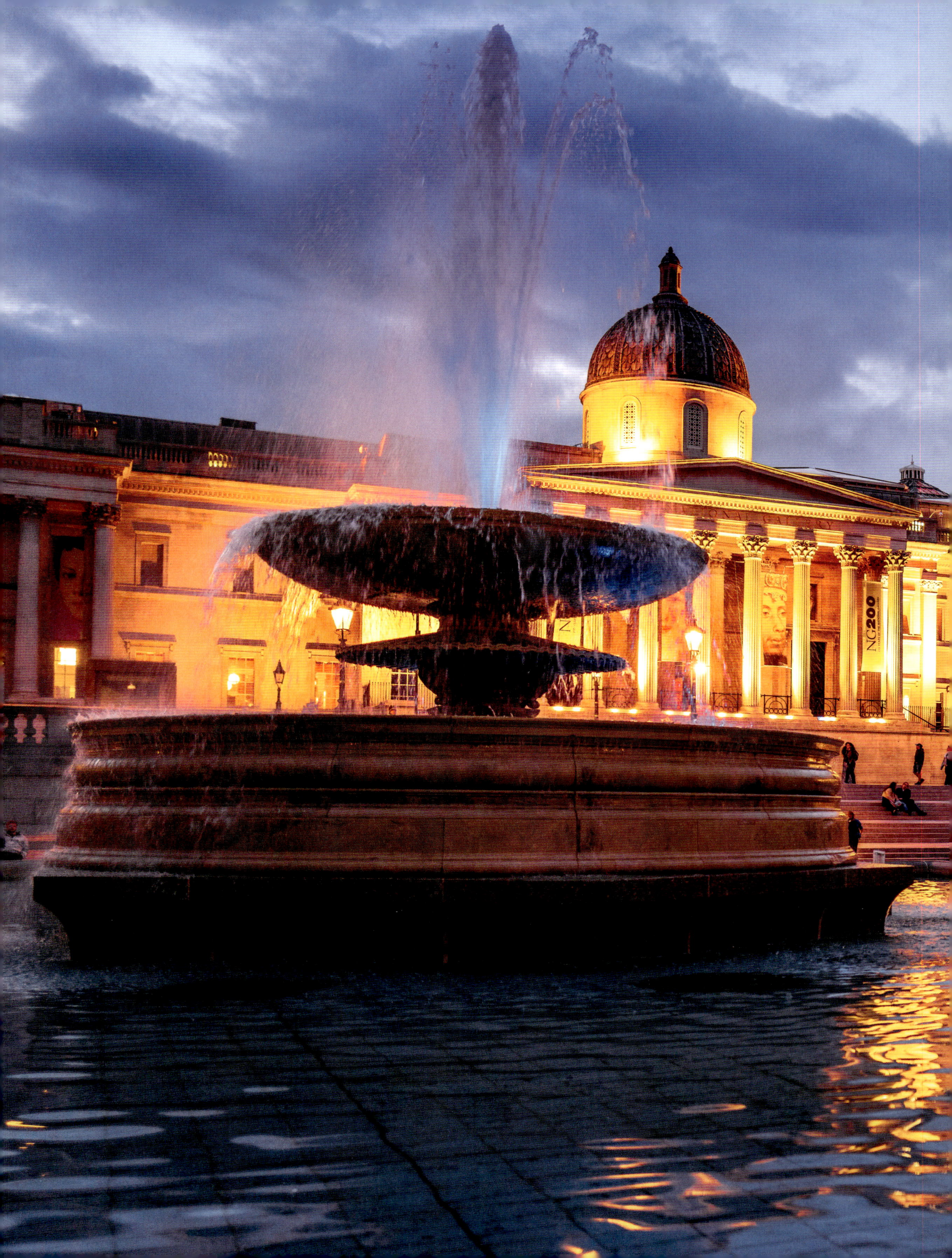
NG200

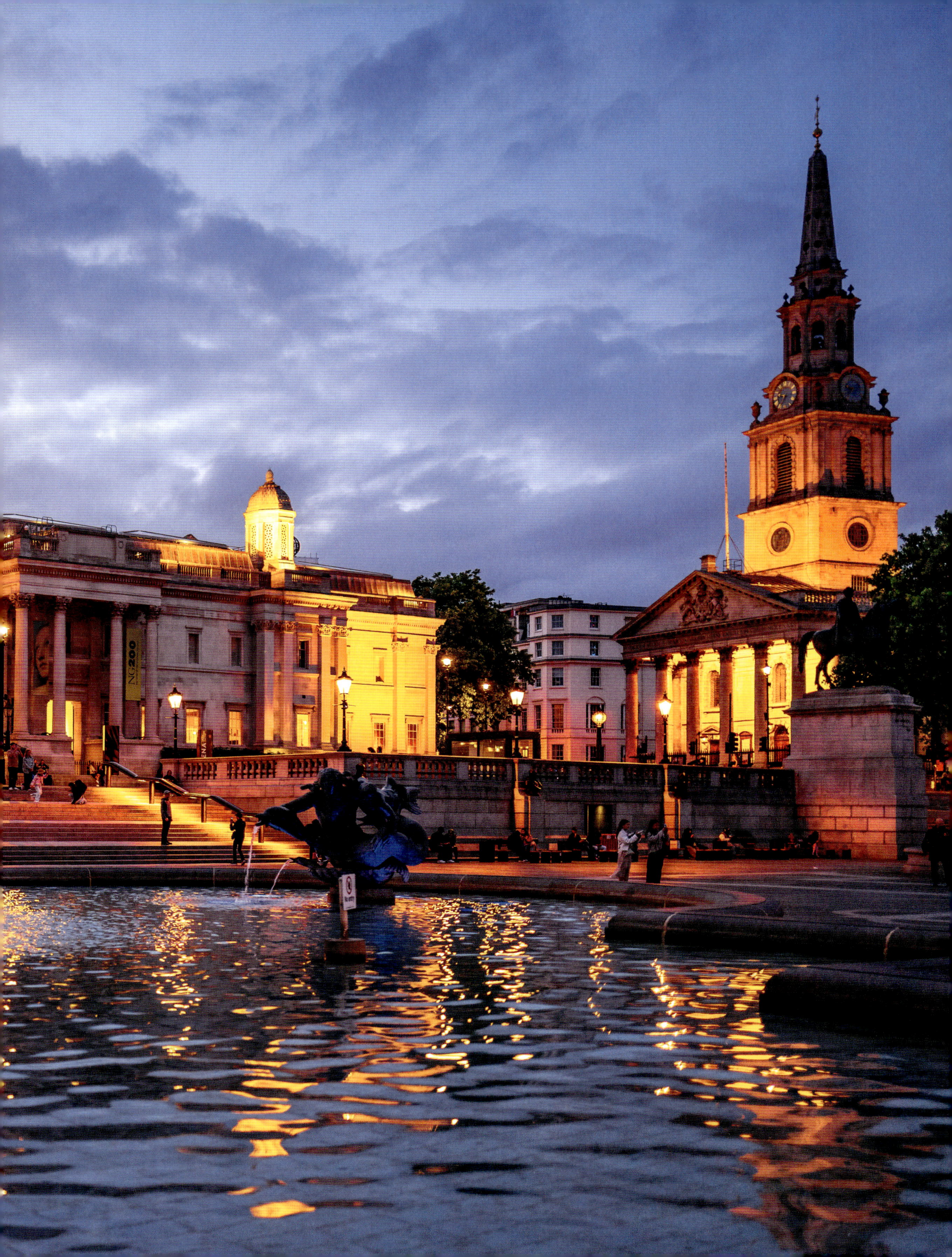

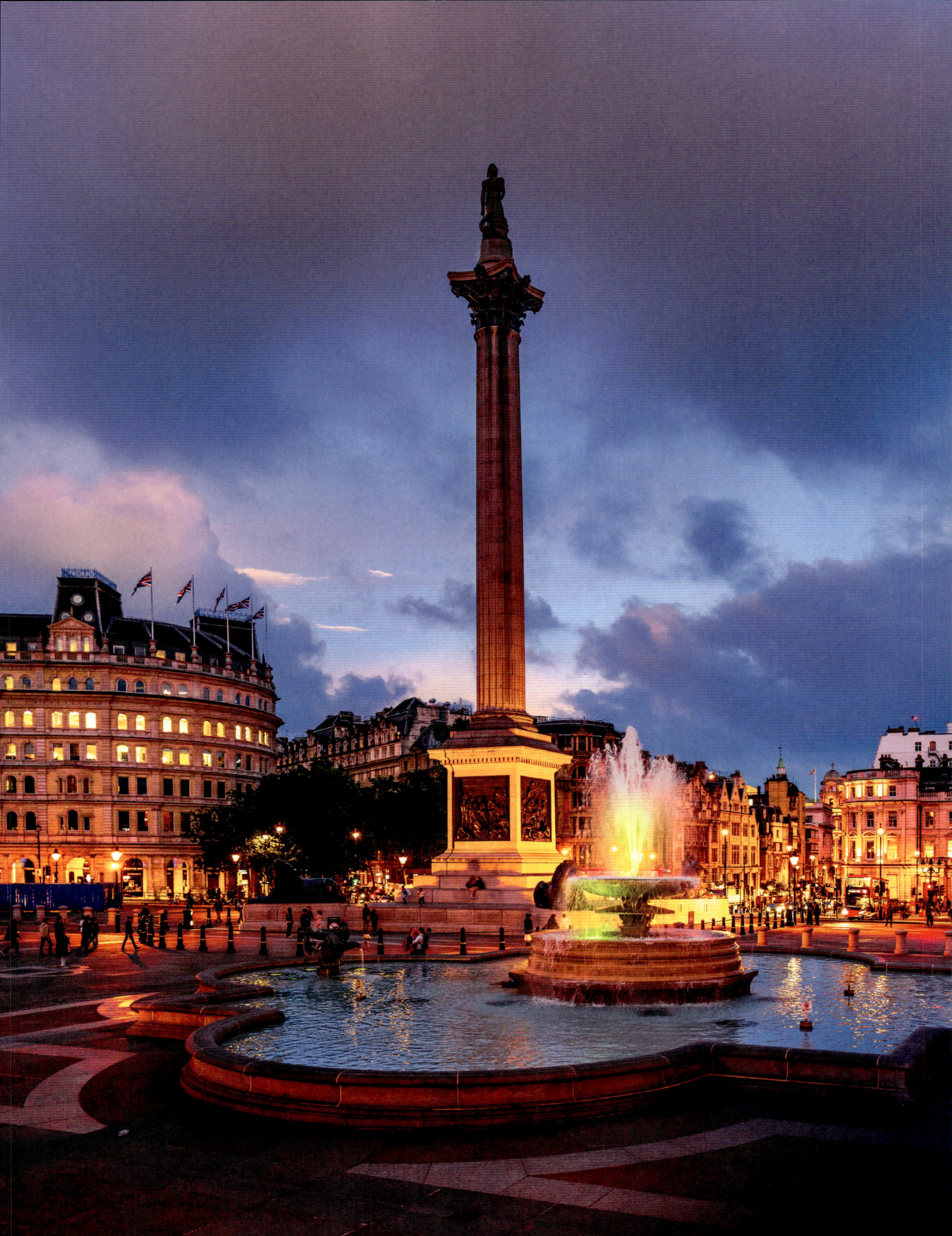

Previous pages and opposite: Trafalgar Square at twilight. London's largest public square, it is home to famous landmarks such as the National Gallery and the 169-foot (52-meter) Nelson's Column.

Vorherige und diese Seite: Trafalgar Square im Dämmerlicht. Auf Londons größtem öffentlichen Platz stehen berühmte Wahrzeichen der Stadt wie die National Gallery und die 52 Meter hohe Nelson's Column.

Cette page et la précédente : Trafalgar Square au crépuscule. La plus grande place de Londres abrite des attractions célèbres comme la National Gallery et la colonne de Nelson haute de 52 mètres.

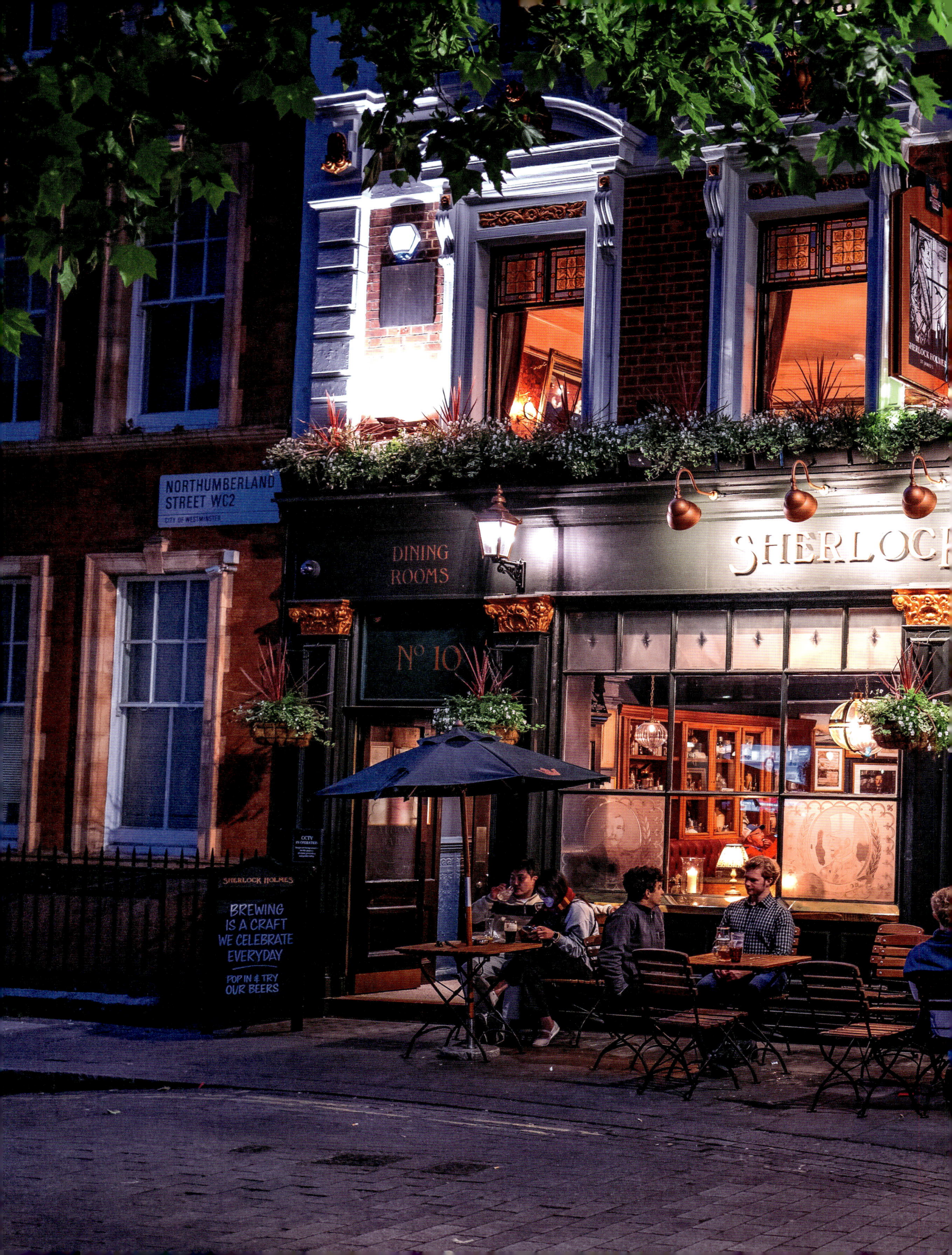
NORTHUMBERLAND
STREET WC2
CITY OF WESTMINSTER
DINING
ROOMS
Nº 10
SHERLOC
SHERLOCK HOLMES
BREWING
IS A CRAFT
WE CELEBRATE
EVERYDAY
POP IN & TRY
OUR BEERS

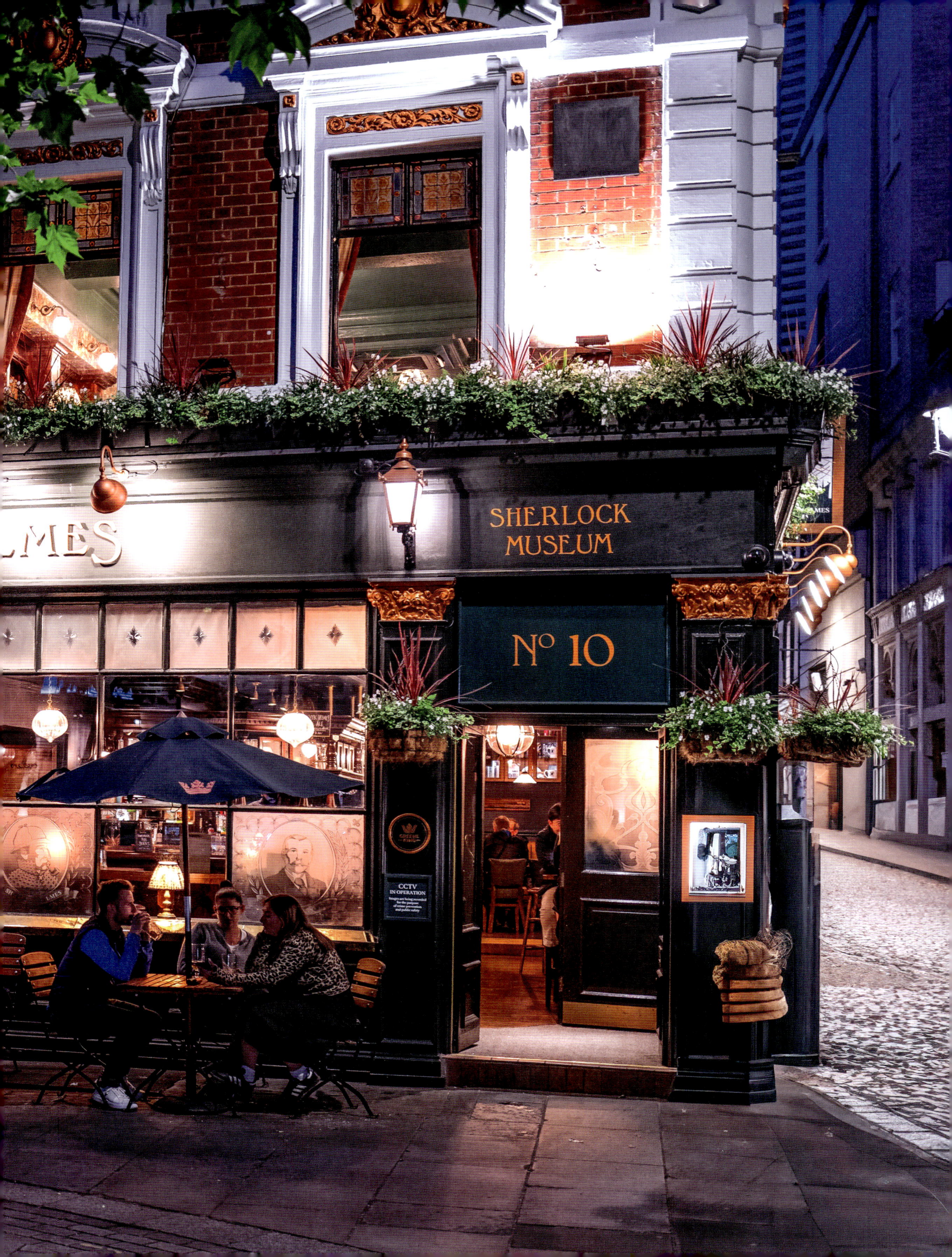
SHERLOCK
MUSEUM
Nº 10
CCTV
IN OPERATION

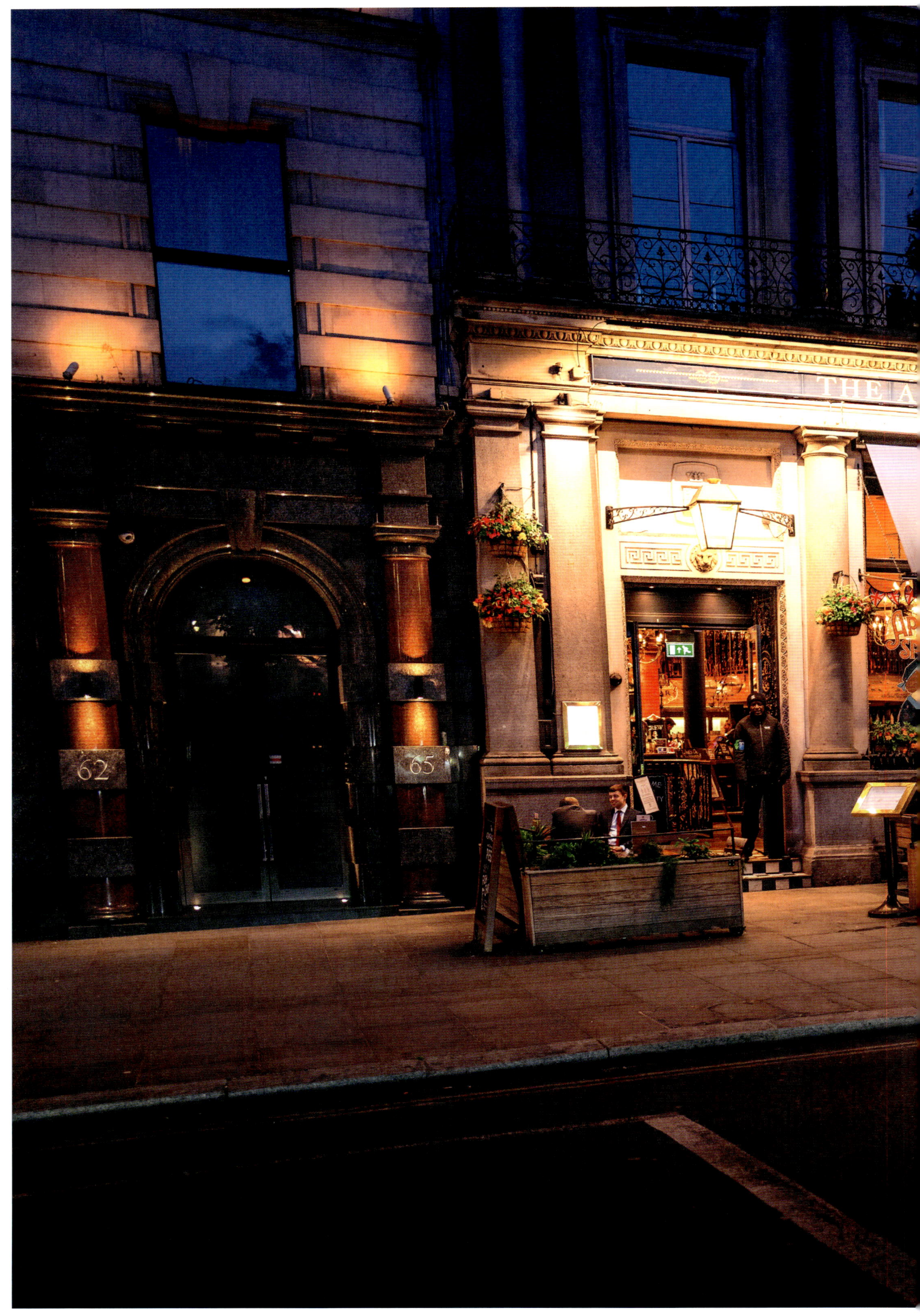
62
65

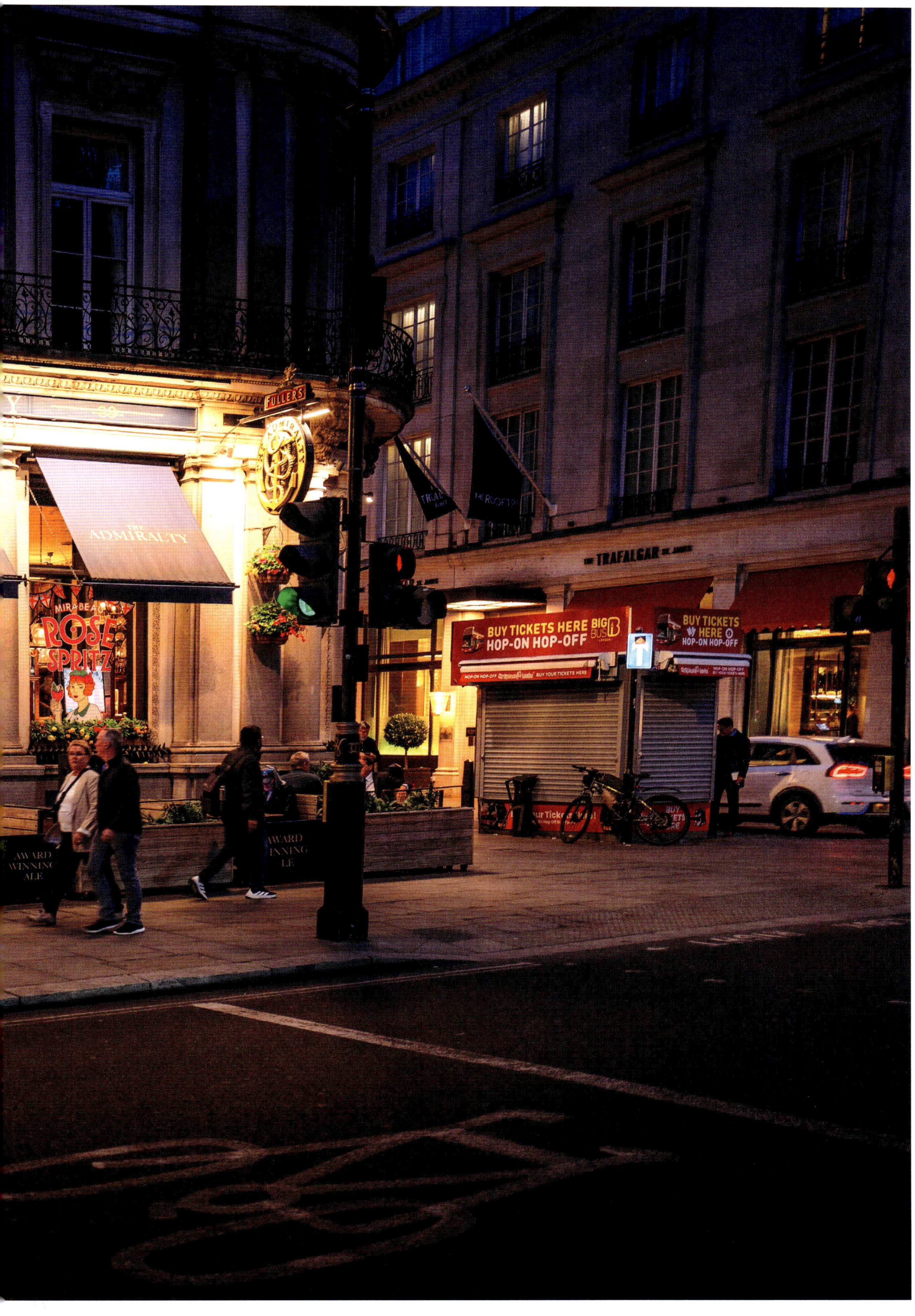
FULLER'S
THE ADMIRALTY
ROSE SPRITZ
THE TRAFALGAR
BUY TICKETS HERE
HOP-ON HOP-OFF
BUY TICKETS HERE
HOP-ON HOP-OFF

Previous pages: Pub culture is a big part of British society, and it's not just about drinking but about socializing.

Opposite and following pages: Trinity Square Gardens at Tower Hill at night.

Vorherige Seite: Pubs sind ein fester Bestandteil des kulturellen Lebens in Großbritannien. Dabei geht es nicht nur ums Trinken, sondern auch um Geselligkeit.

Diese und nächste Seite: Trinity Square Gardens in Tower Hill bei Nacht.

Page précédente : Parmi les piliers de la culture britannique, les pubs ne sont pas de simples débits de boisson, ils créent aussi du lien social.

Cette page et la suivante : Les jardins de Trinity Square à Tower Hill de nuit.

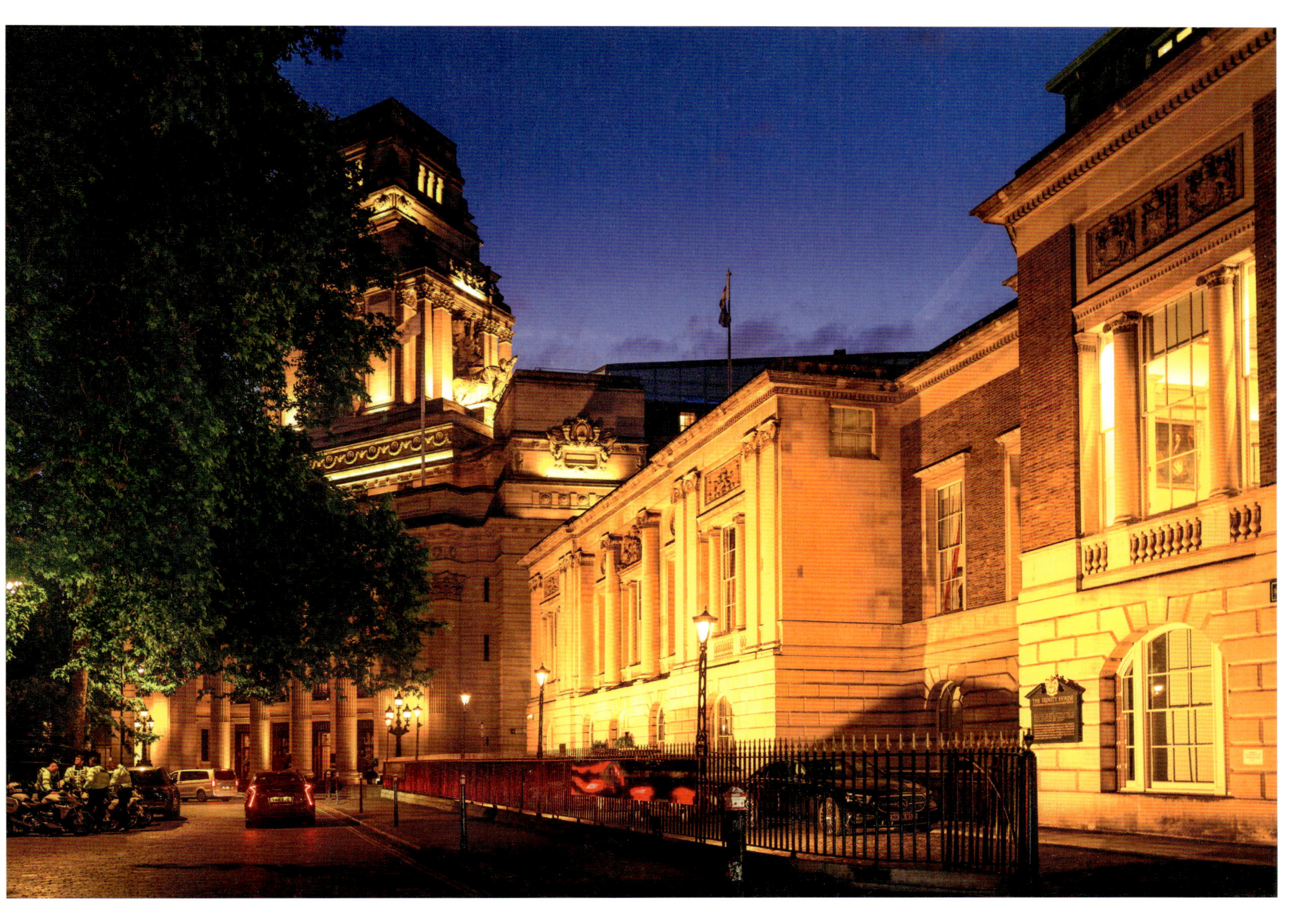

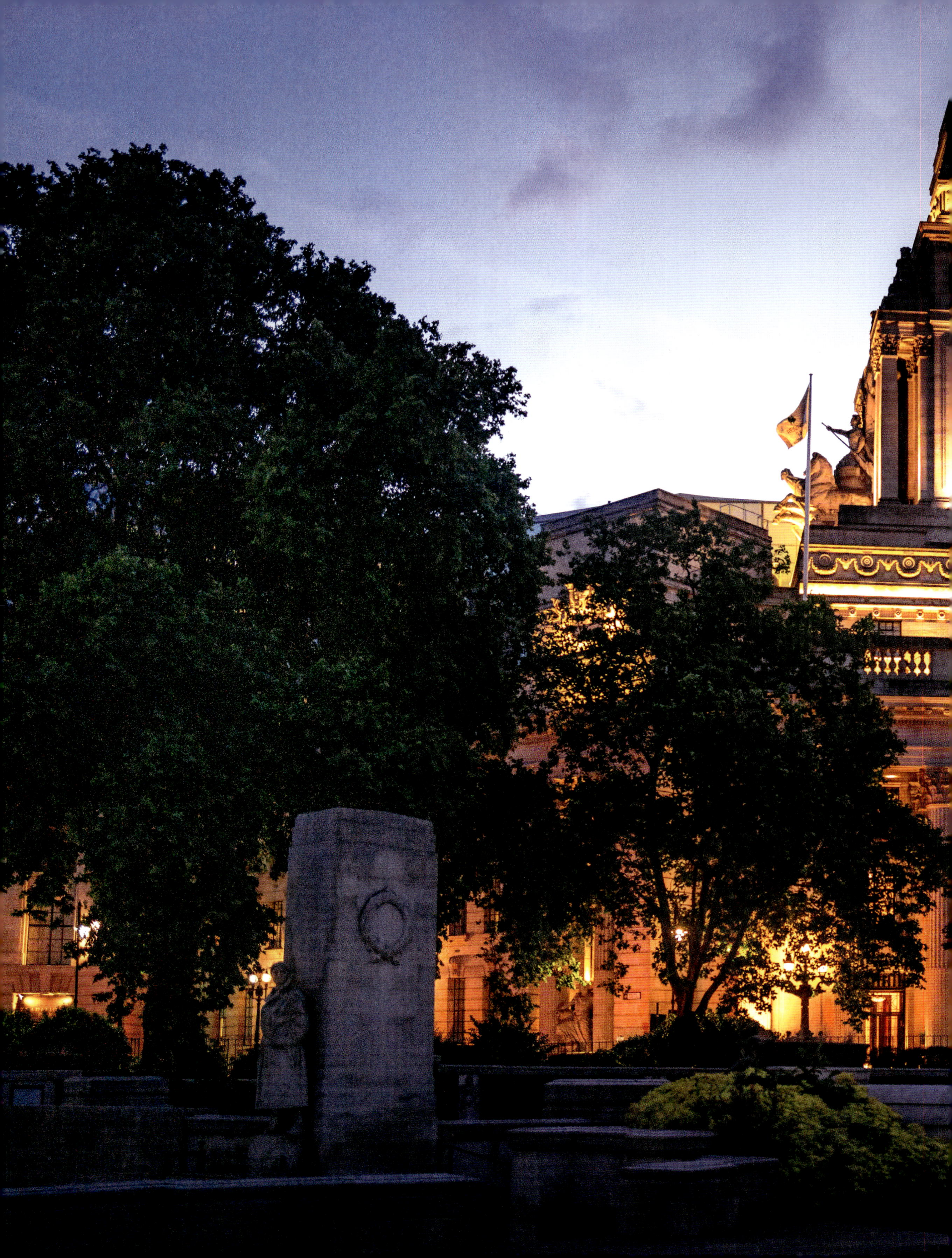

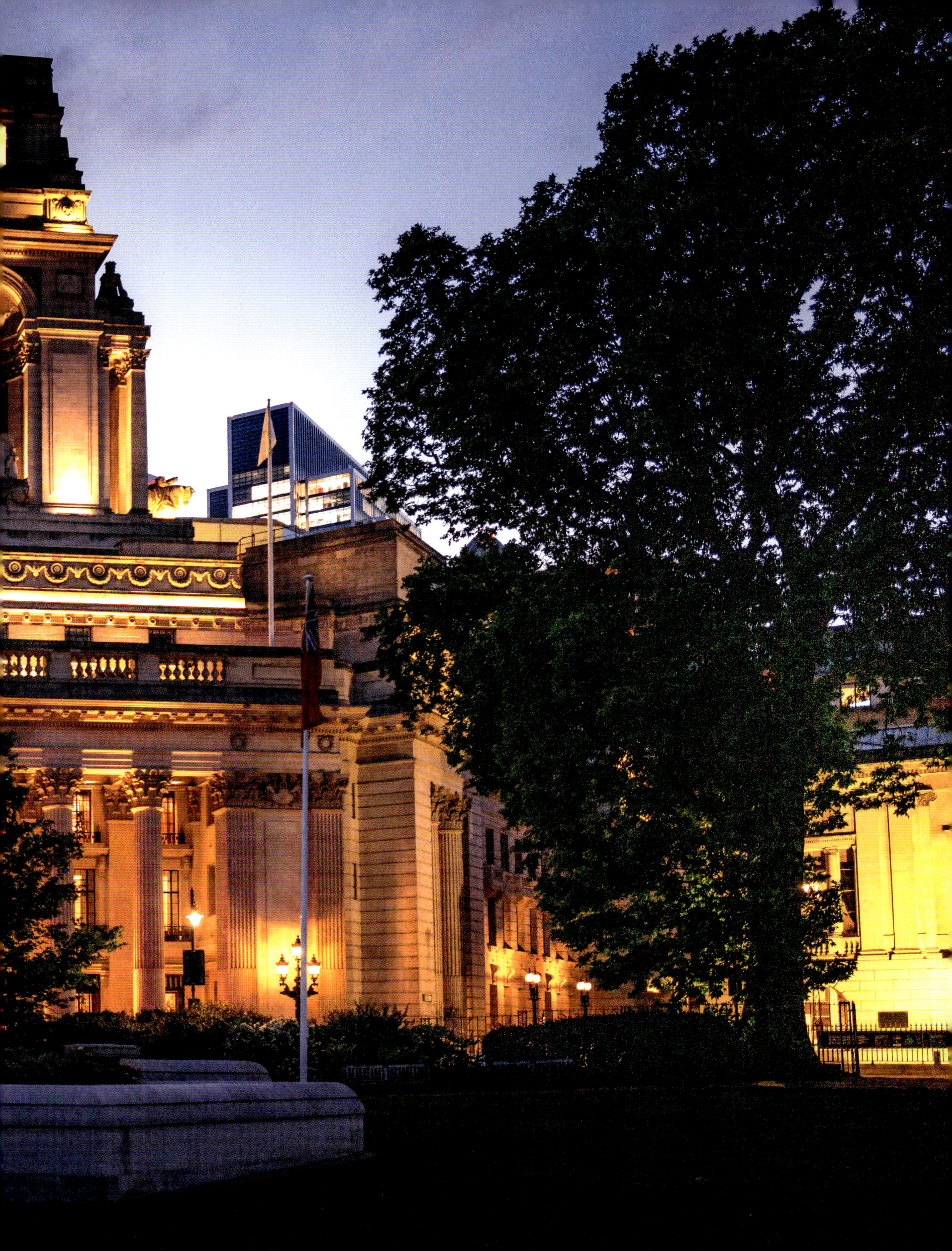

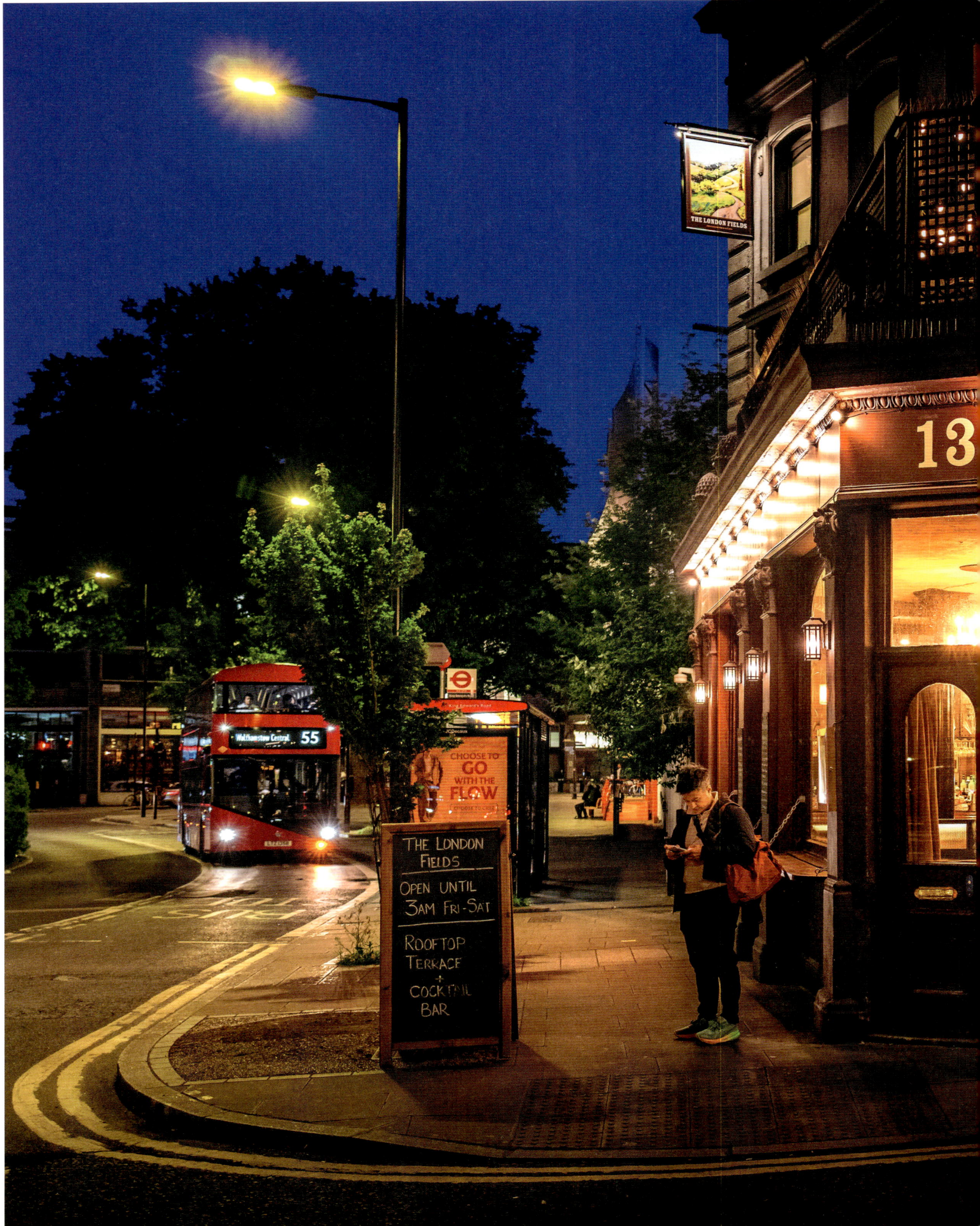
THE LONDON FIELDS
Walthamstow Central 55
CHOOSE TO
GO
WITH THE
FLOW
THE LONDON FIELDS
OPEN UNTIL 3AM FRI-SAT
ROOFTOP TERRACE + COCKTAIL BAR
13

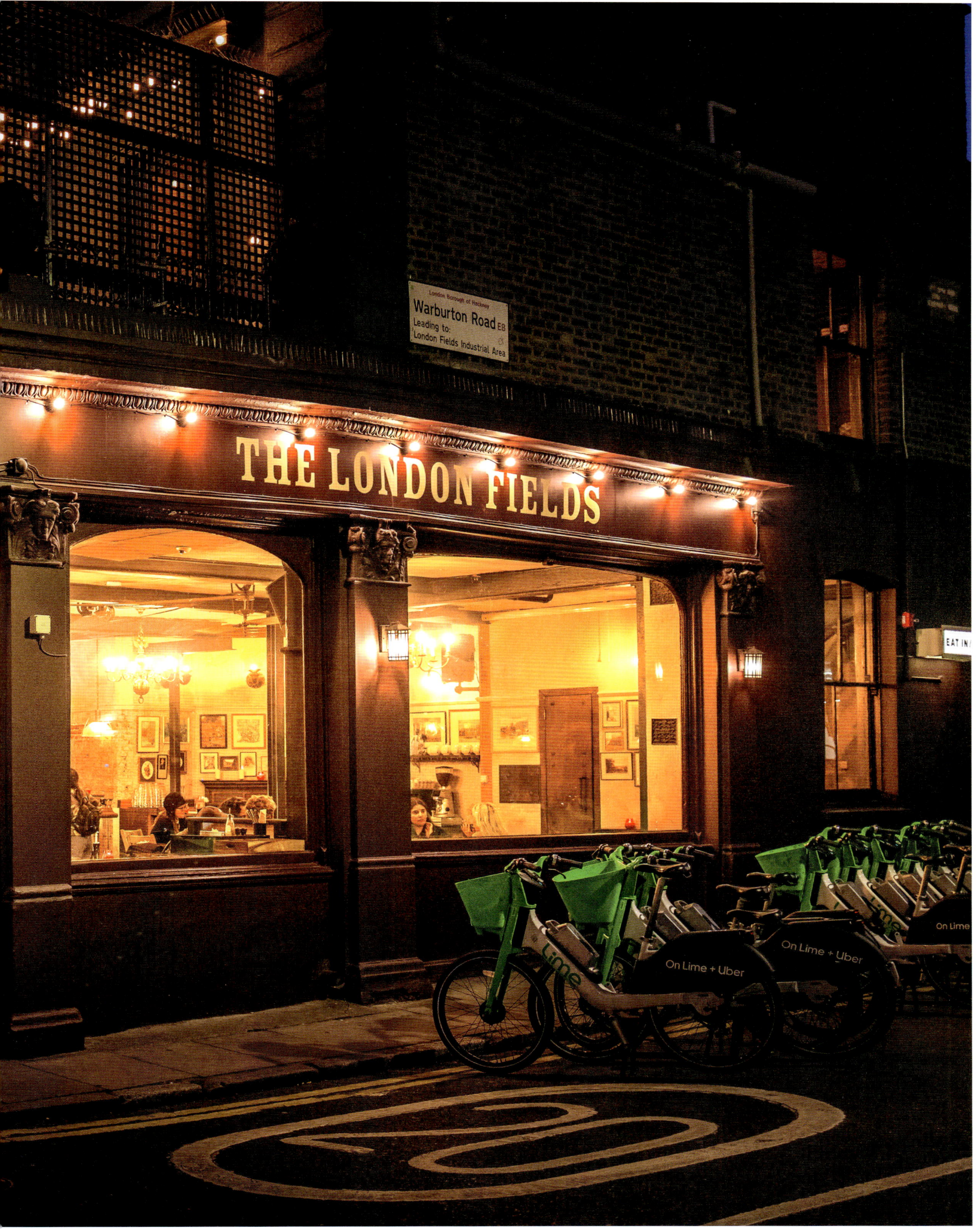
THE LONDON FIELDS
London Borough of Hackney
Warburton Road E8
Leading to:
London Fields Industrial Area
On Lime + Uber
On Lime + Uber
On Lime
Lime

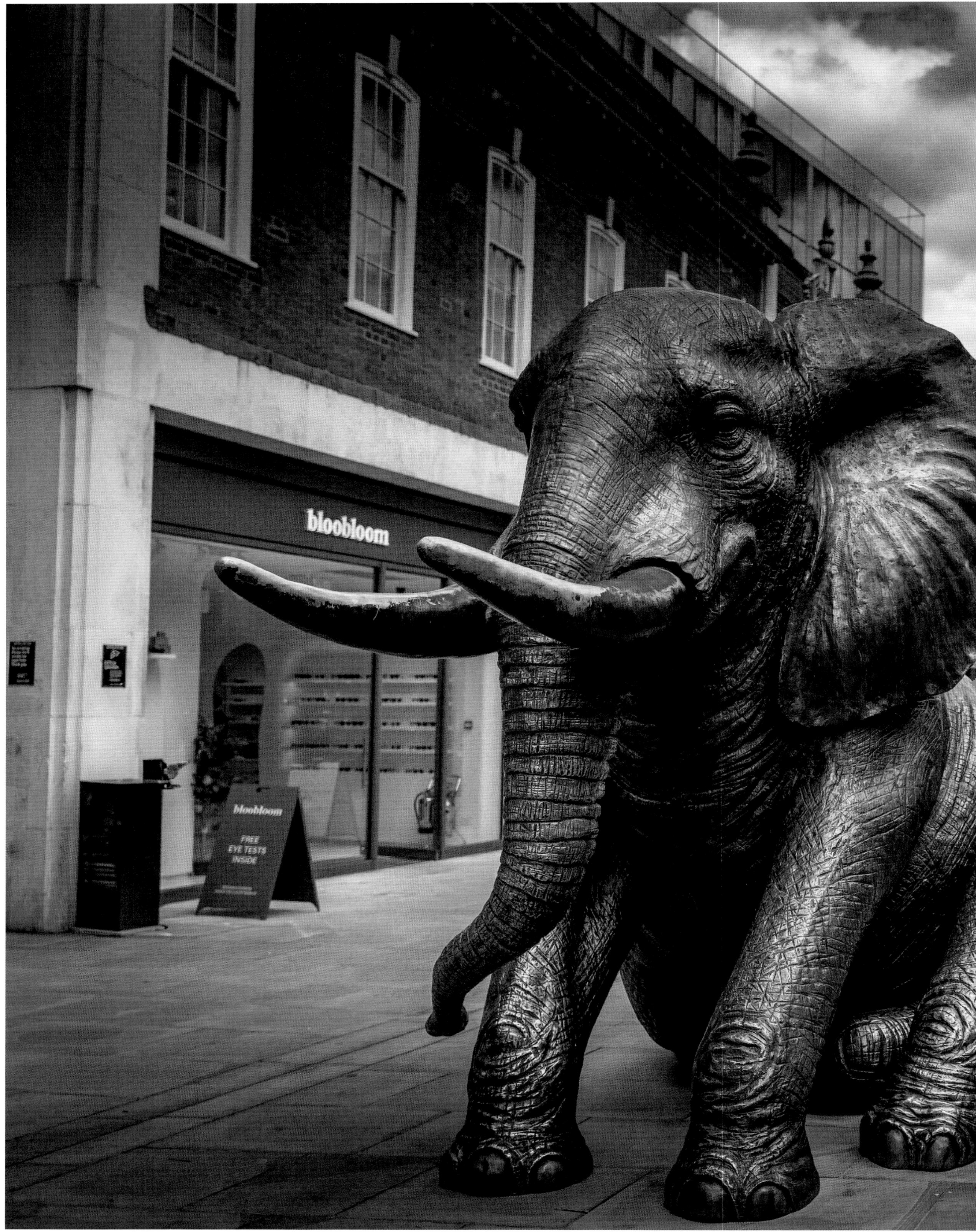
bloobloom
bloobloom
FREE
EYE TESTS
INSIDE

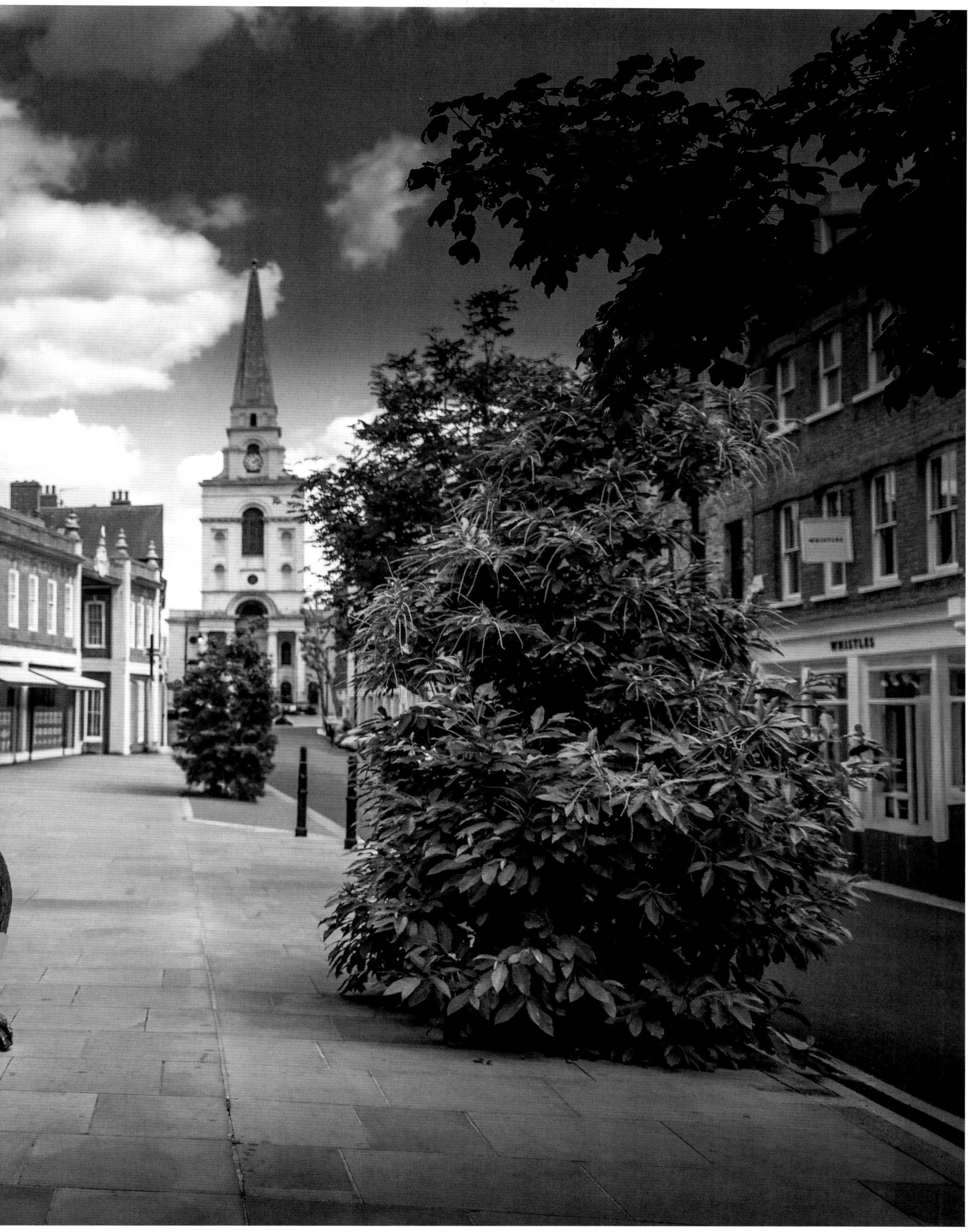
WHISTLES

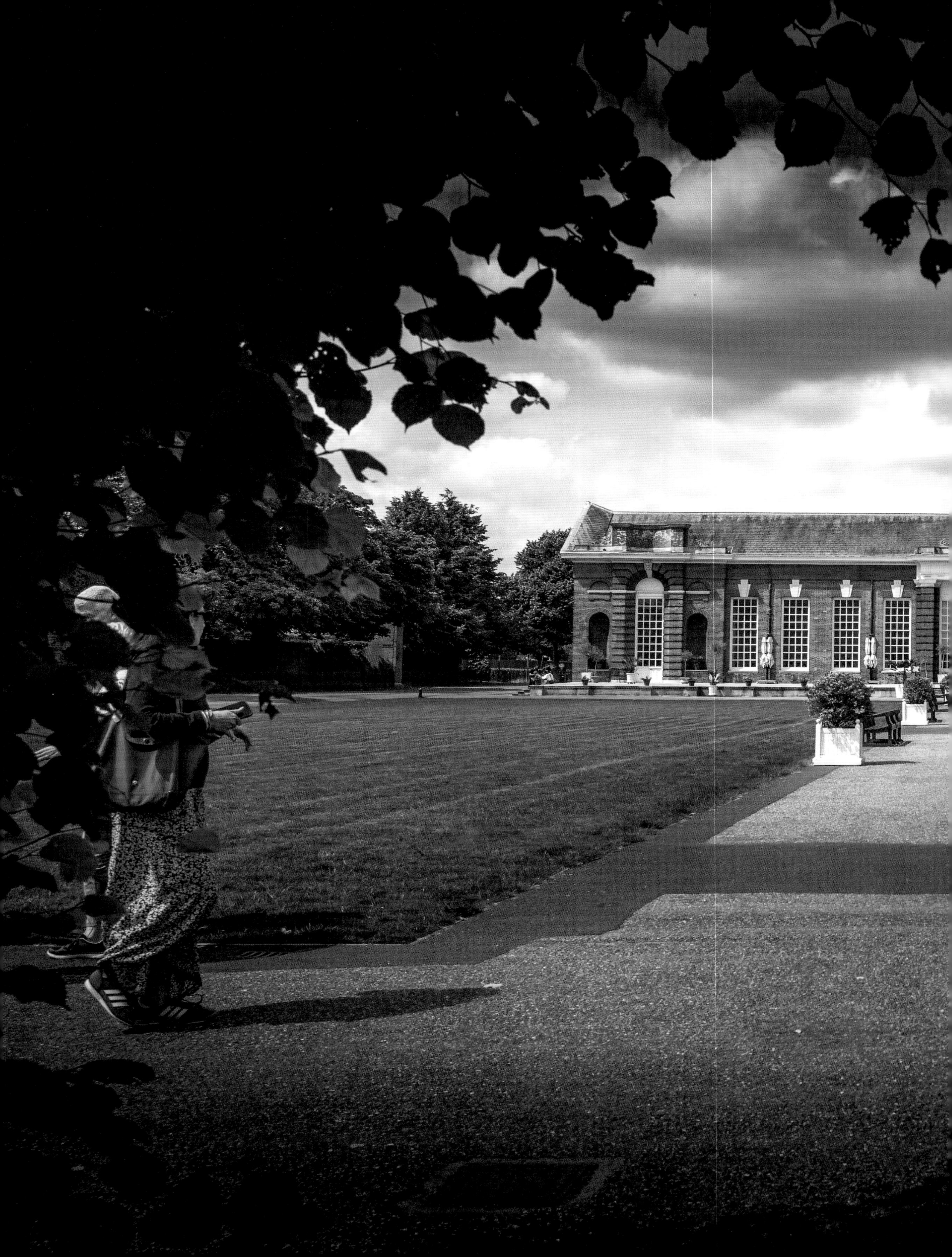

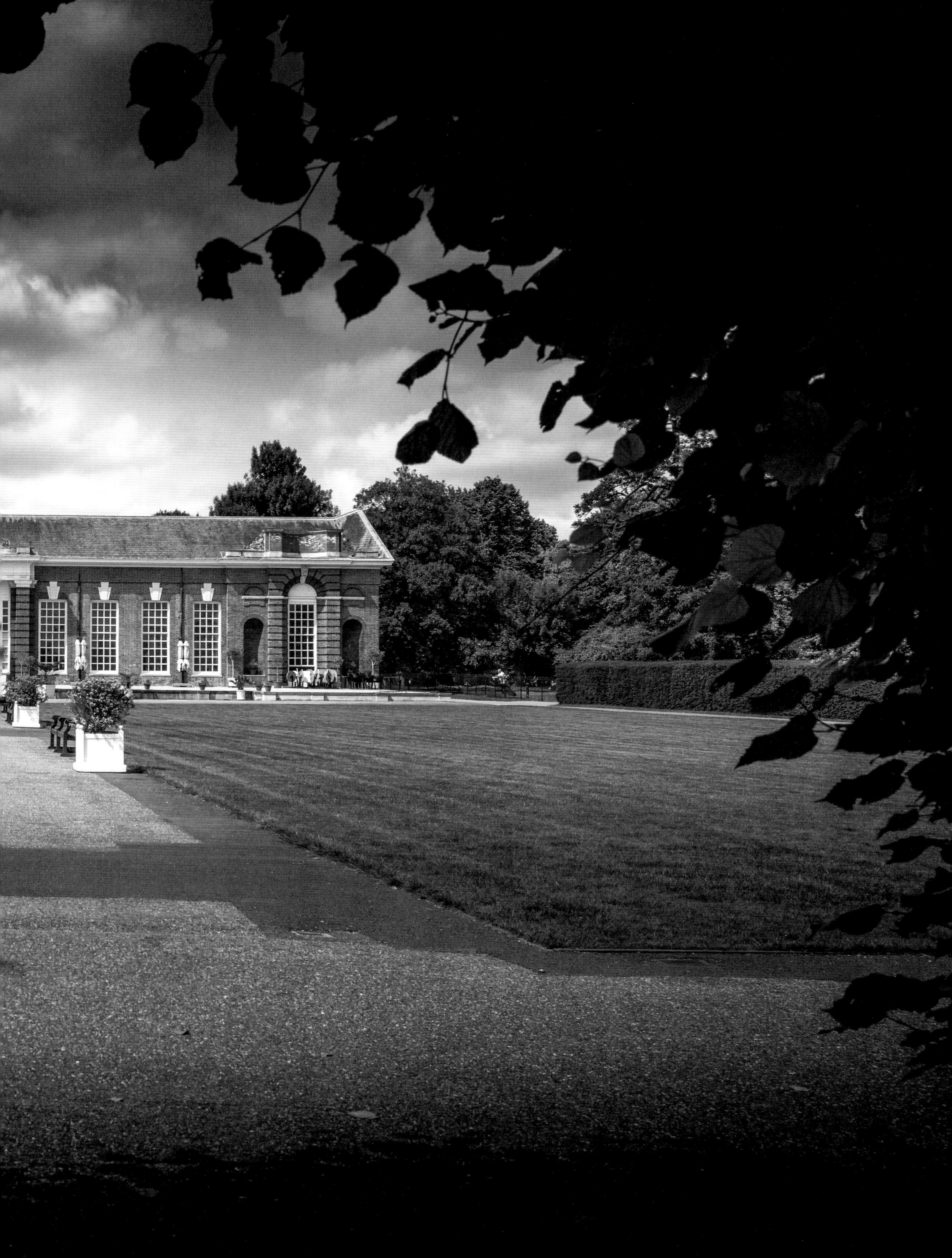

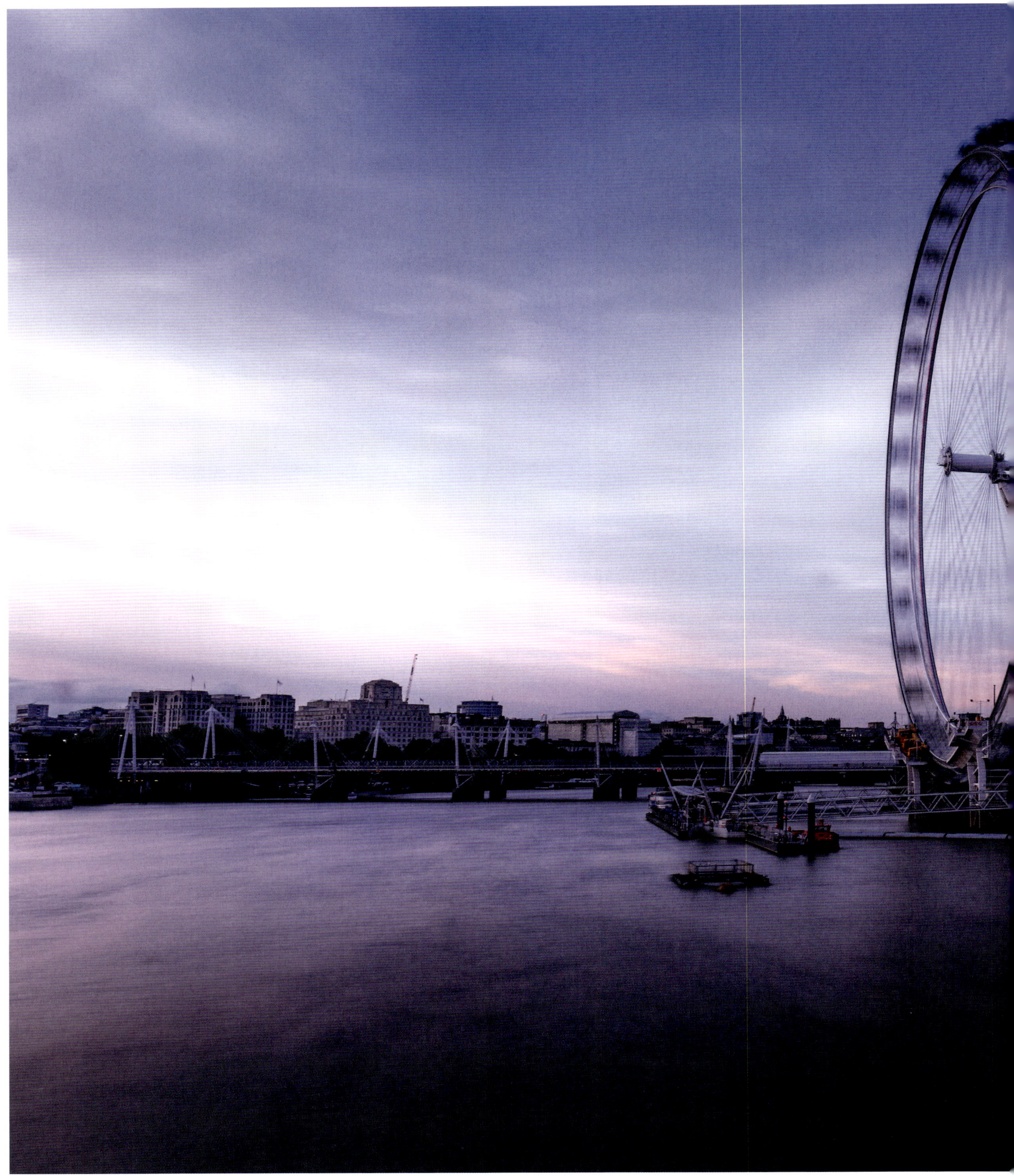

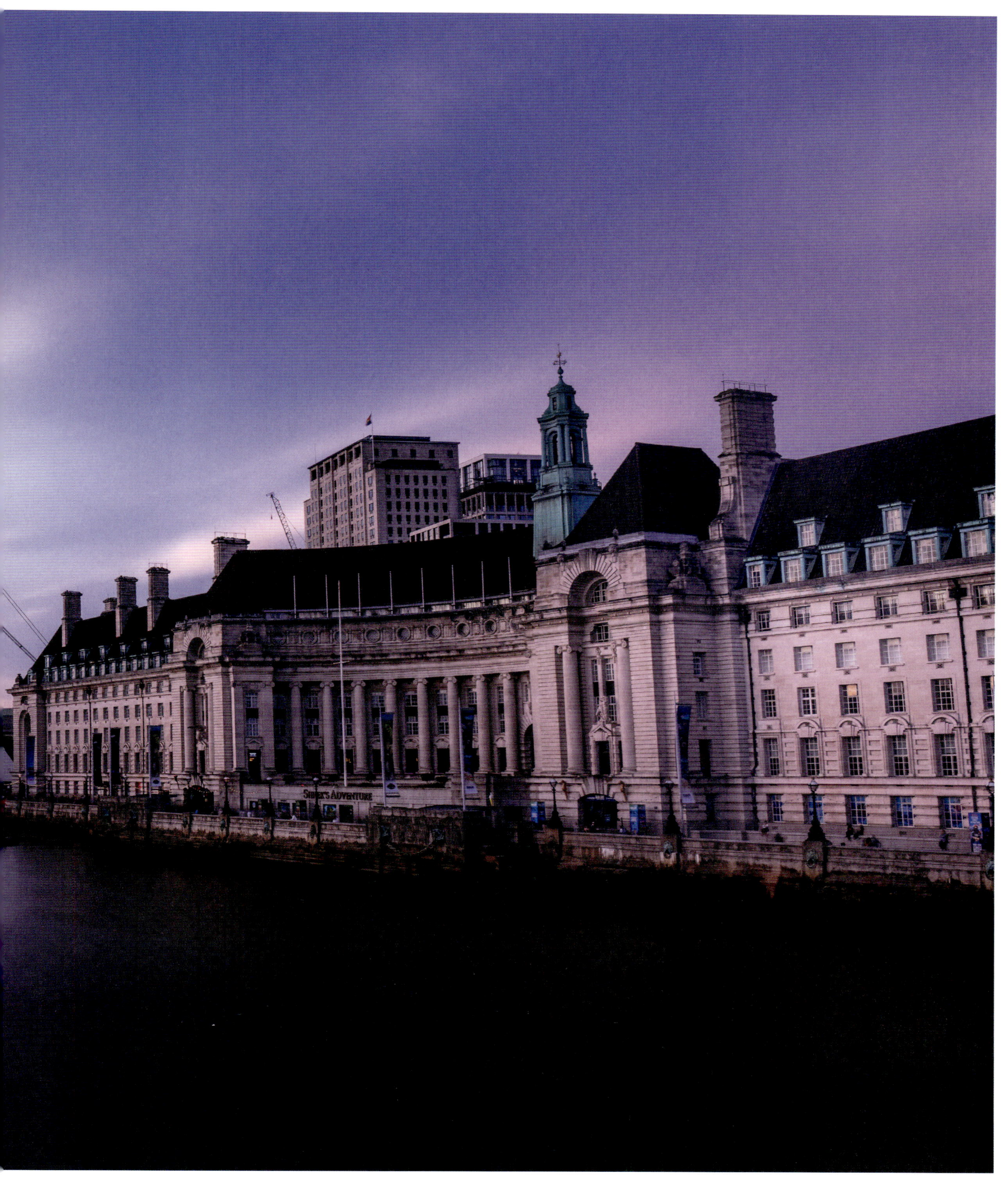
ADVENTURE

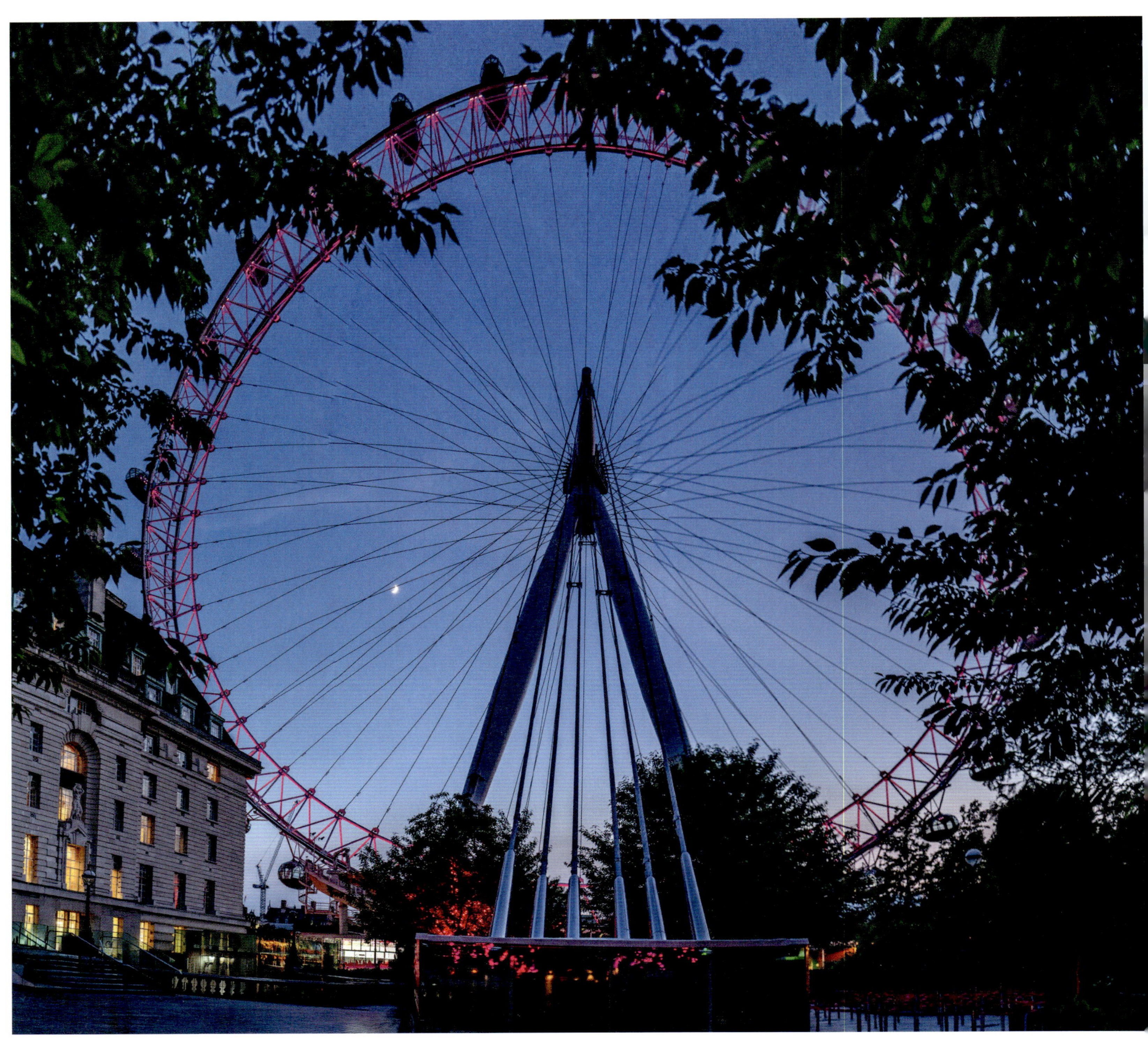

Previous pages and opposite: The London Eye captured at different times of day.
When completed in 2000, this 443-foot-tall (135-meter) structure was the tallest Ferris wheel in the world.

Pages 118–119: The distinctive MI6 (Secret Intelligence Service) building stands by the River Thames at Vauxhall Cross.

Vorherige und diese Seite: Das London Eye zu unterschiedlichen Tageszeiten.
Bei ihrer Fertigstellung im Jahr 2000 war die 135 Meter hohe Konstruktion das höchste Riesenrad der Welt.

Seiten 118–119: Das auffällige Gebäude des britischen Auslandsgeheimdienstes MI6 steht bei Vauxhall Cross an der Themse.

Cette page et la précédente : Le London Eye à différentes heures de la journée.
À son achèvement en l'an 2000, cette grande roue de 135 mètres de hauteur était la plus haute du monde.

Pages 118–119 : Le bâtiment caractéristique du MI6, les services secrets britanniques, se trouve au bord de la Tamise, à Vauxhall Cross.

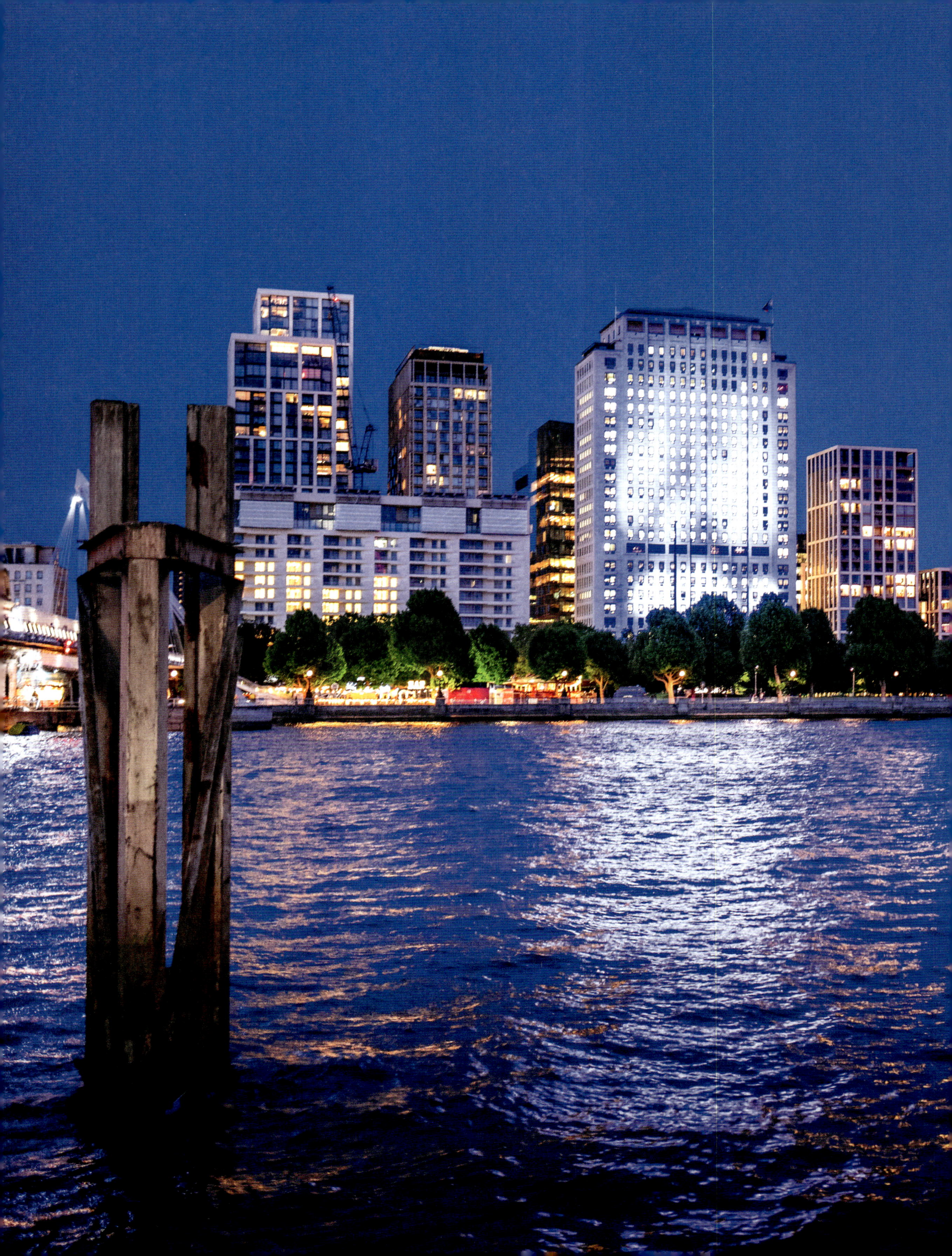

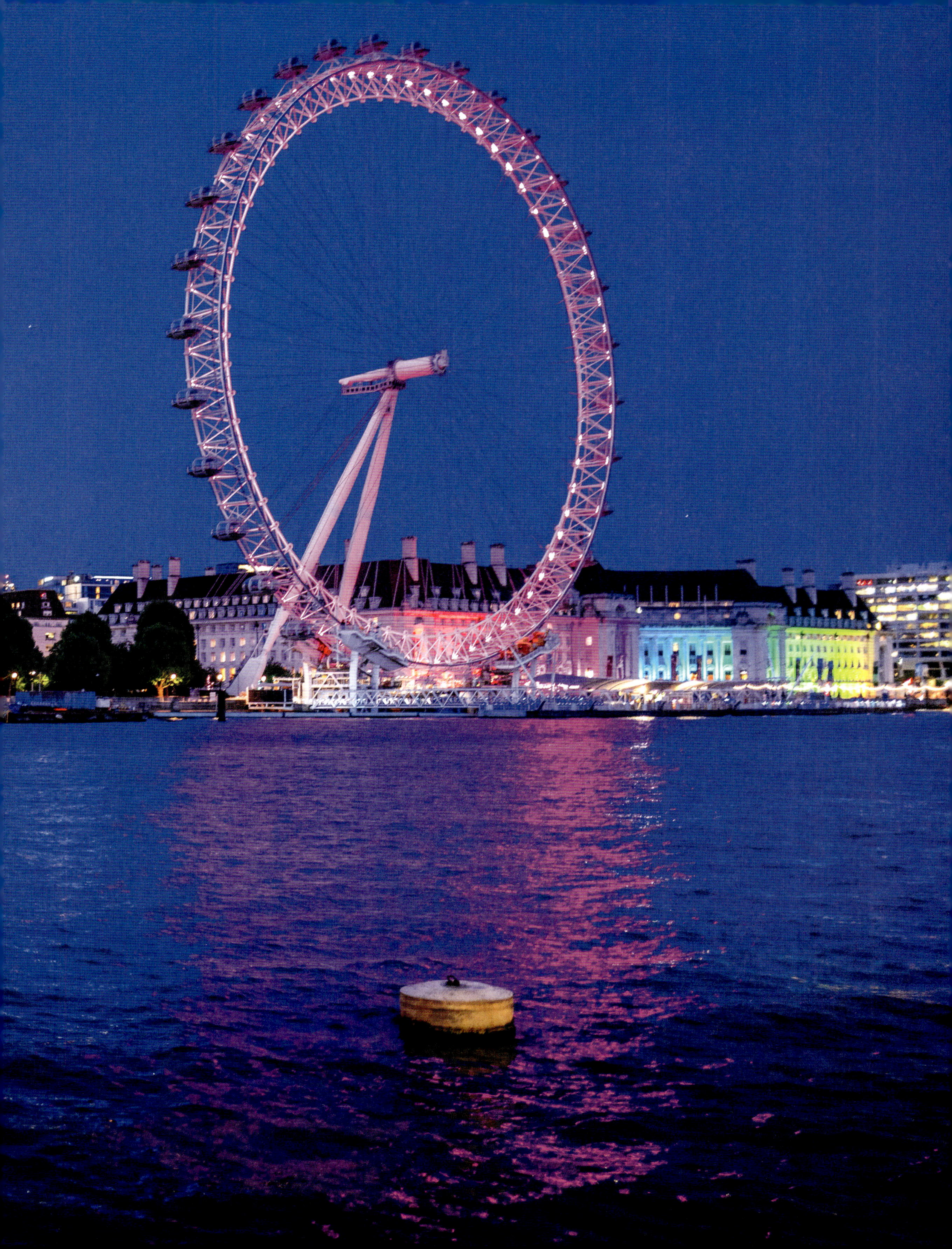

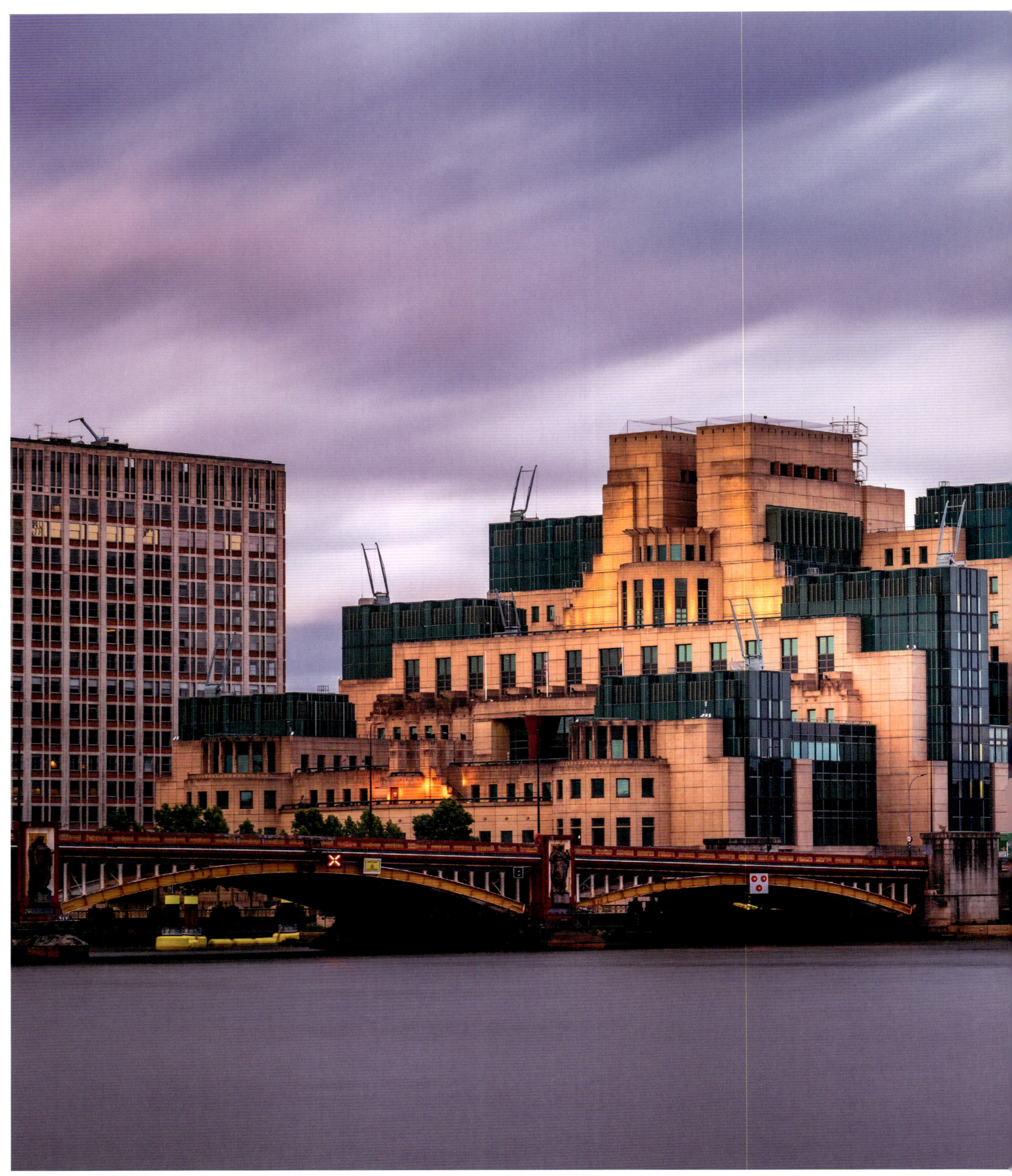

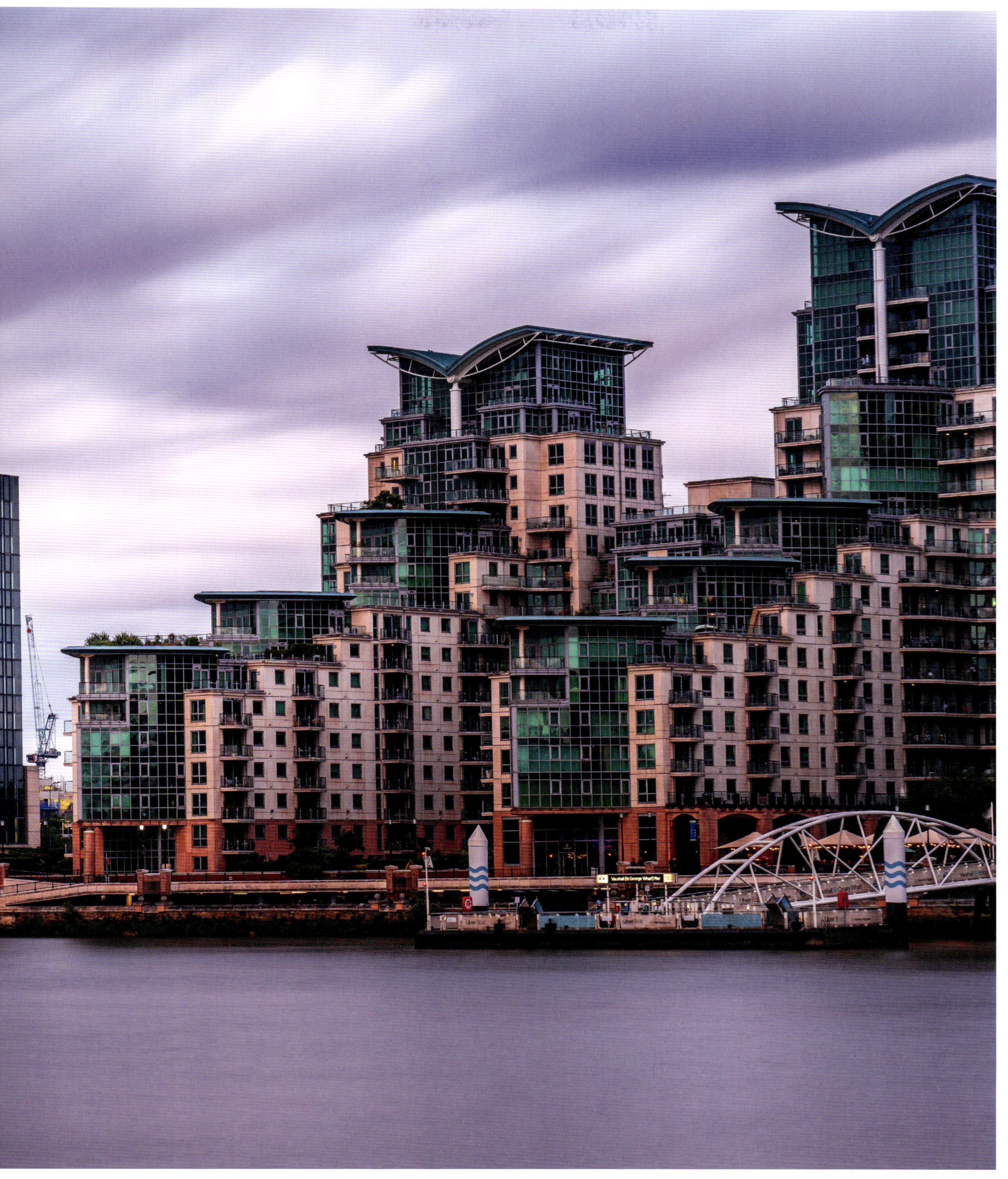
Vauxhall (St George Wharf) Pier

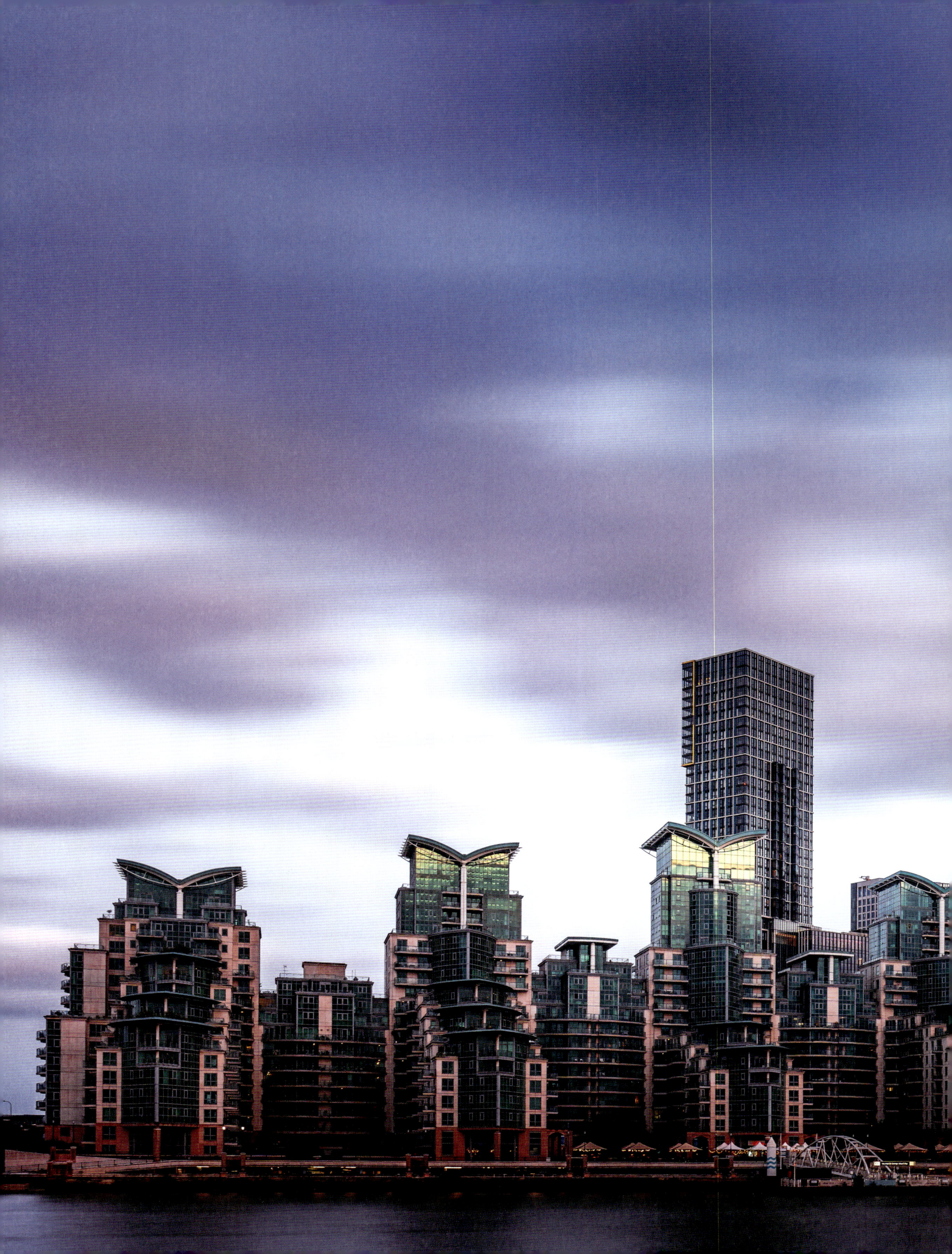

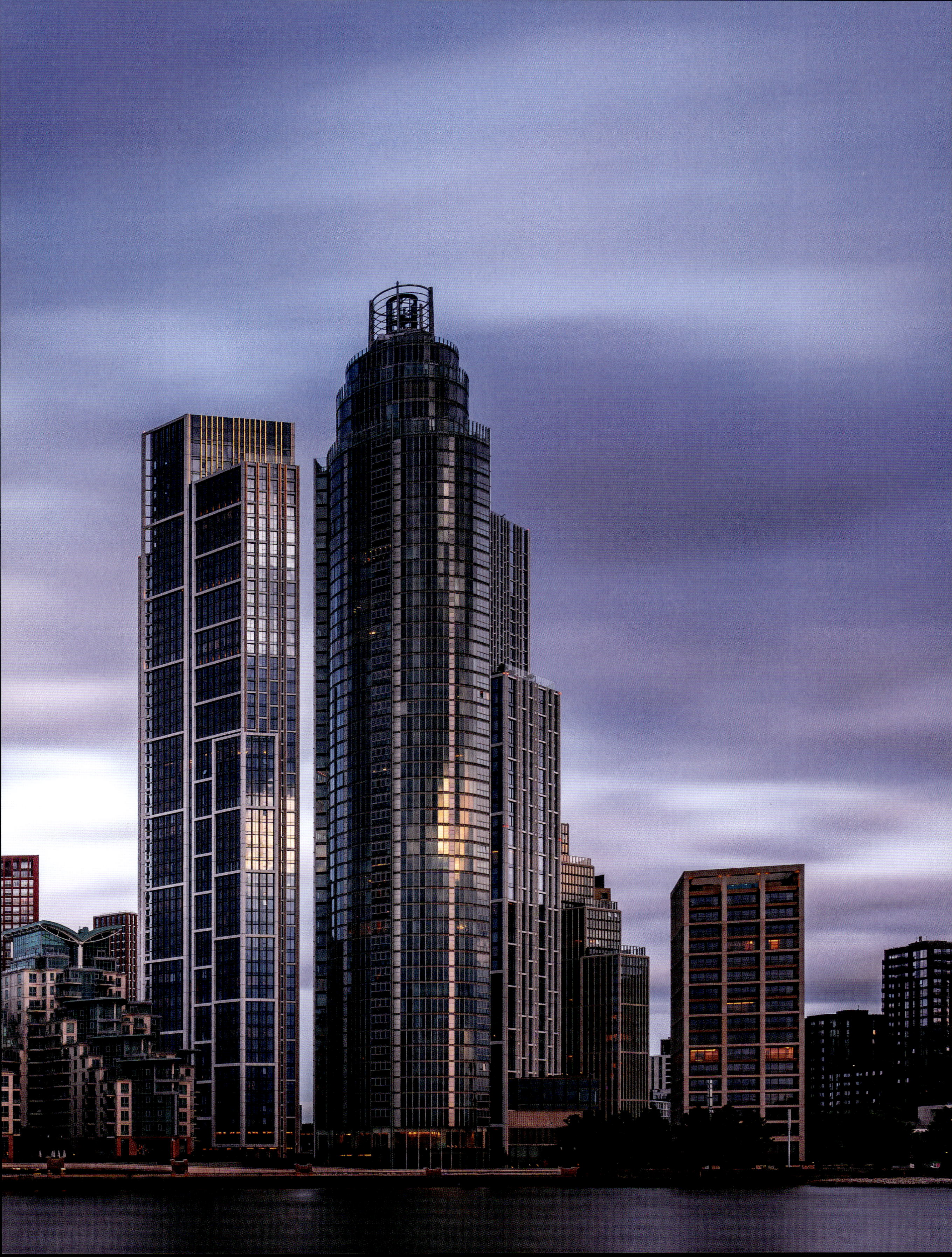

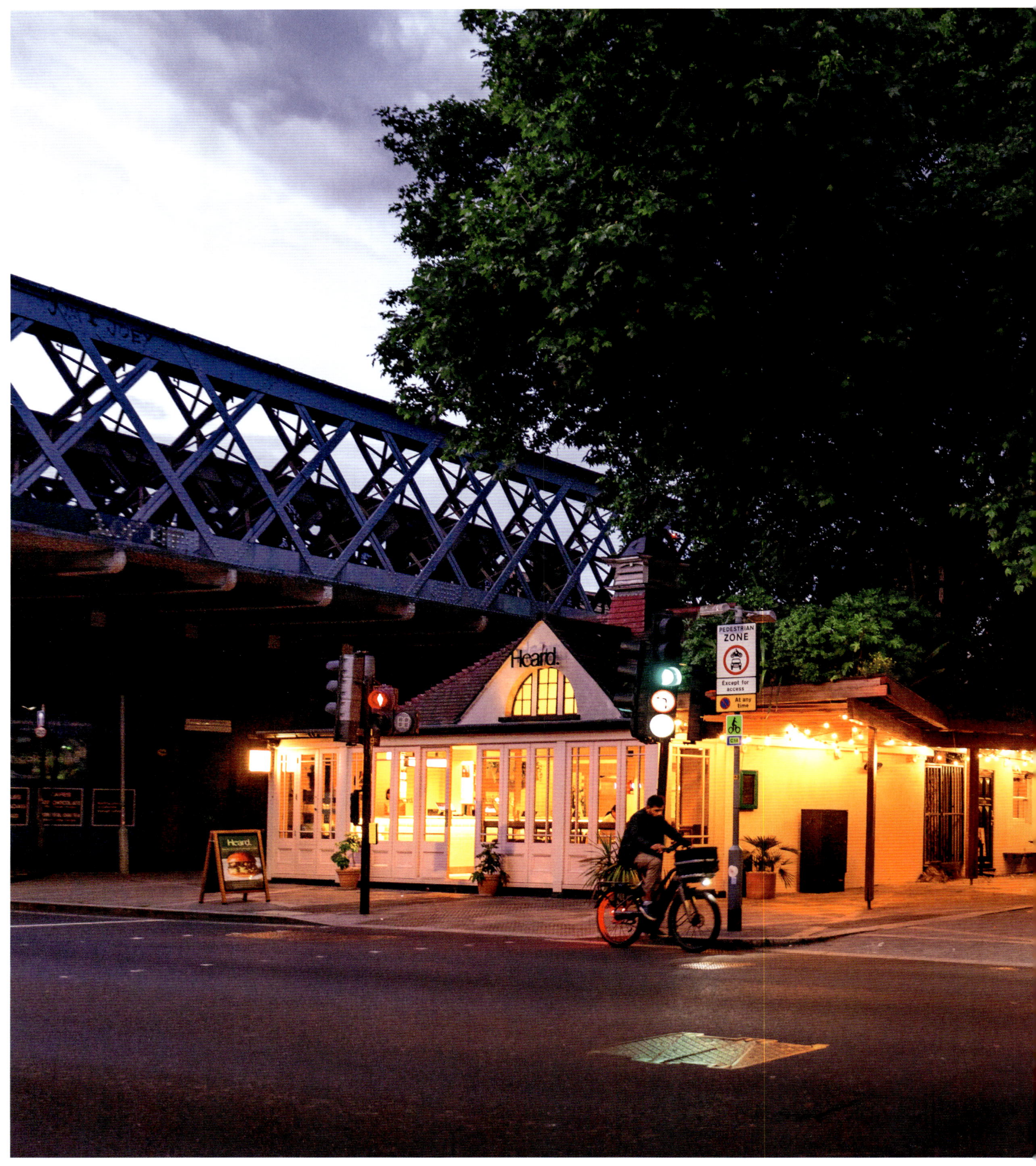
Heard.
PEDESTRIAN
ZONE
Except for
access
At any
time
Heard.

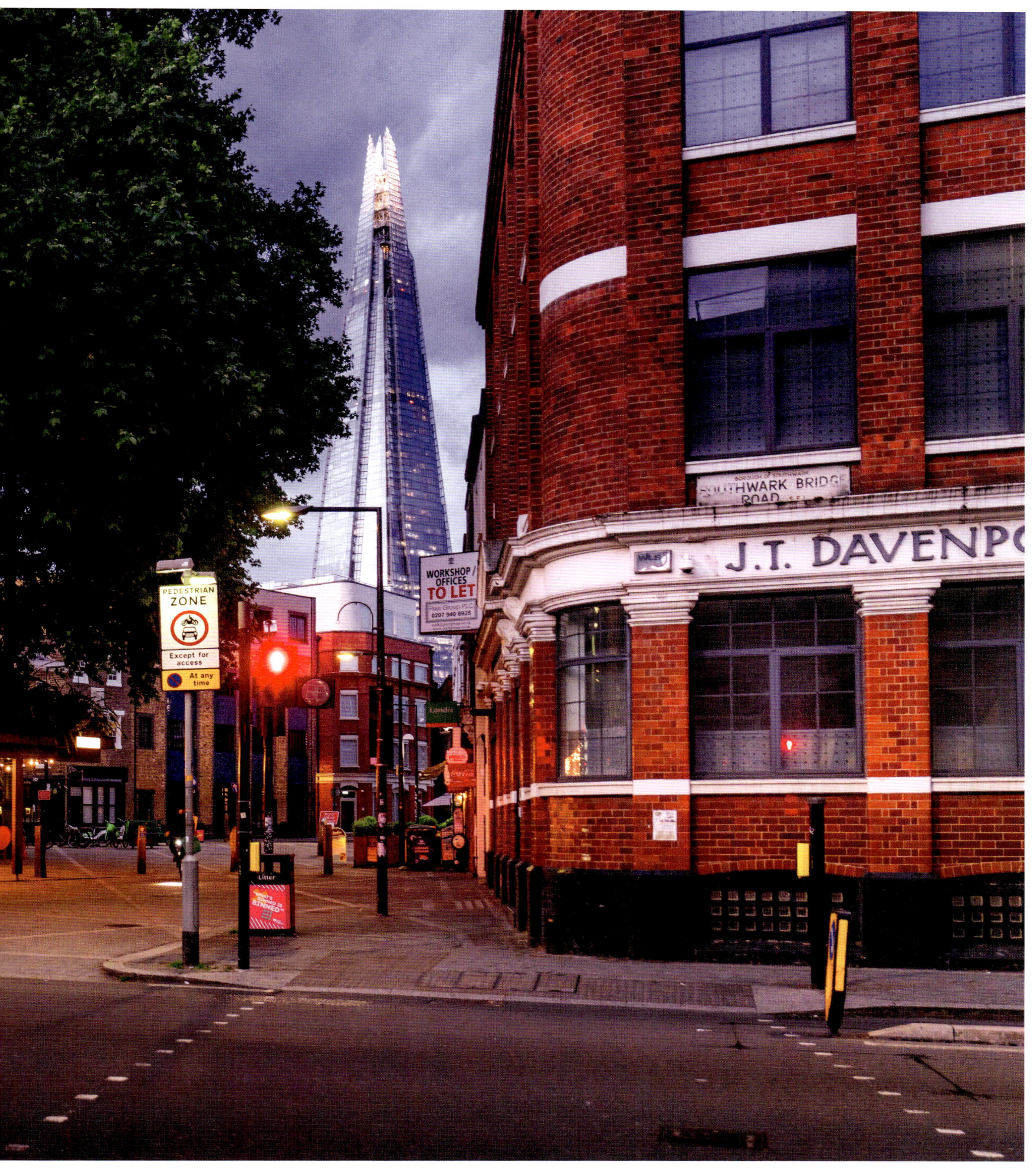
PEDESTRIAN ZONE
Except for access
At any time
WORKSHOP / OFFICES
TO LET
0207 940 8925
Litter
SOUTHWARK BRIDGE ROAD
J.T. DAVENP

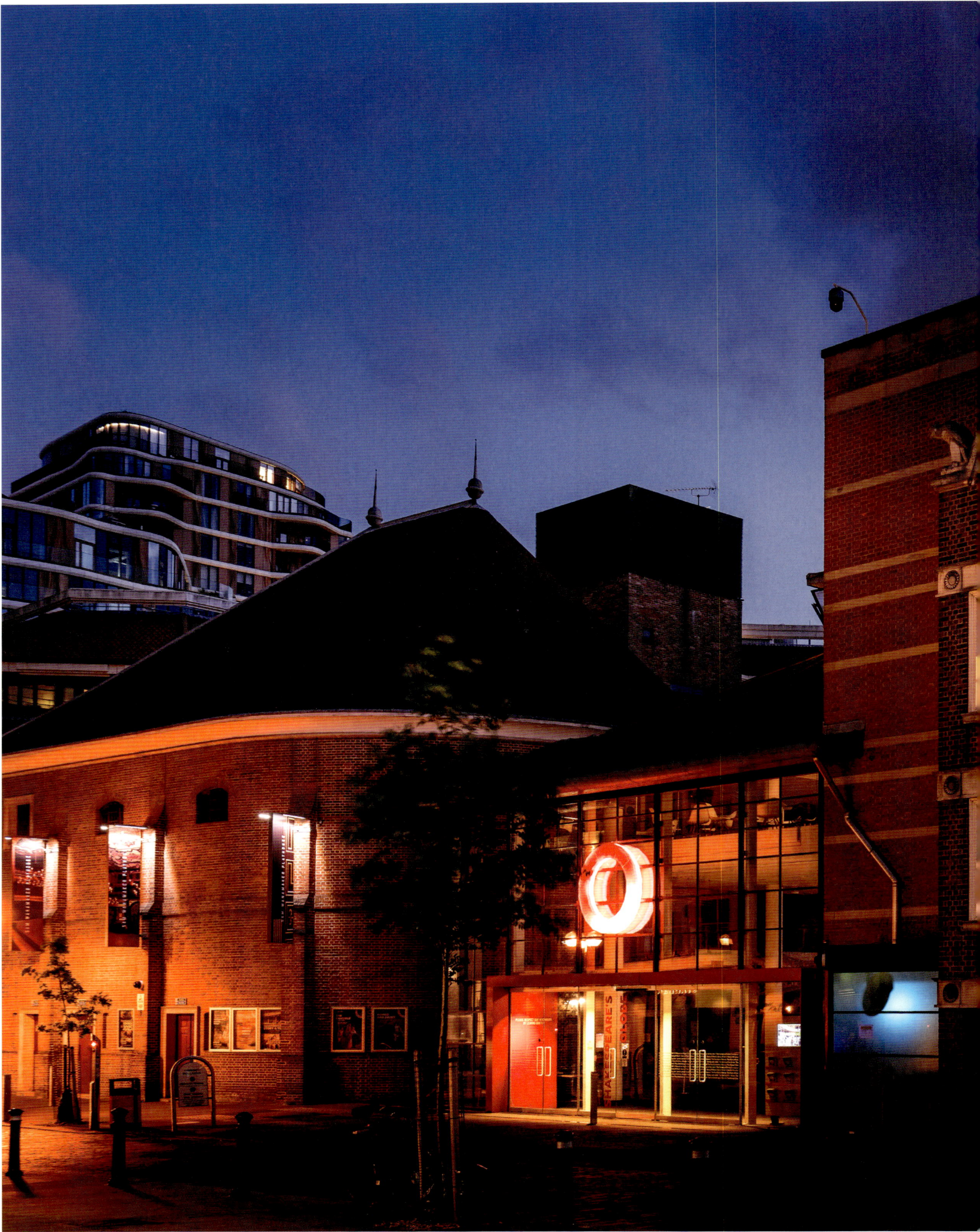
SHAKESPEARE'S
GLOBE

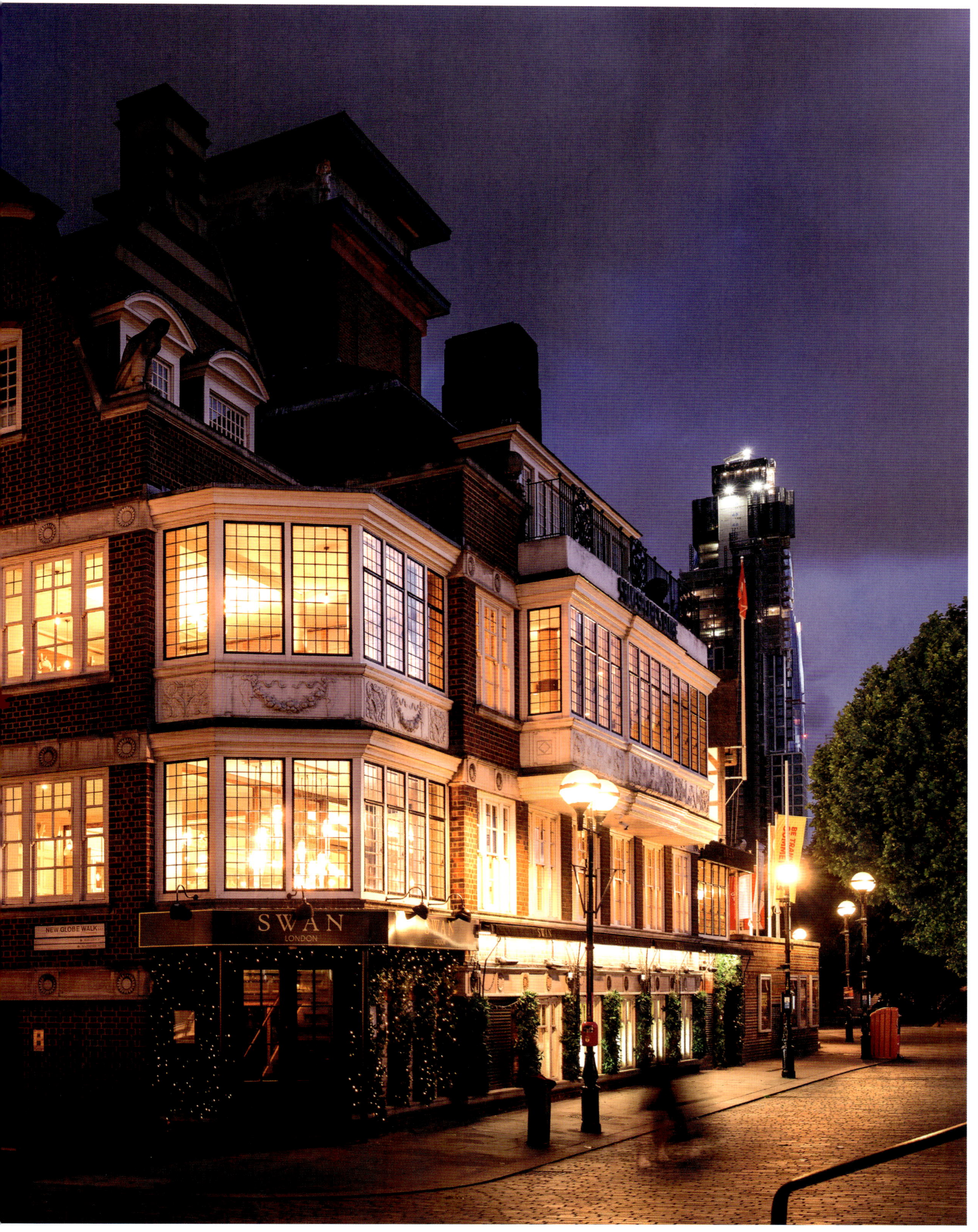
NEW GLOBE WALK
SWAN
LONDON

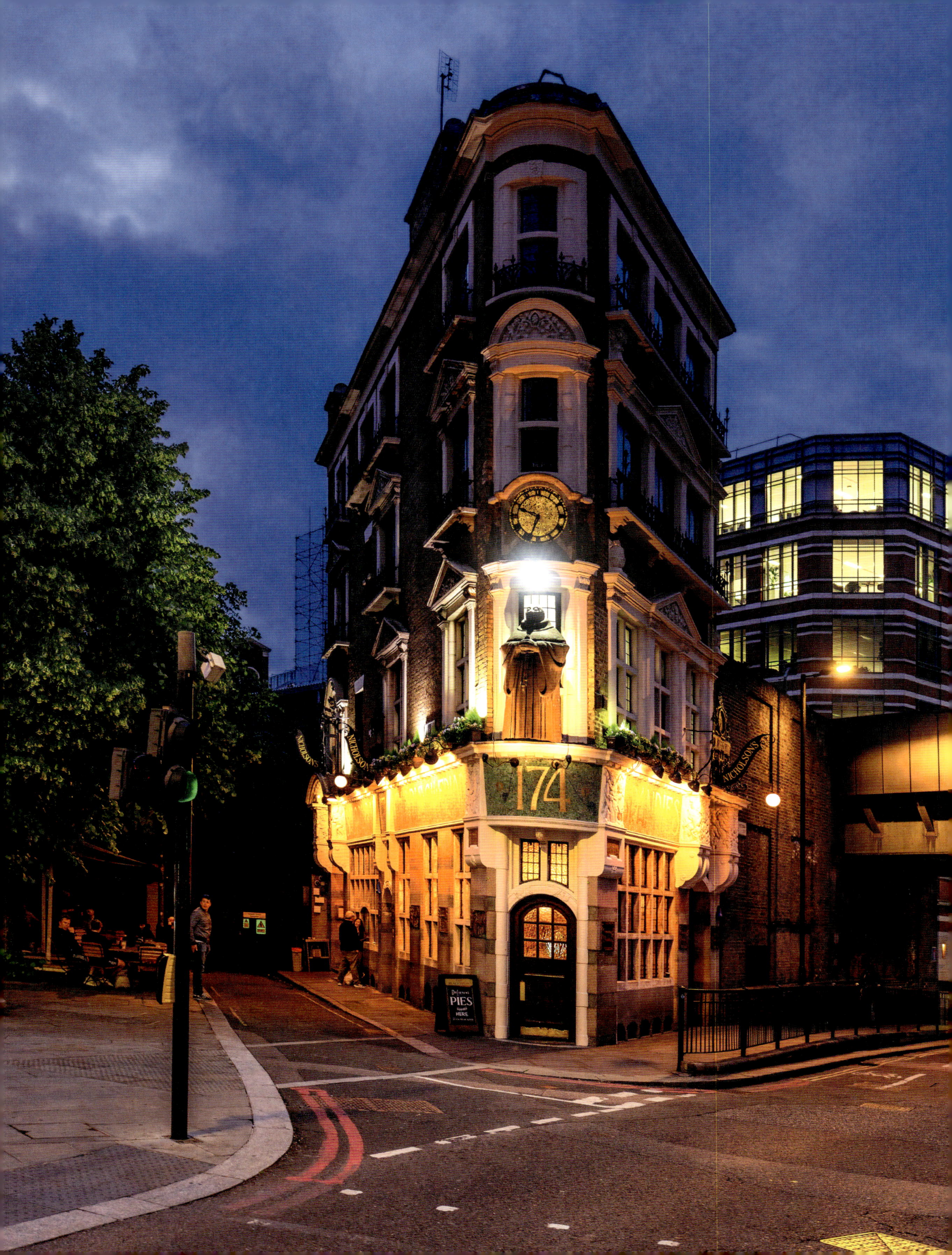
174
NICHOLSON'S
NICHOLSON'S
PIES
HERE

Previous pages: The illuminated Shakespeare's Globe. The theater is a reconstruction of the original Globe Theatre, which burned down in 1613.

Opposite: A charming historic corner building in Blackfriars.

Vorherige Seite: Shakespeare's Globe bei Nacht. Das Theater ist ein Nachbau des ursprünglichen Globe Theatre, das 1613 abbrannte.

Diese Seite: Ein charmantes historisches Eckhaus in Blackfriars.

Page précédente : Le théâtre du Globe illuminé. Il s'agit d'une réplique du théâtre de Shakespeare ravagé par un incendie en 1613.

Cette page : Charmant immeuble d'angle ancien à Blackfriars.

The building that now houses the Mad Hatter Hotel in Southwark was originally a hat-making factory. The name also references the fictional character from Lewis Carroll's *Alice in Wonderland*.

Pages 130–133: The restored railway arches of Borough Yards are home to stores, cafés, and other leisure facilities.

Pages 134–135: The historic Shad Thames street, with old brick warehouses connected by overhead walkways.

Das Gebäude in Southwark, das heutzutage das Mad Hatter Hotel beherbergt, war ursprünglich eine Hutfabrik. Der Name des Hotels spielt auch auf eine fiktionale Figur in Lewis Carrolls Roman *Alice im Wunderland* an.

Seiten 130–133: Unter den restaurierten Eisenbahnbögen von Borough Yards befinden sich heute Geschäfte, Cafés und andere Freizeiteinrichtungen.

Seiten 134–135: Die historische Straße Shad Thames mit ihren alten Ziegel-Lagerhäusern, die durch Fußgänger-Überwege miteinander verbunden sind.

Le bâtiment qui abrite aujourd'hui le Mad Hatter Hotel, à Southwark, était à l'origine une chapellerie. Le nom de l'hôtel fait aussi référence au personnage du chapelier fou dans *Alice au pays des merveilles* de Lewis Carroll.

Pages 130–133 : Sous ses arcades restaurées, le viaduc ferroviaire de Borough Yards abrite des commerces, des cafés et autres lieux de détente.

Pages 134–135 : Shad Thames est une rue historique bordée de vieux entrepôts en briques reliés par des passerelles.

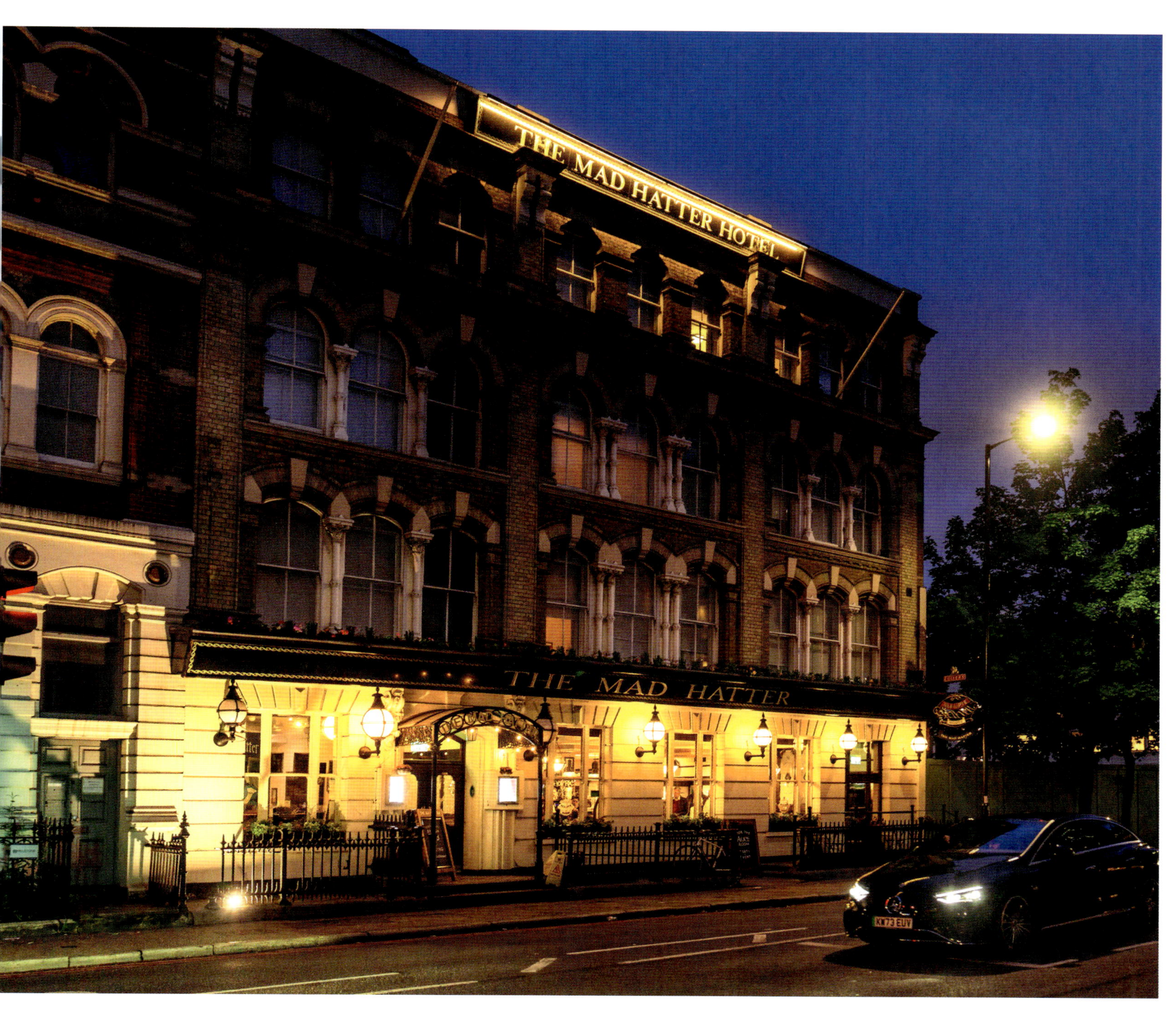
THE MAD HATTER HOTEL
THE MAD HATTER

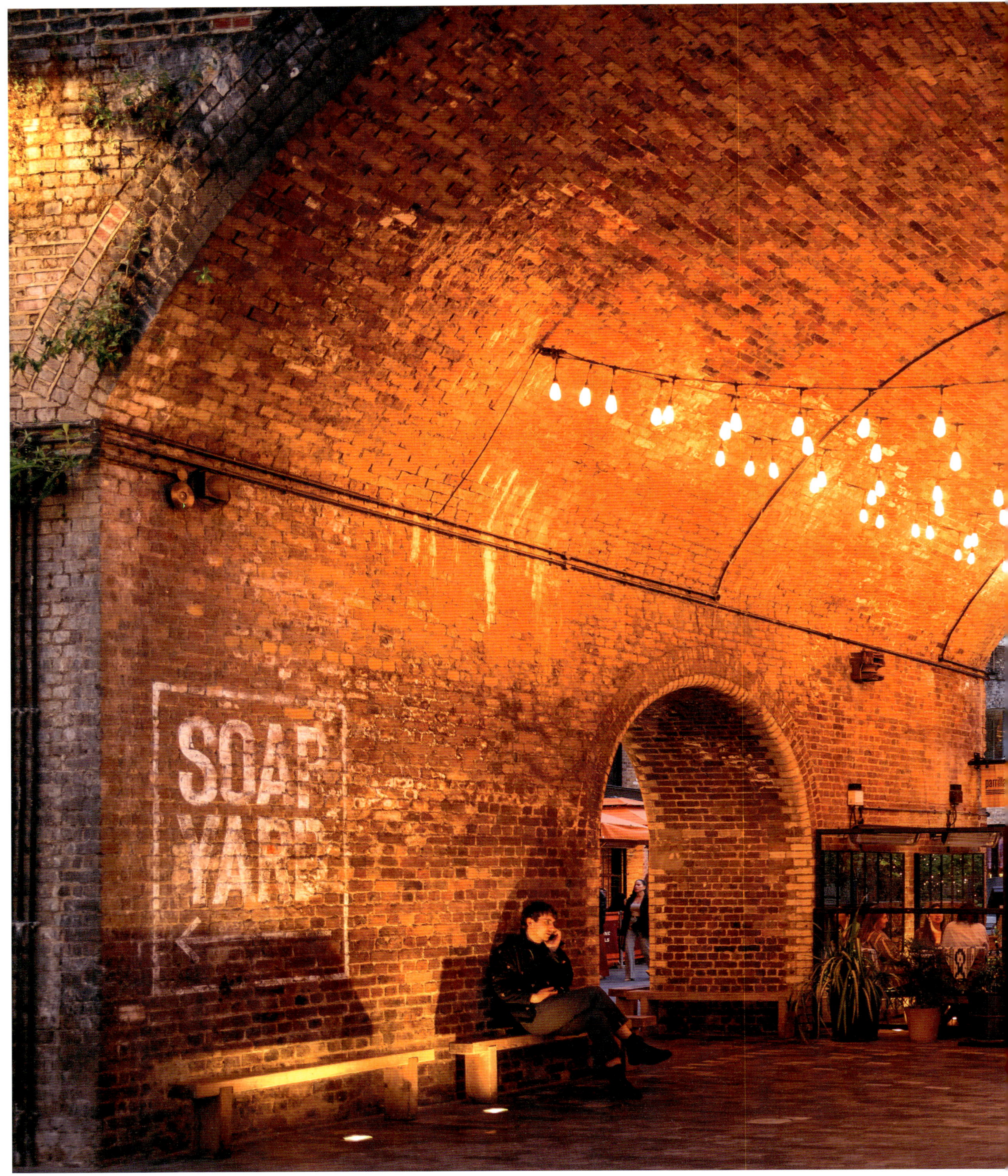
SOAP
YARD

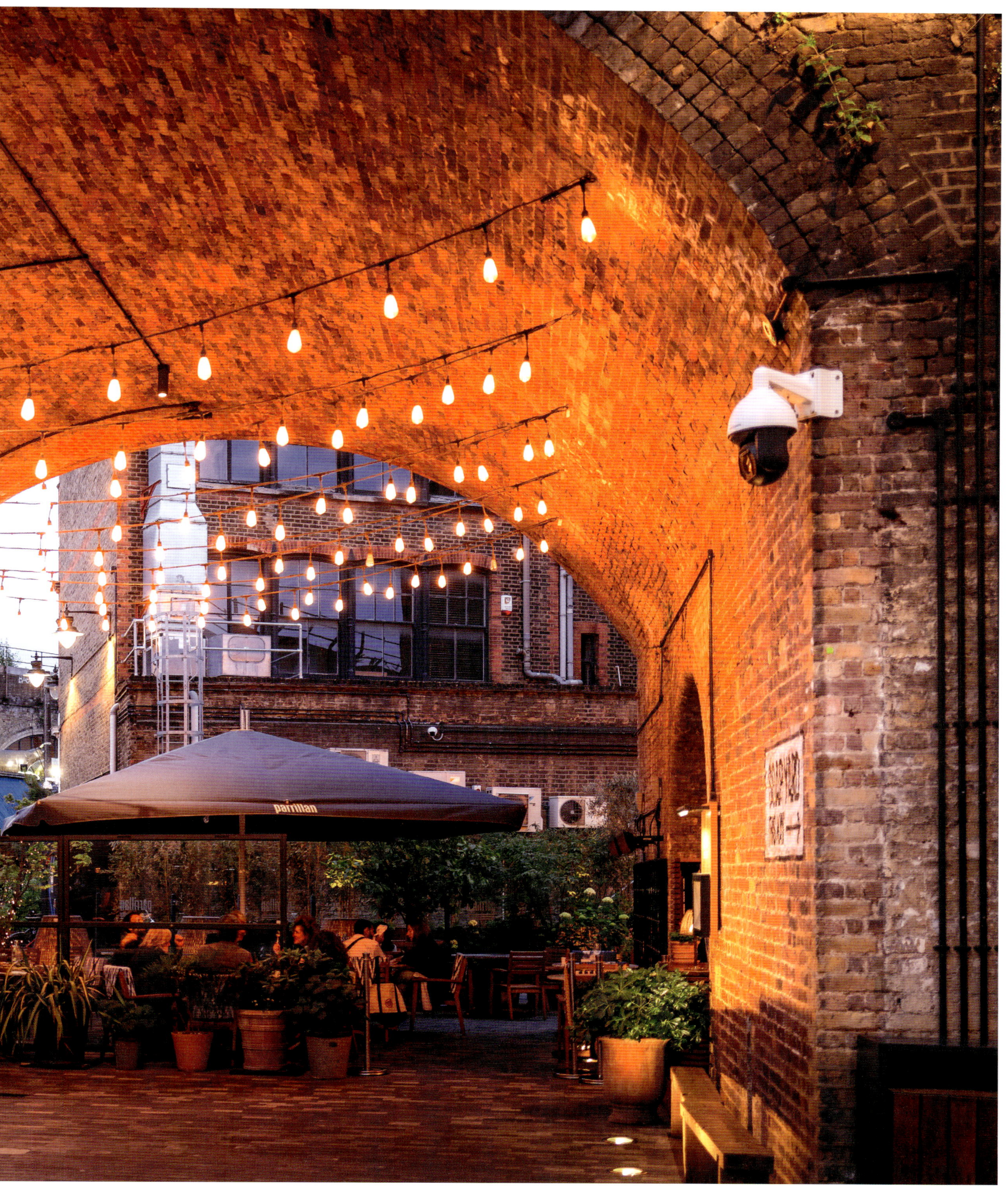
parrillan

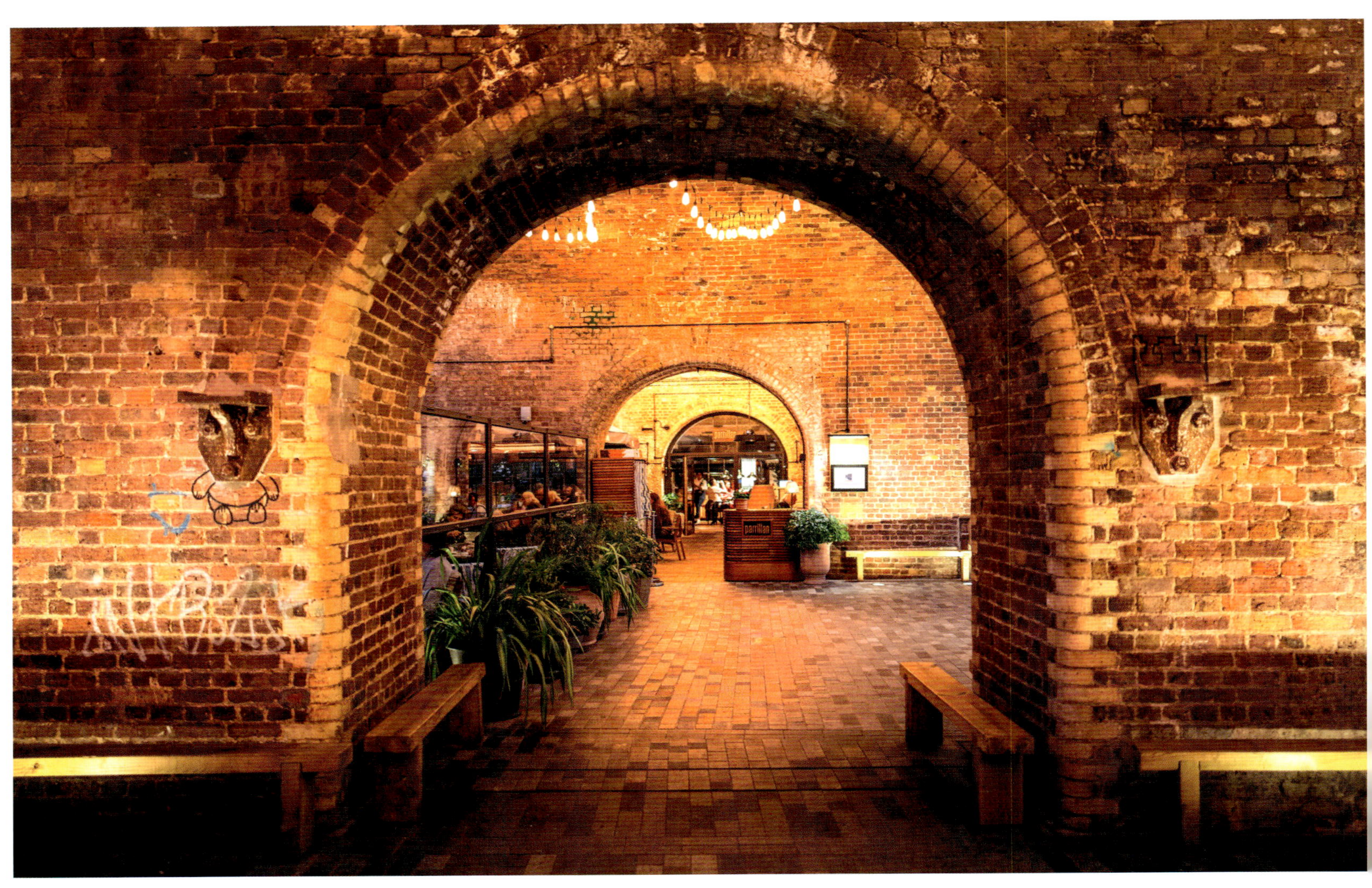

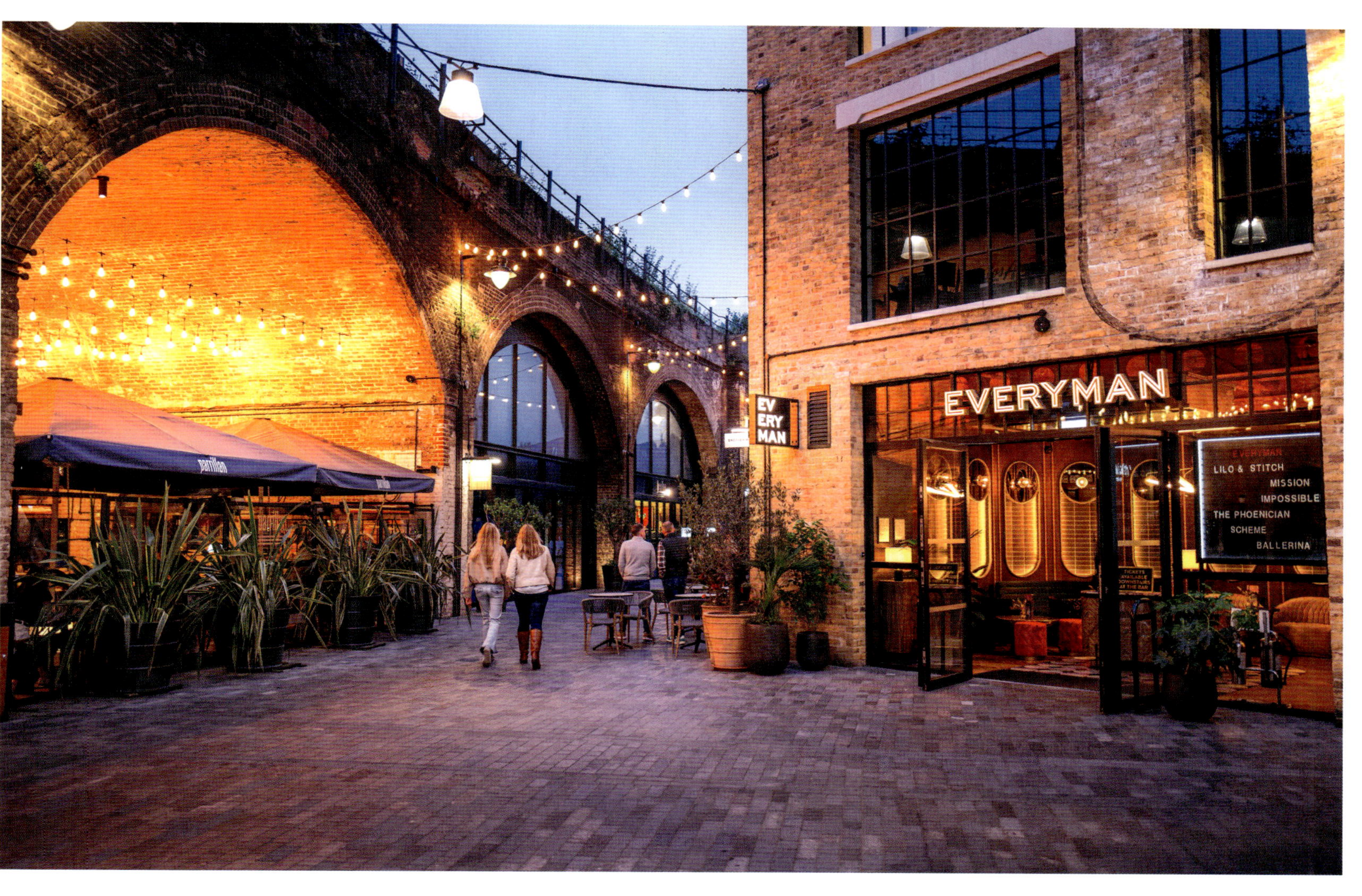
EVERYMAN
EV
ERY
MAN
EVERYMAN
LILO & STITCH
MISSION
IMPOSSIBLE
THE PHOENICIAN
SCHEME
BALLERINA

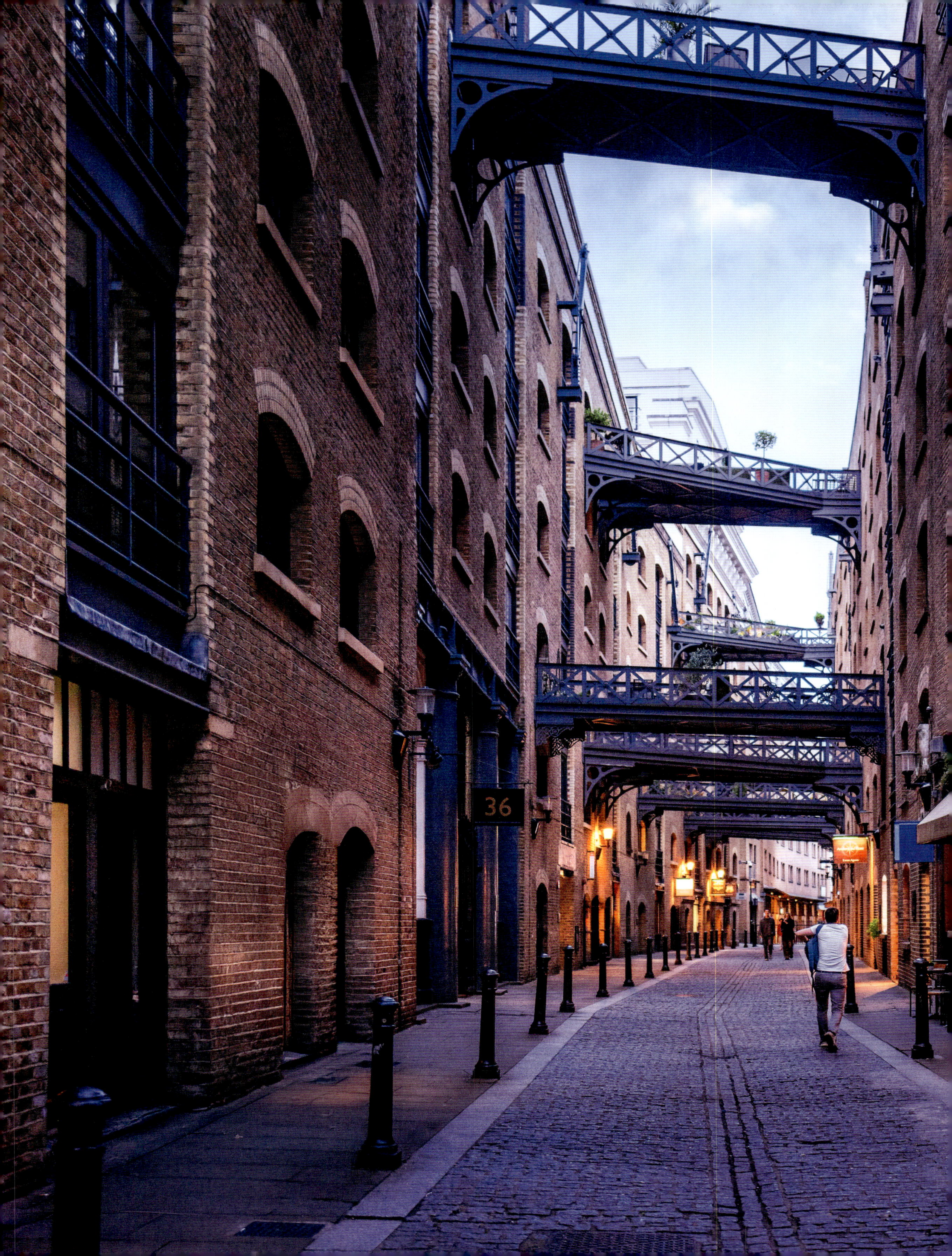
36

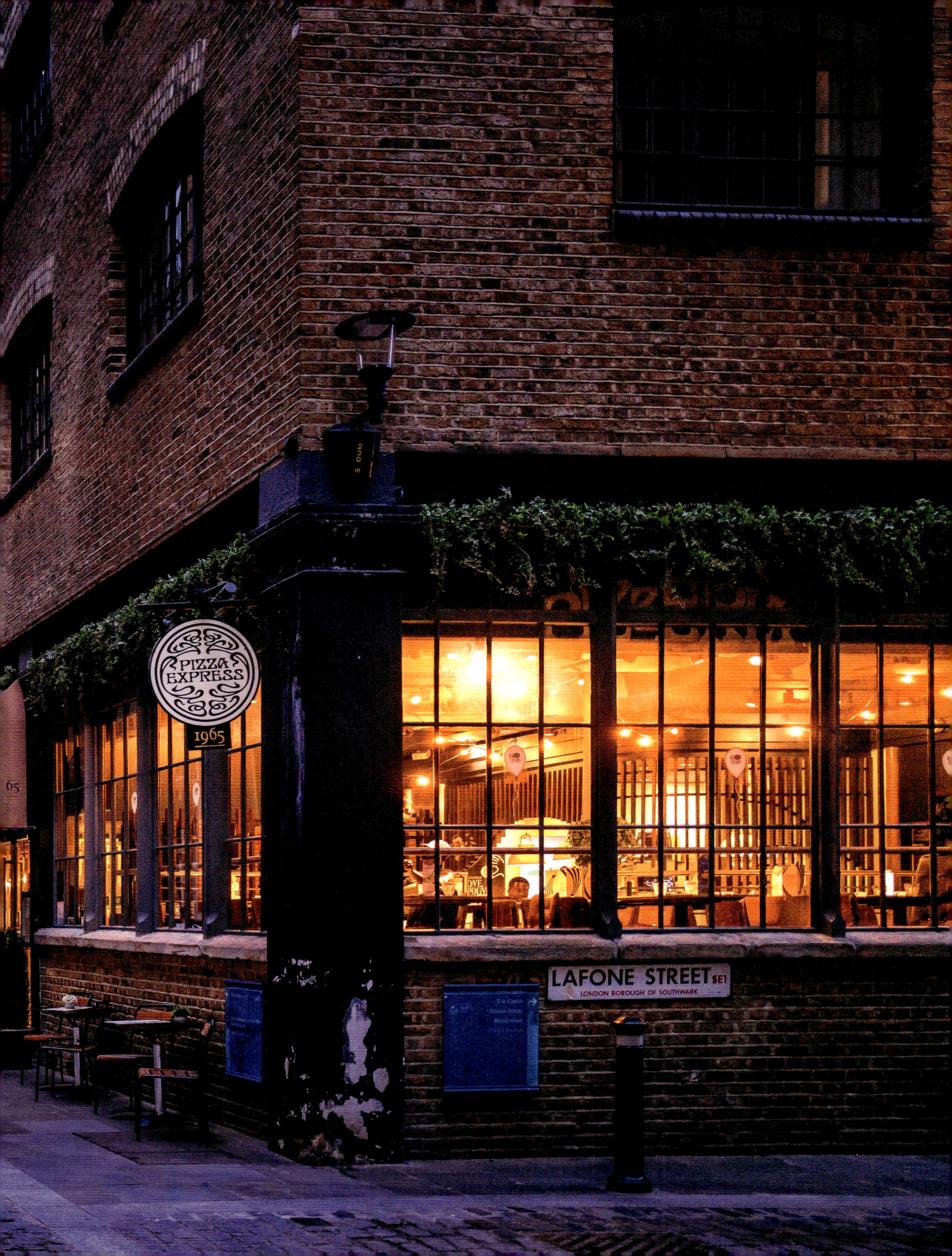
PIZZA EXPRESS
1965
LAFONE STREET SE1
LONDON BOROUGH OF SOUTHWARK

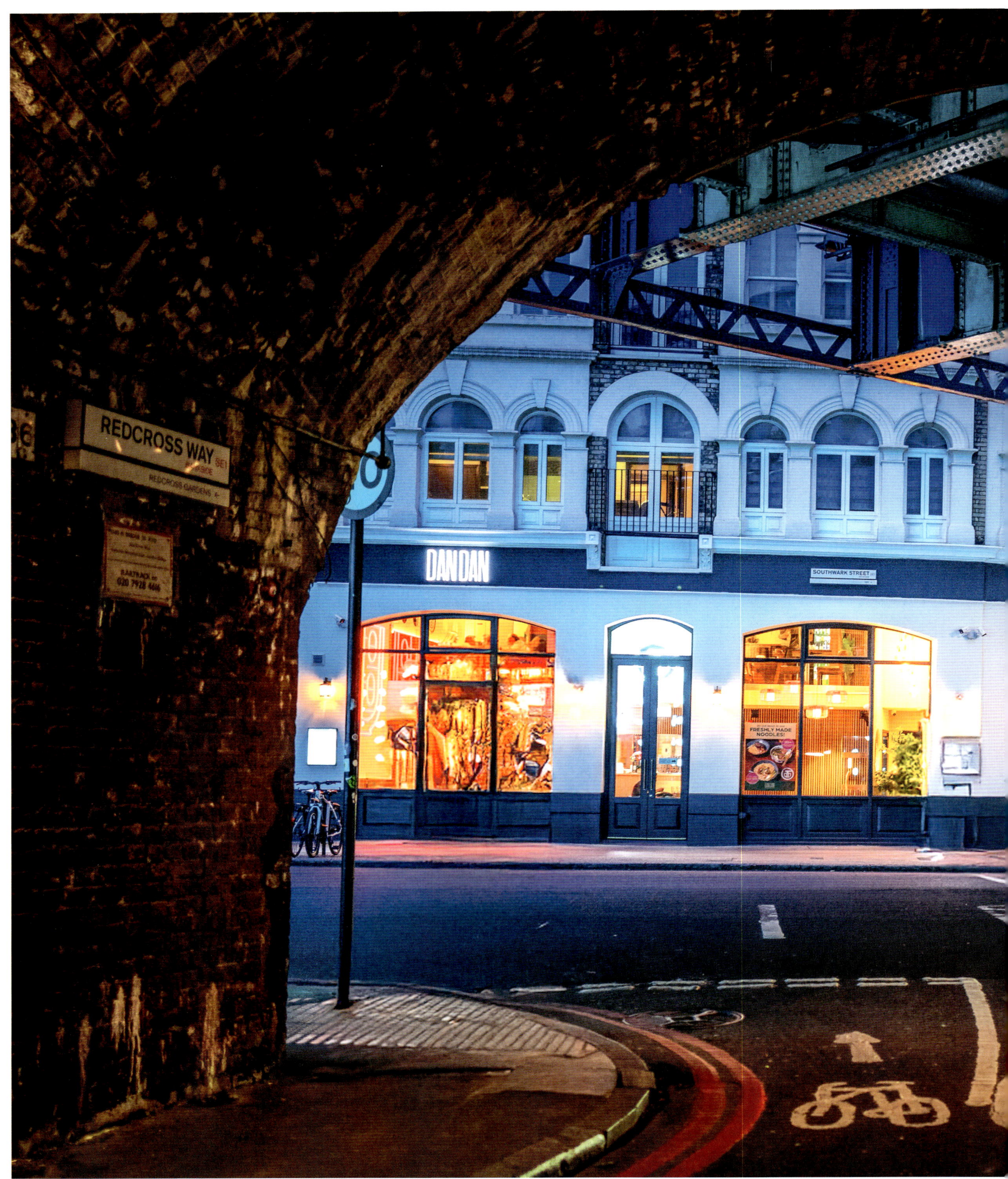
REDCROSS WAY SE1
REDCROSS GARDENS
DAN DAN
SOUTHWARK STREET
FRESHLY MADE NOODLES!

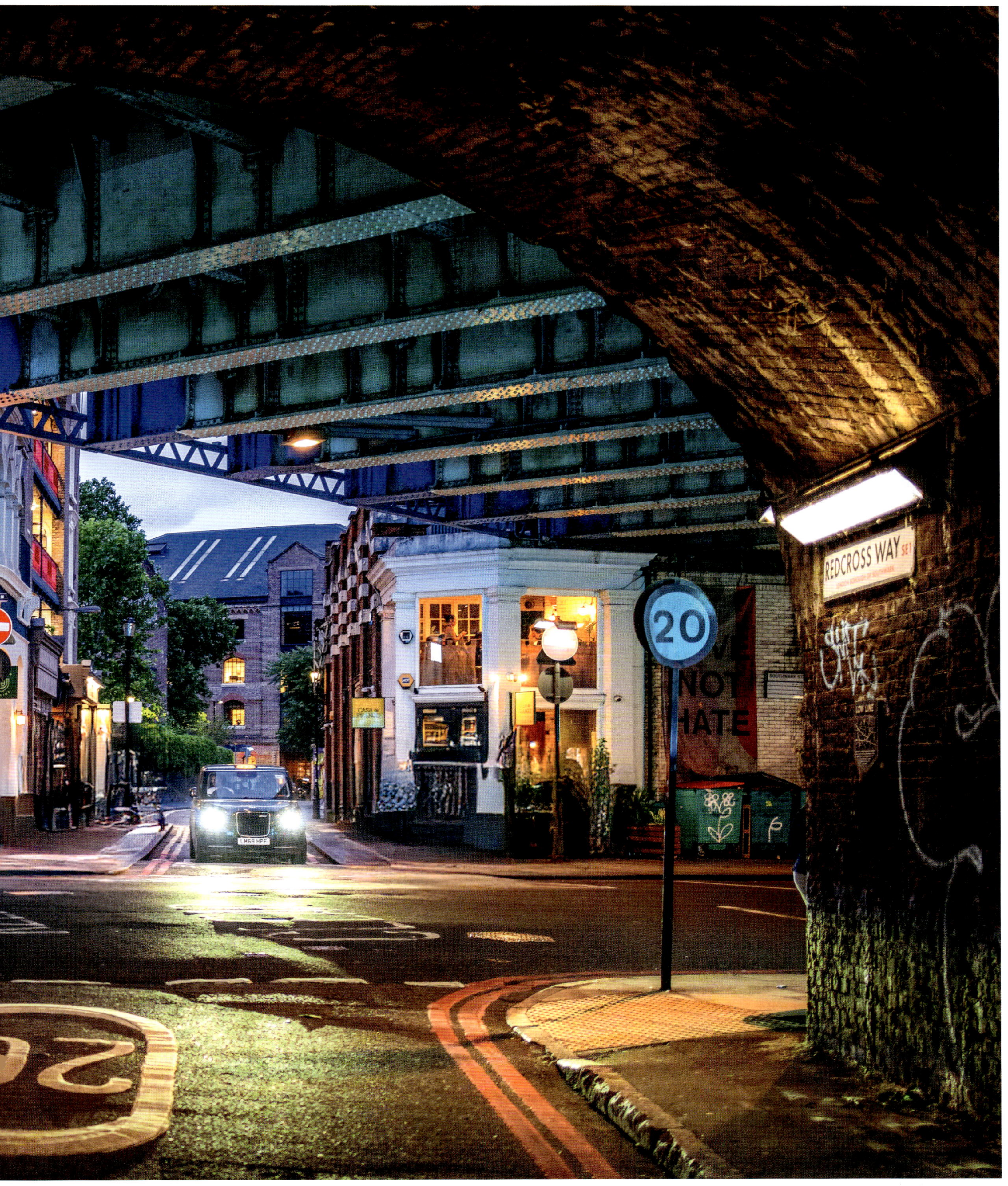
REDCROSS WAY SE1
20
NOT
HATE
LM68 HPF

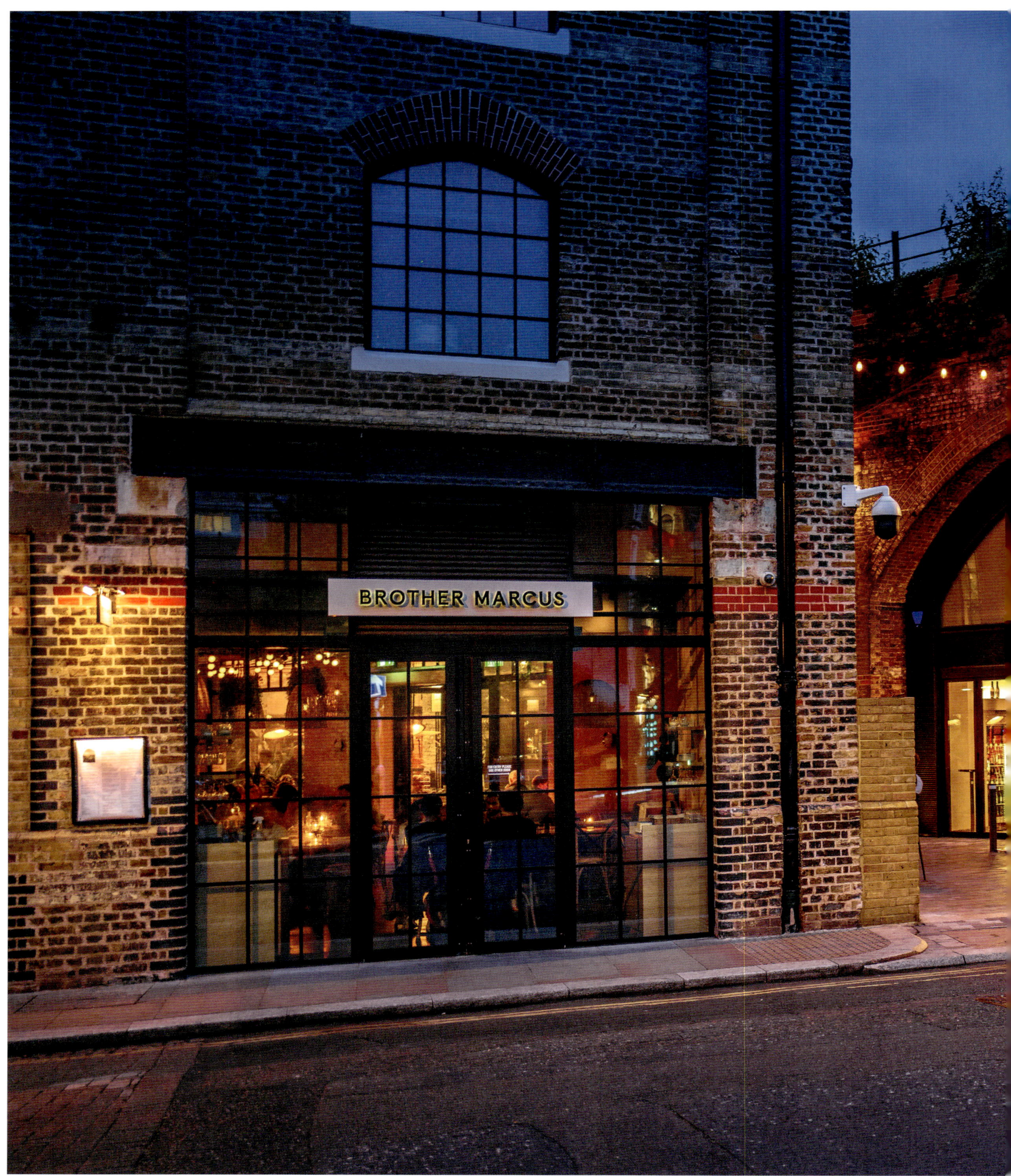
BROTHER MARCUS

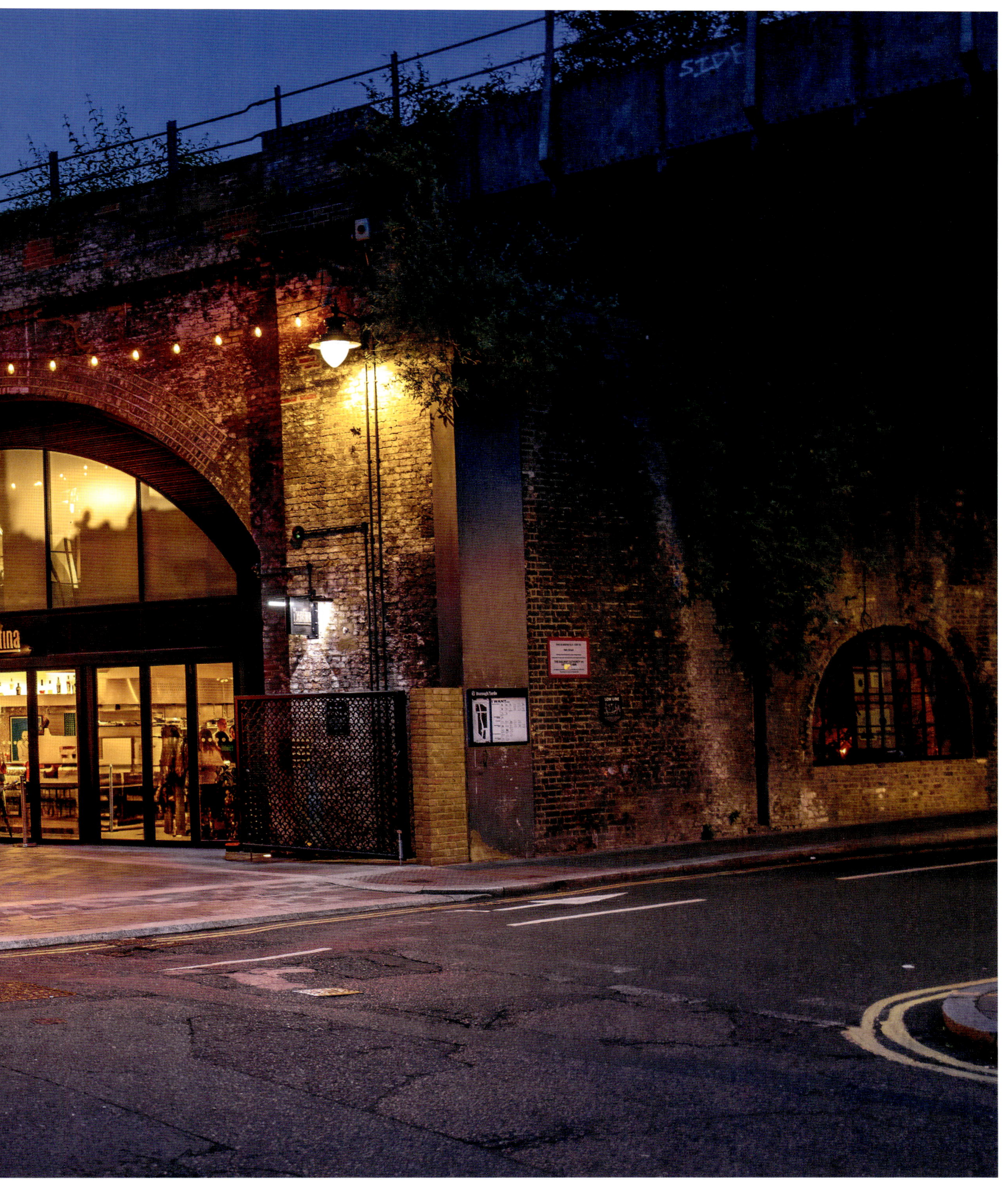

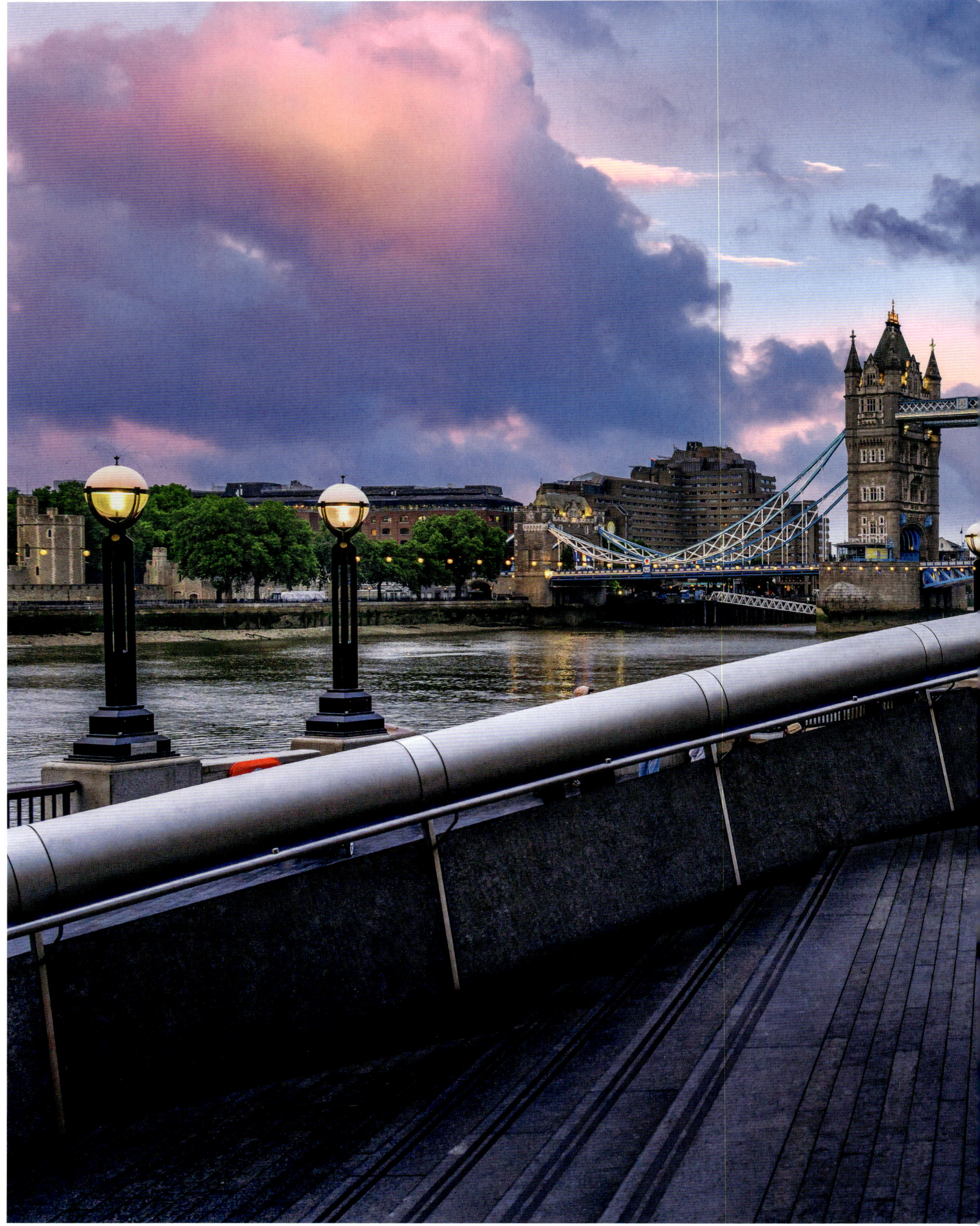

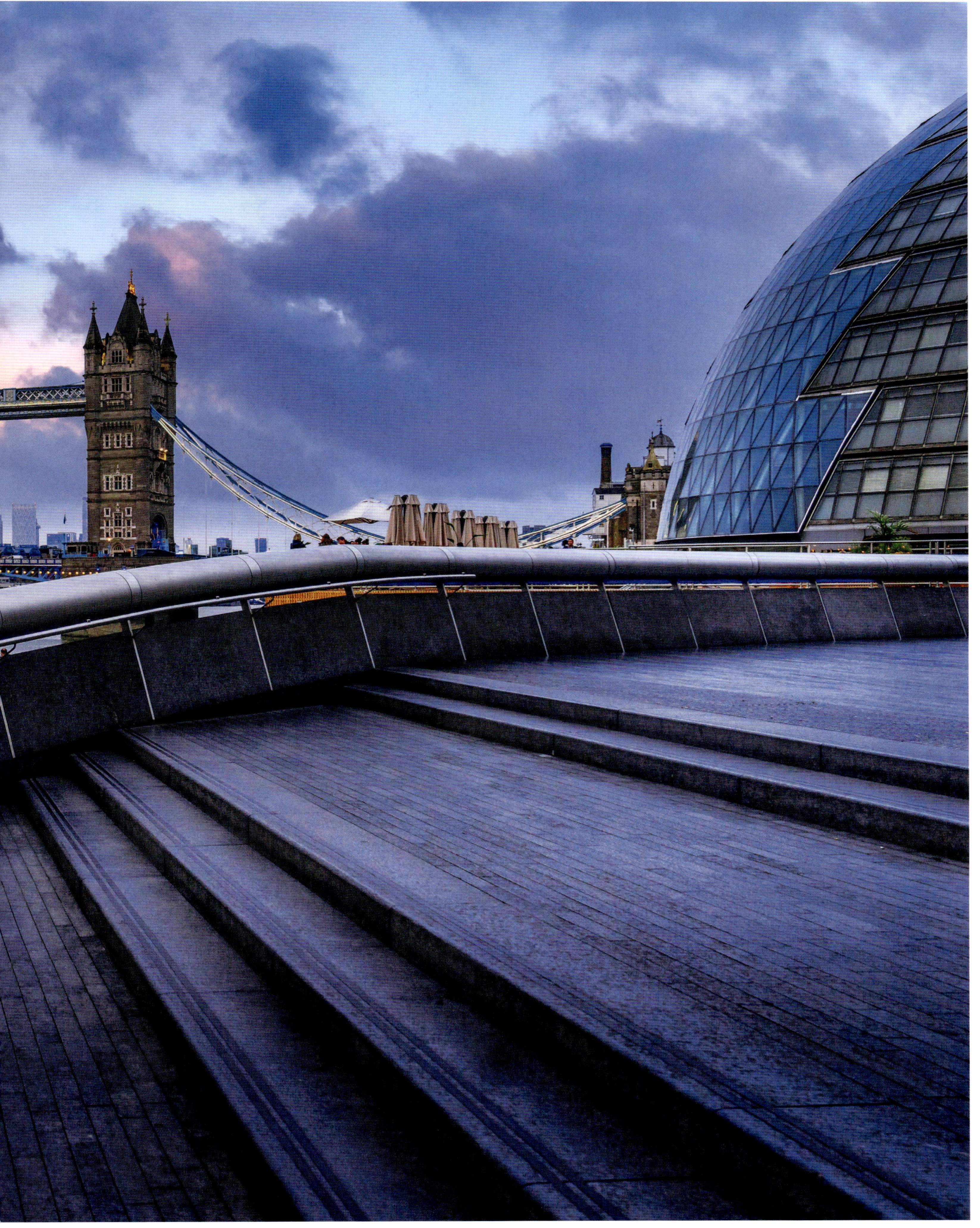

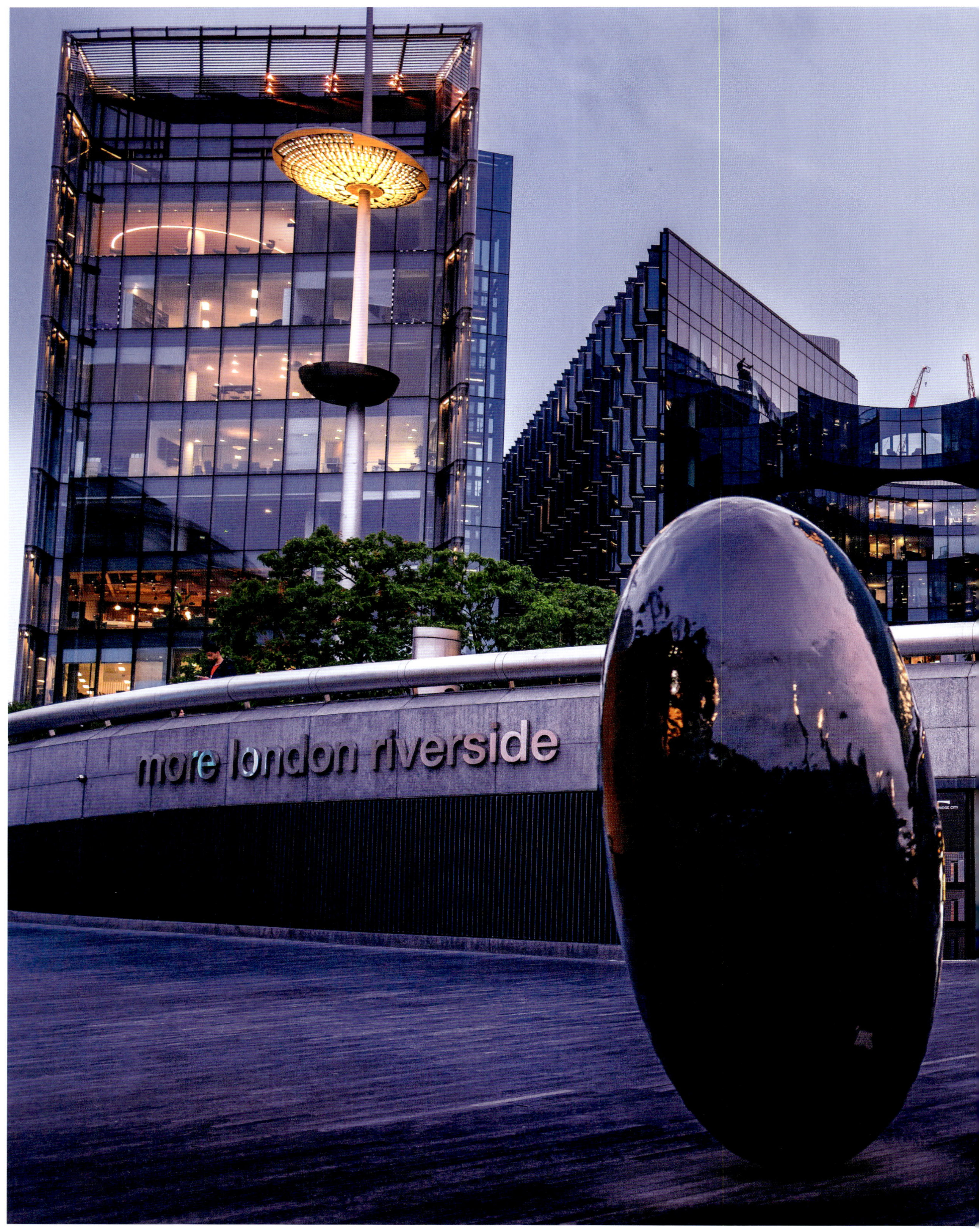
more london riverside

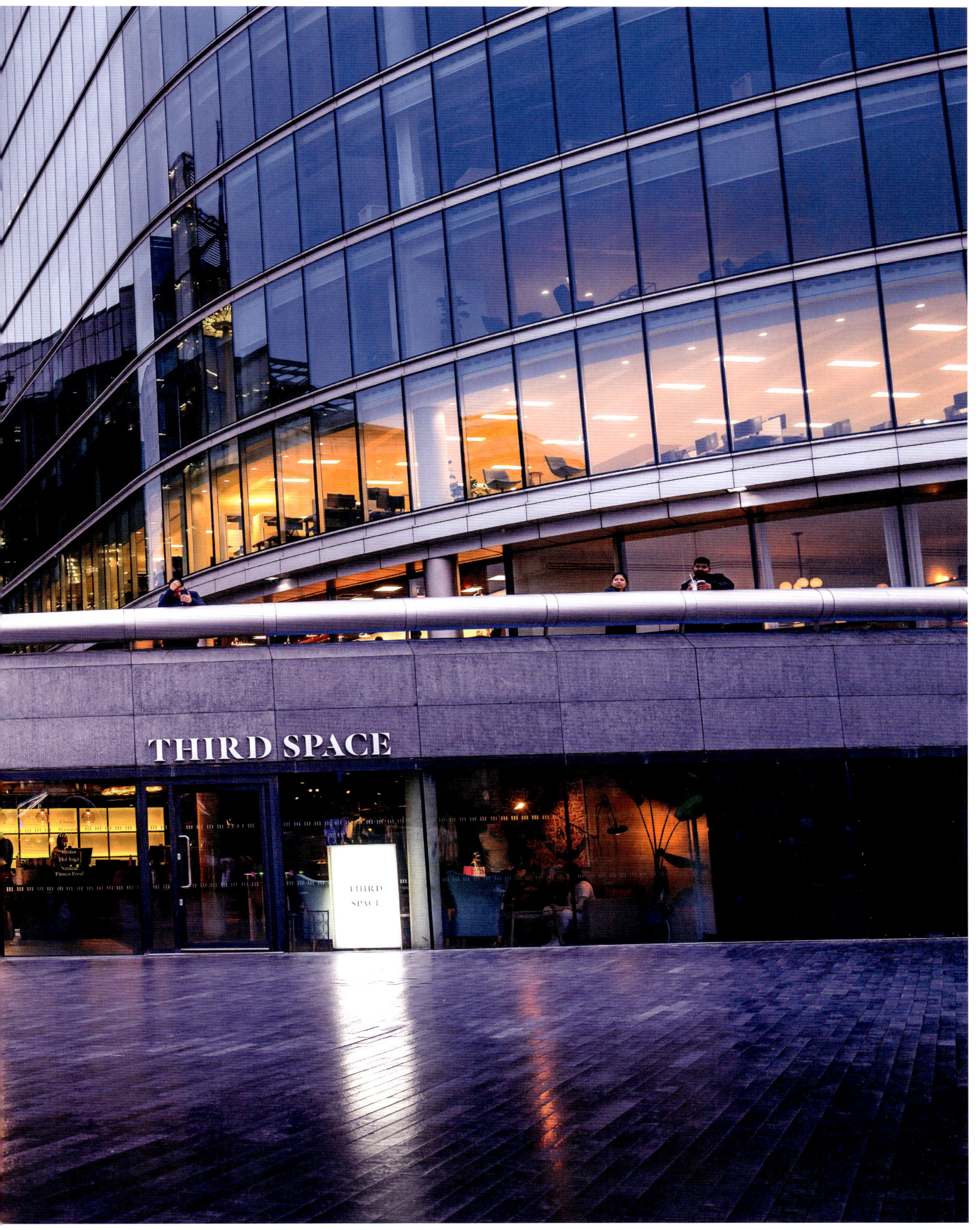
THIRD SPACE
THIRD
SPACE

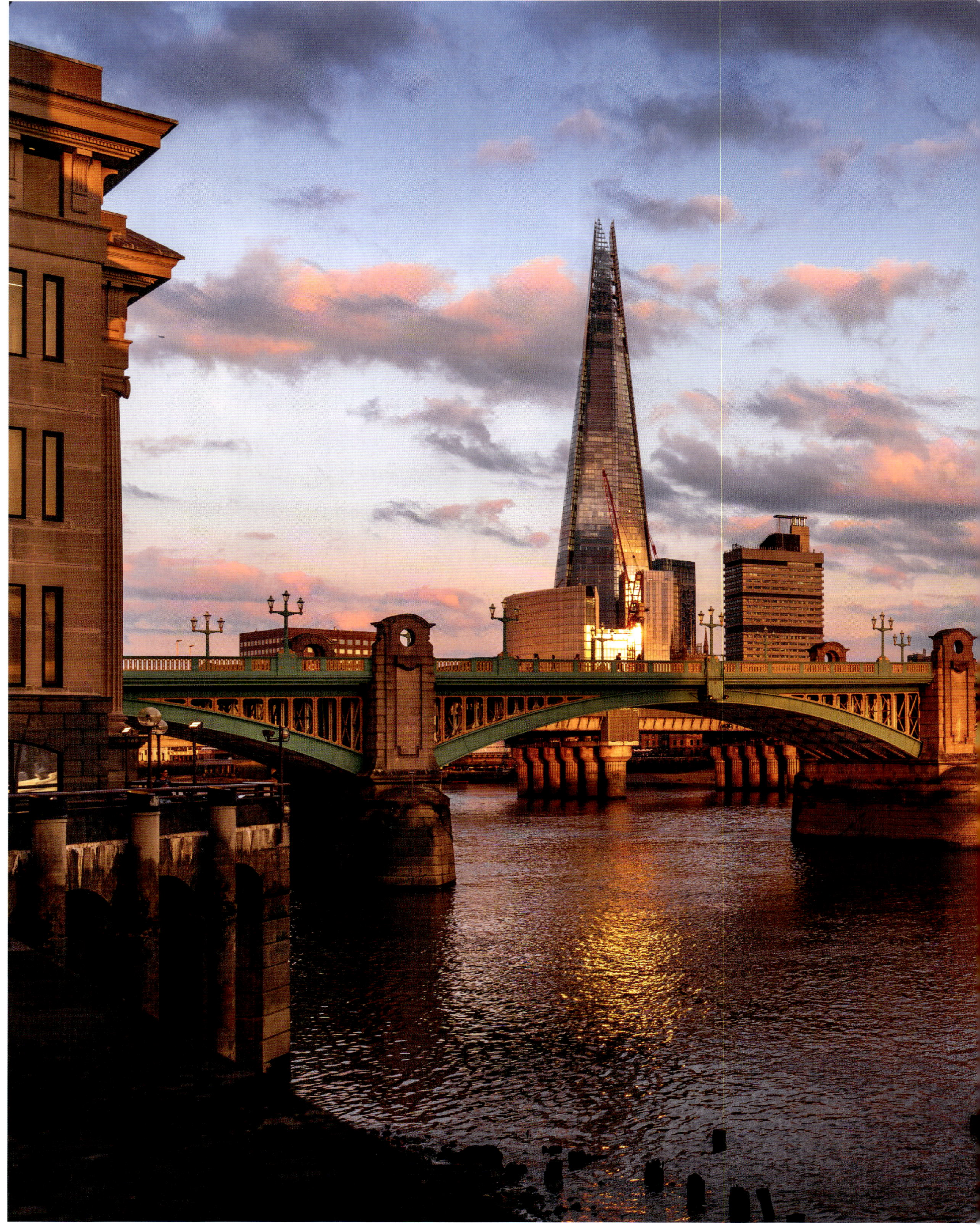

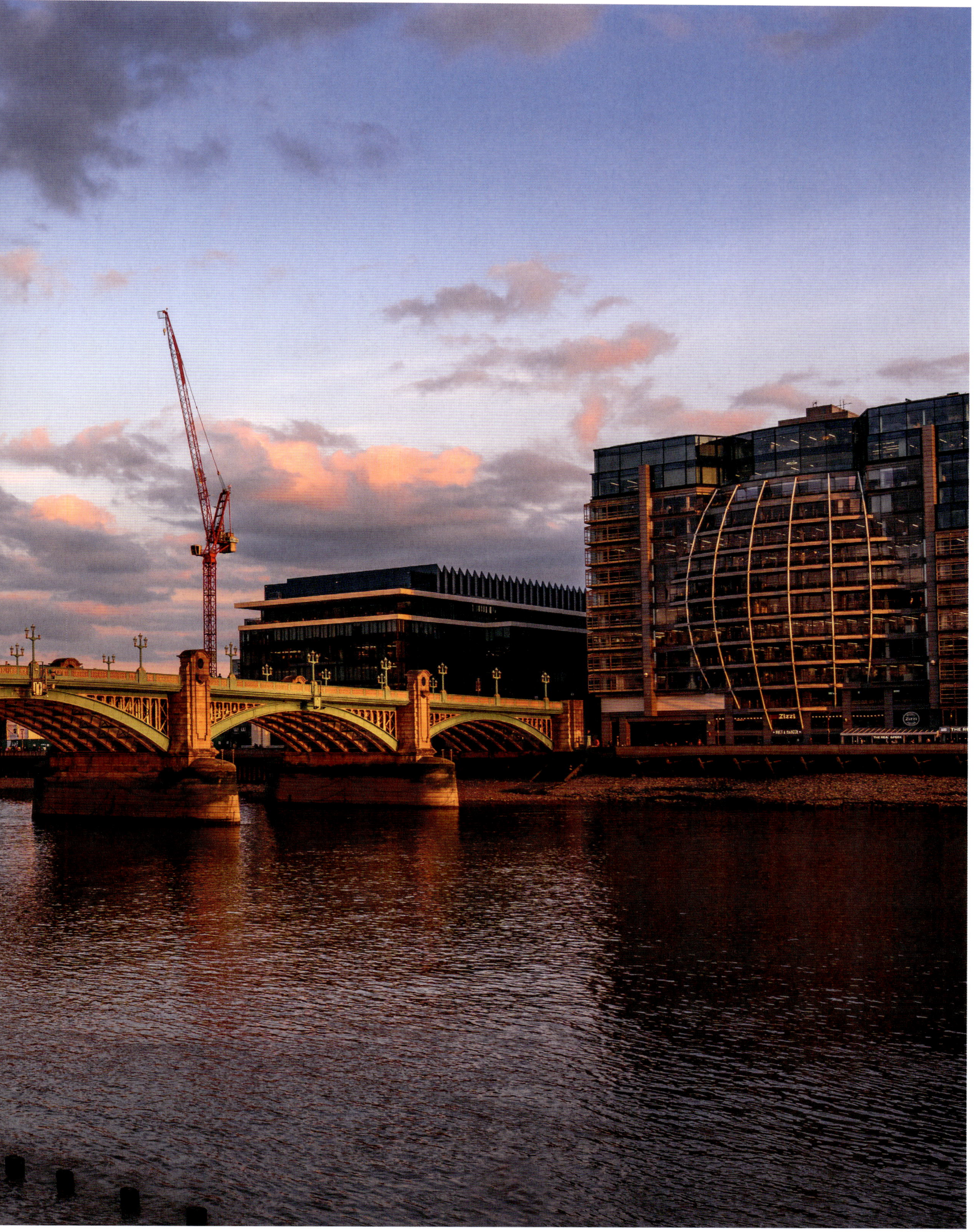

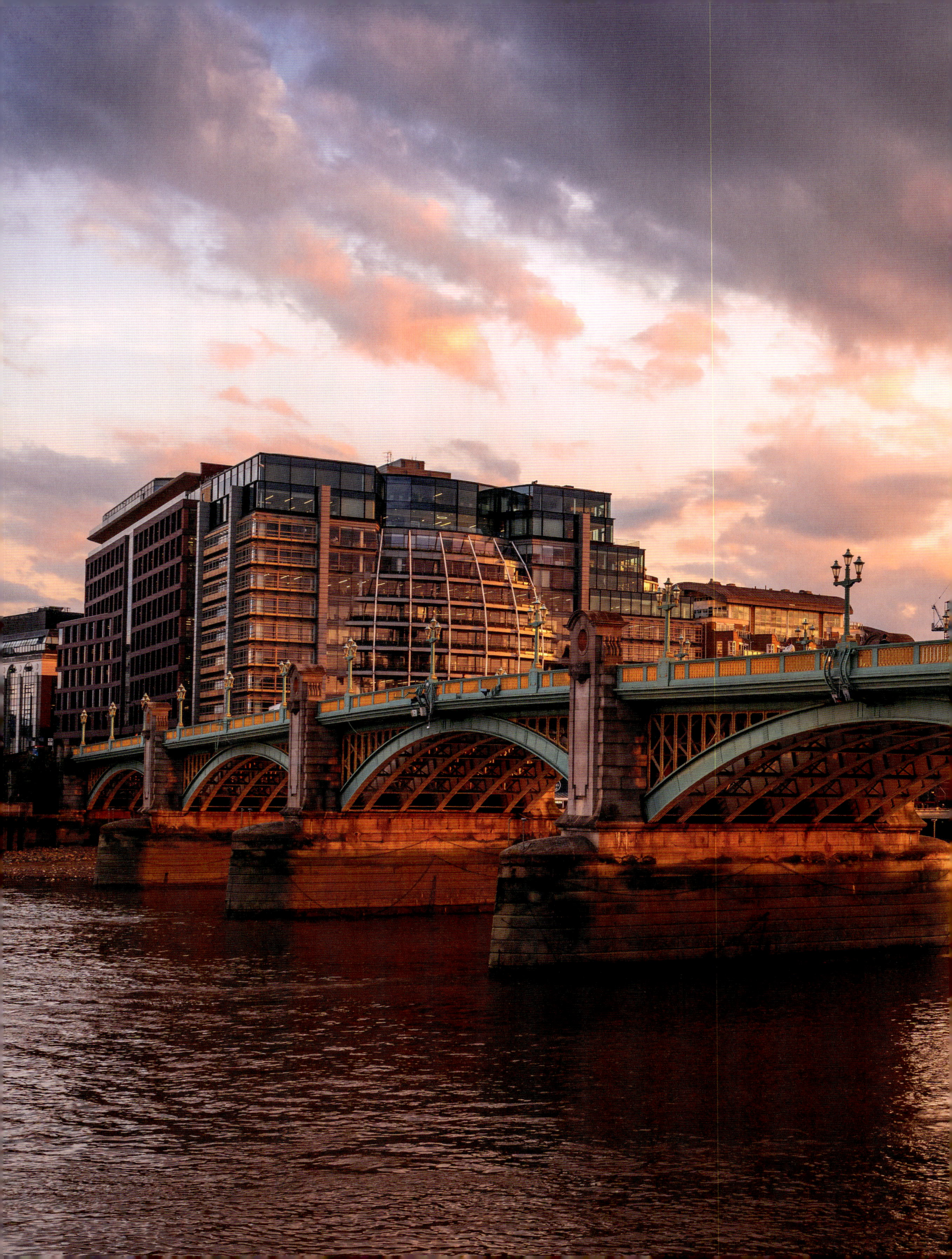

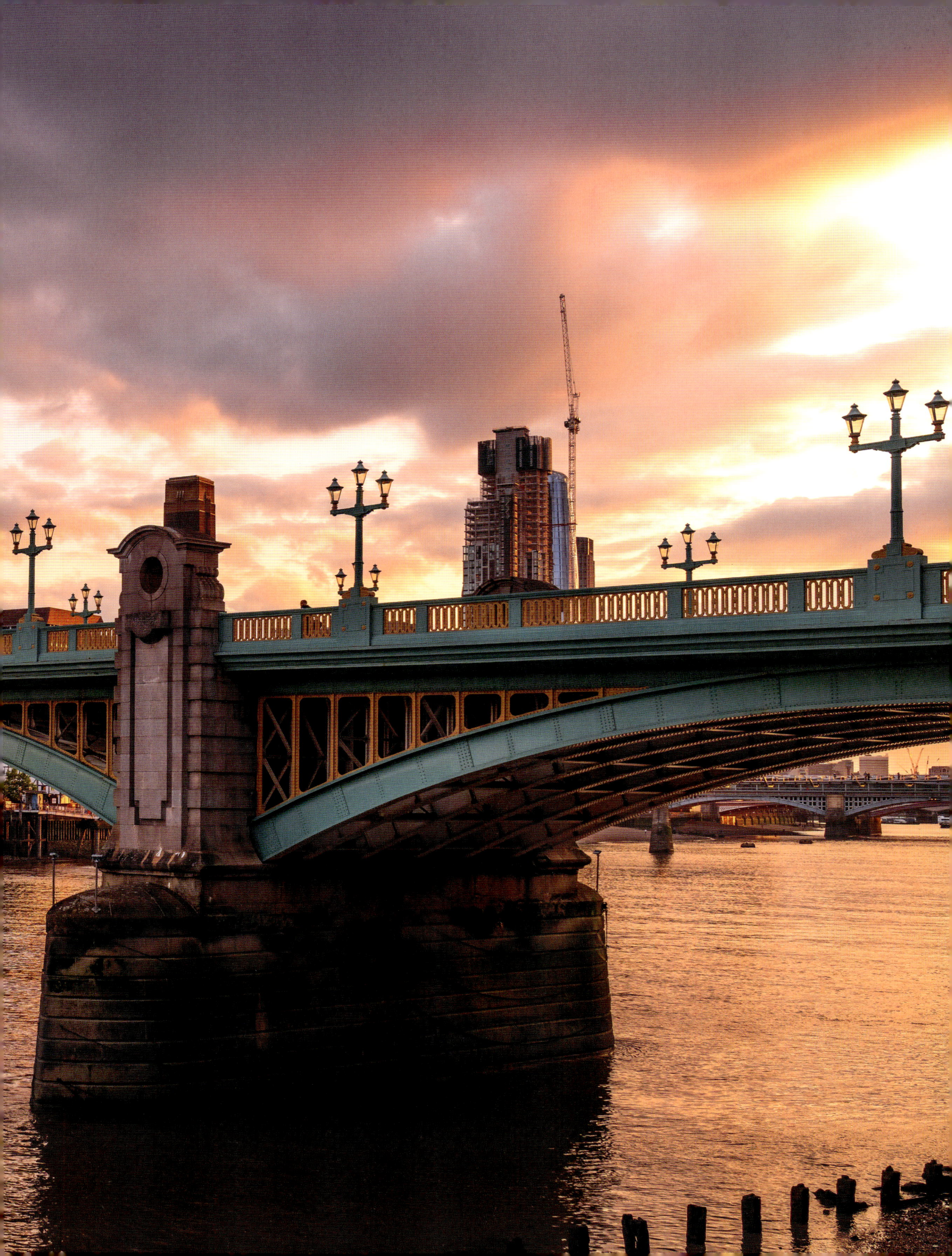

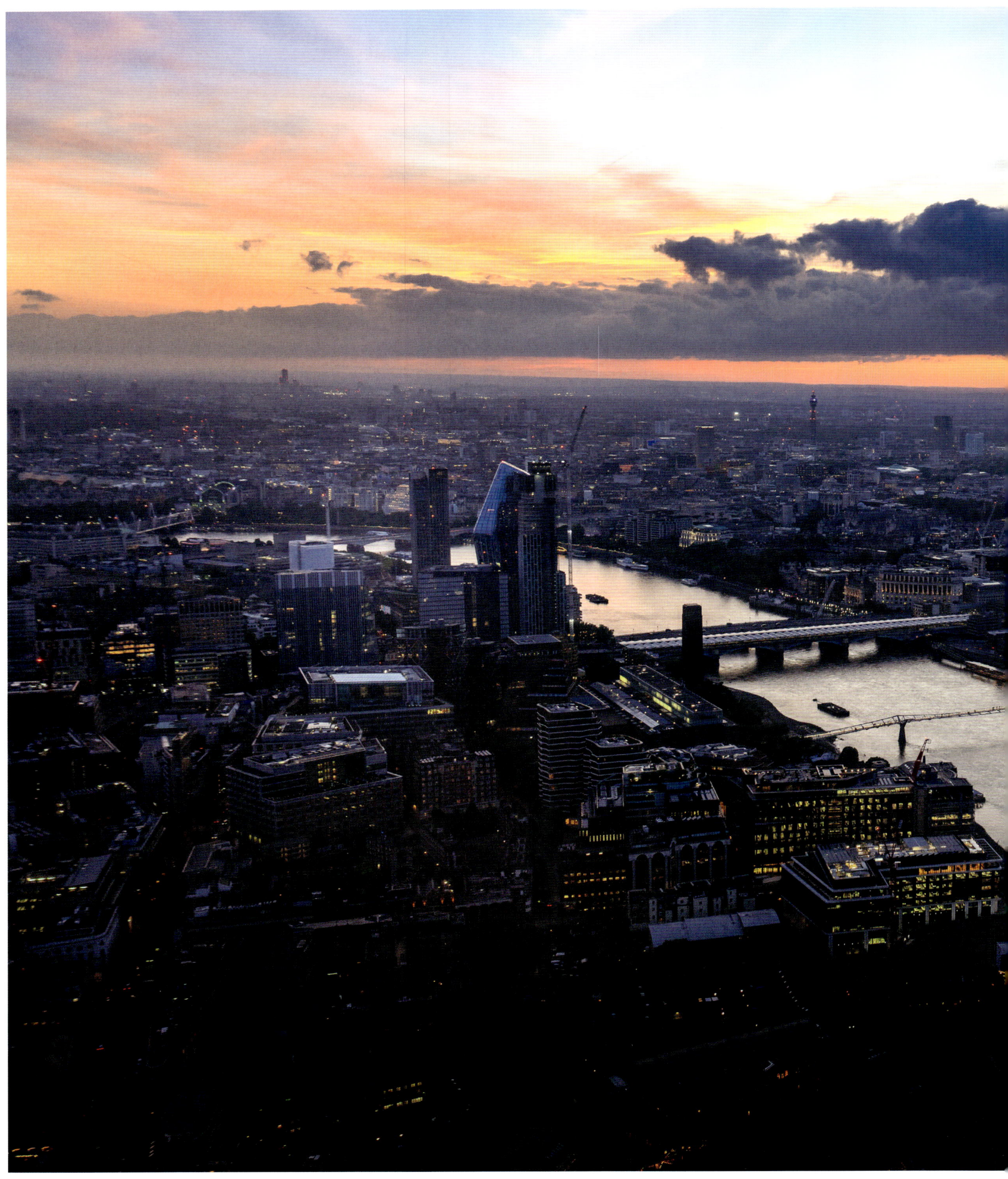

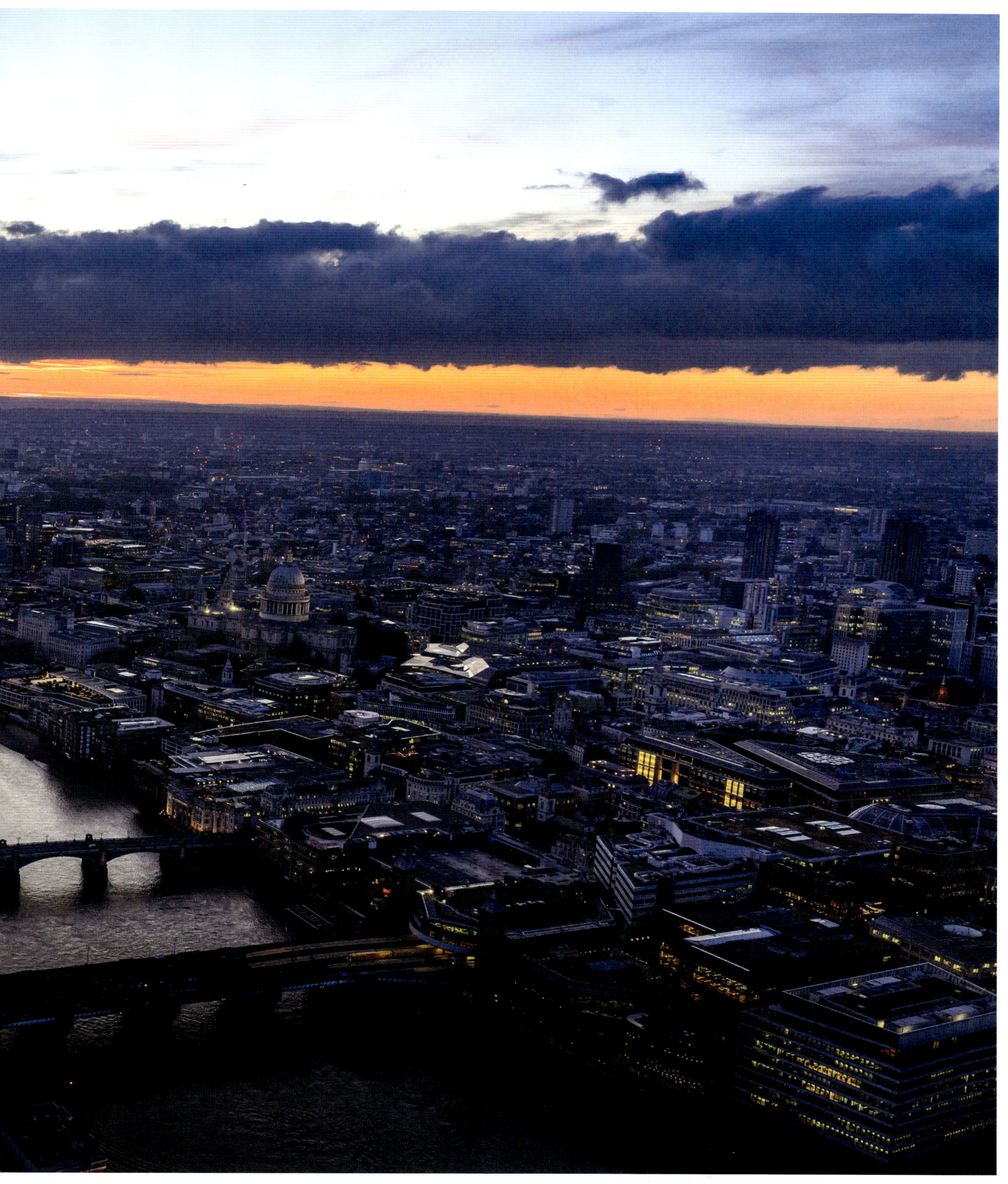

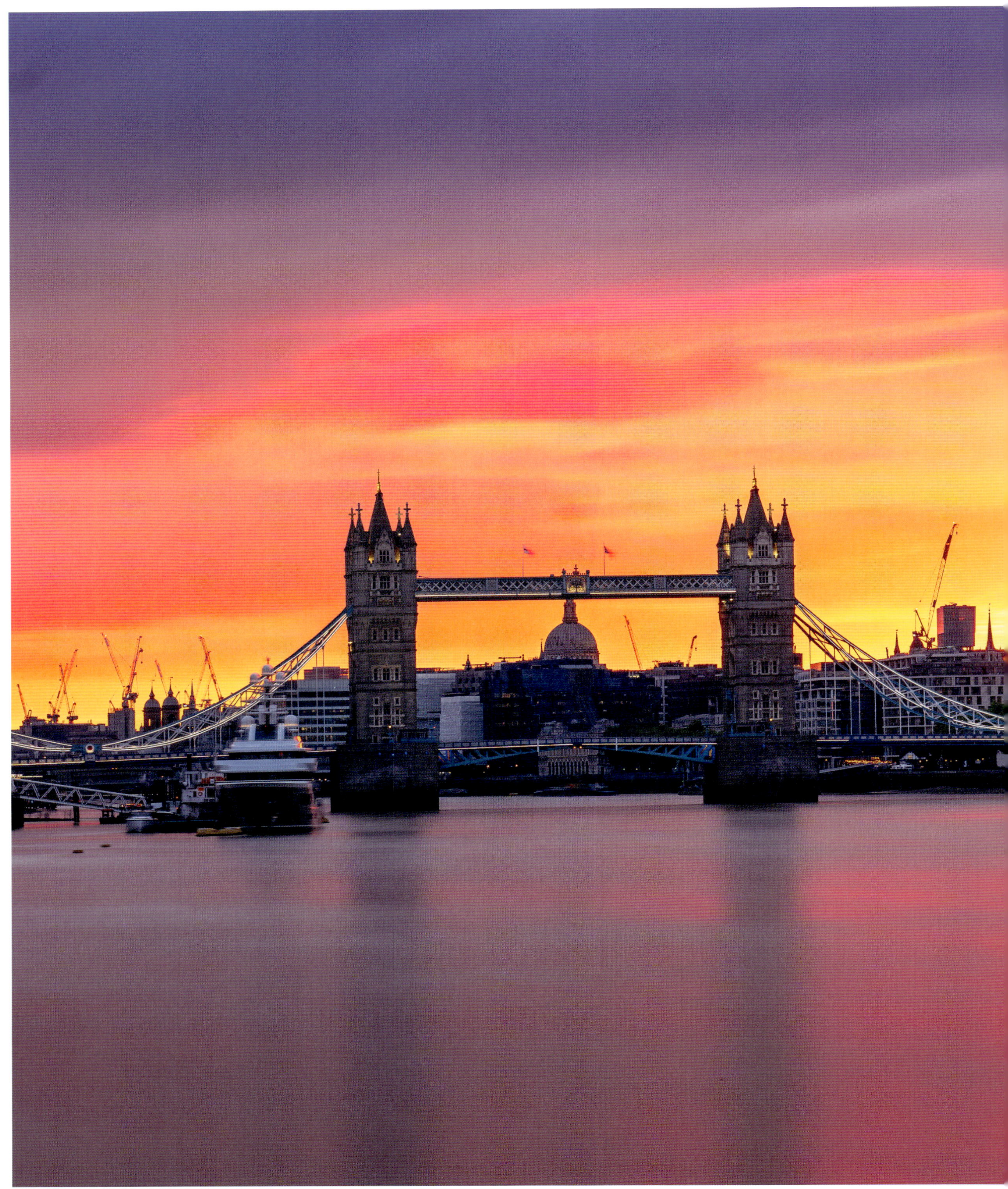

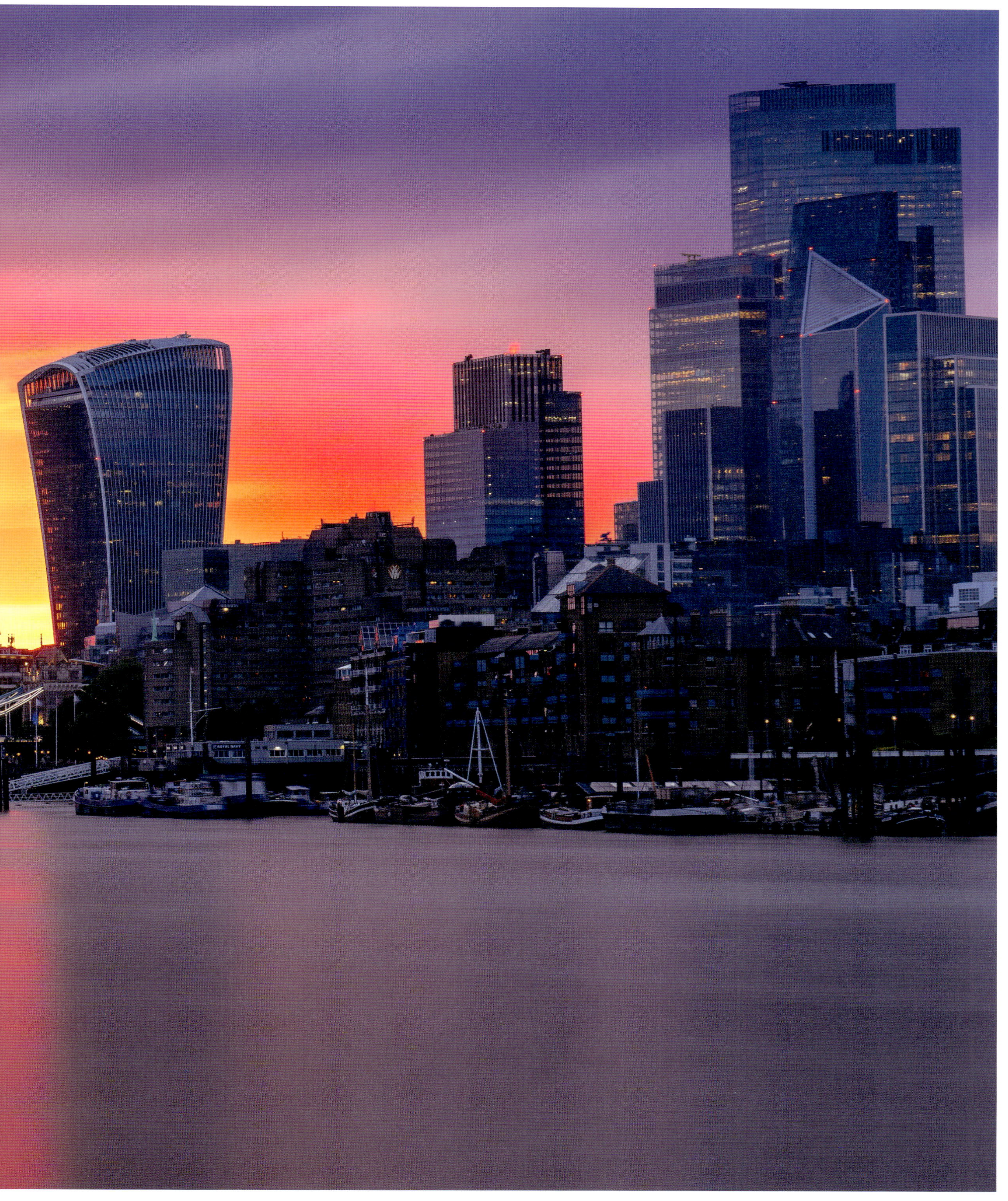

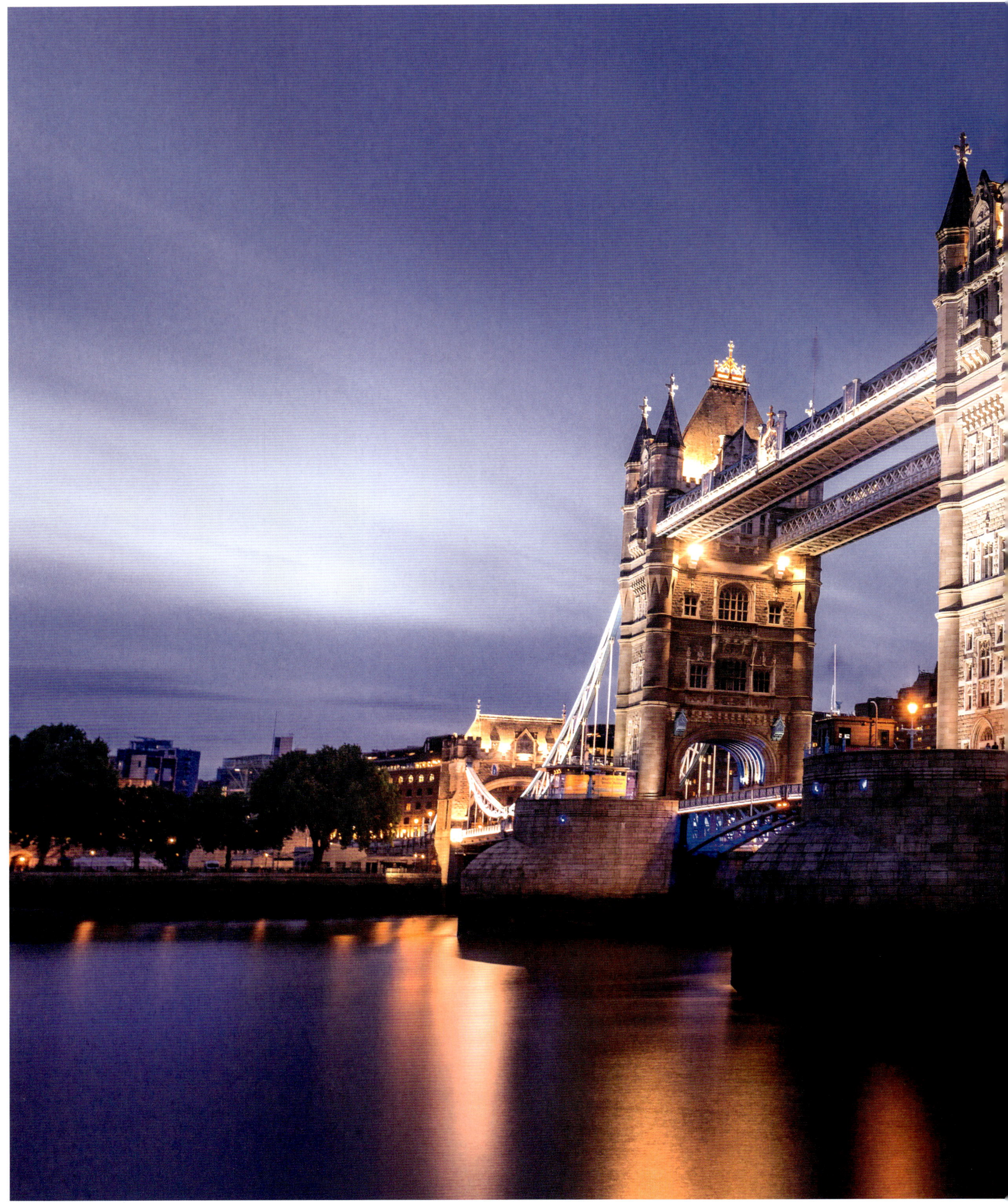

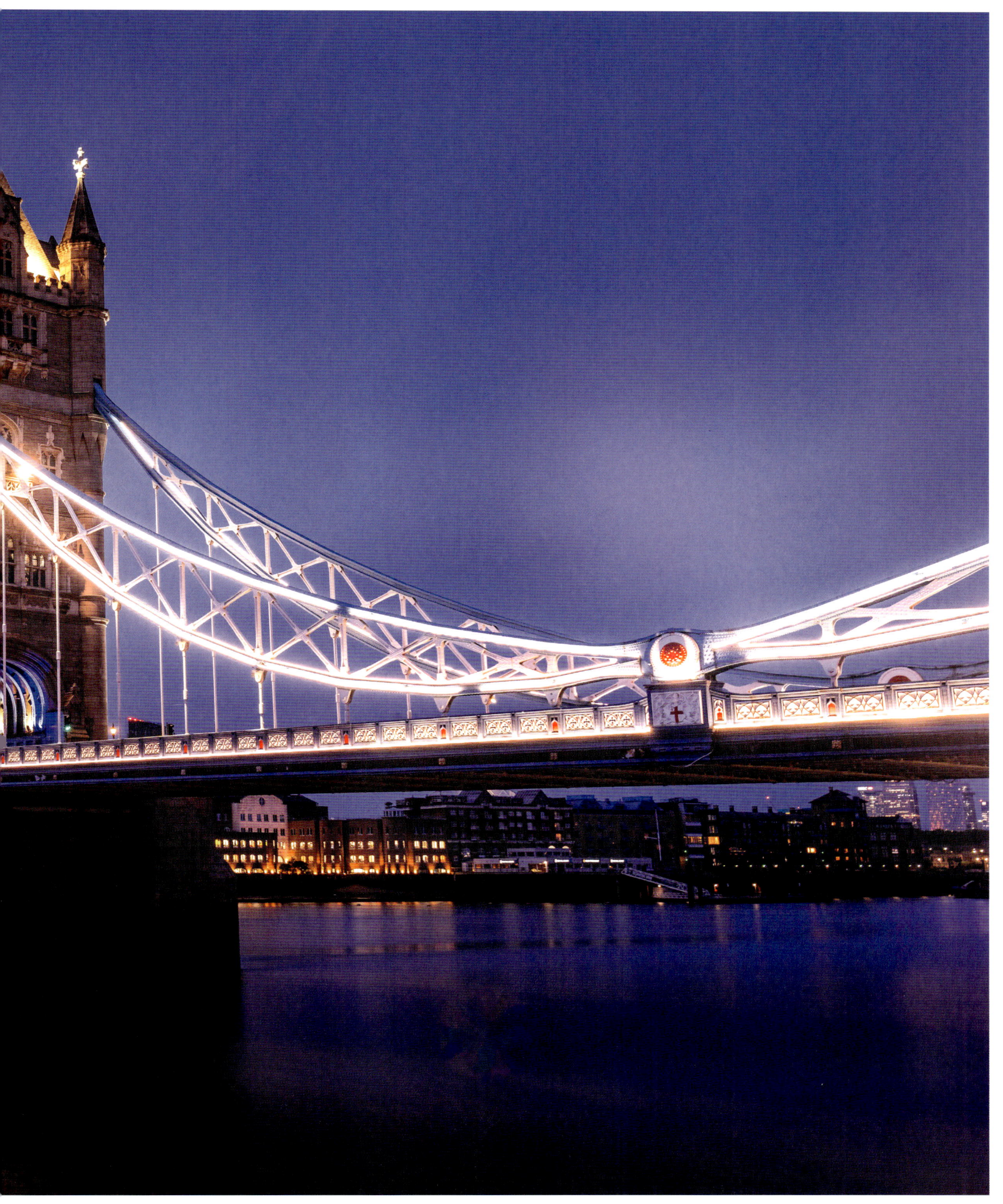

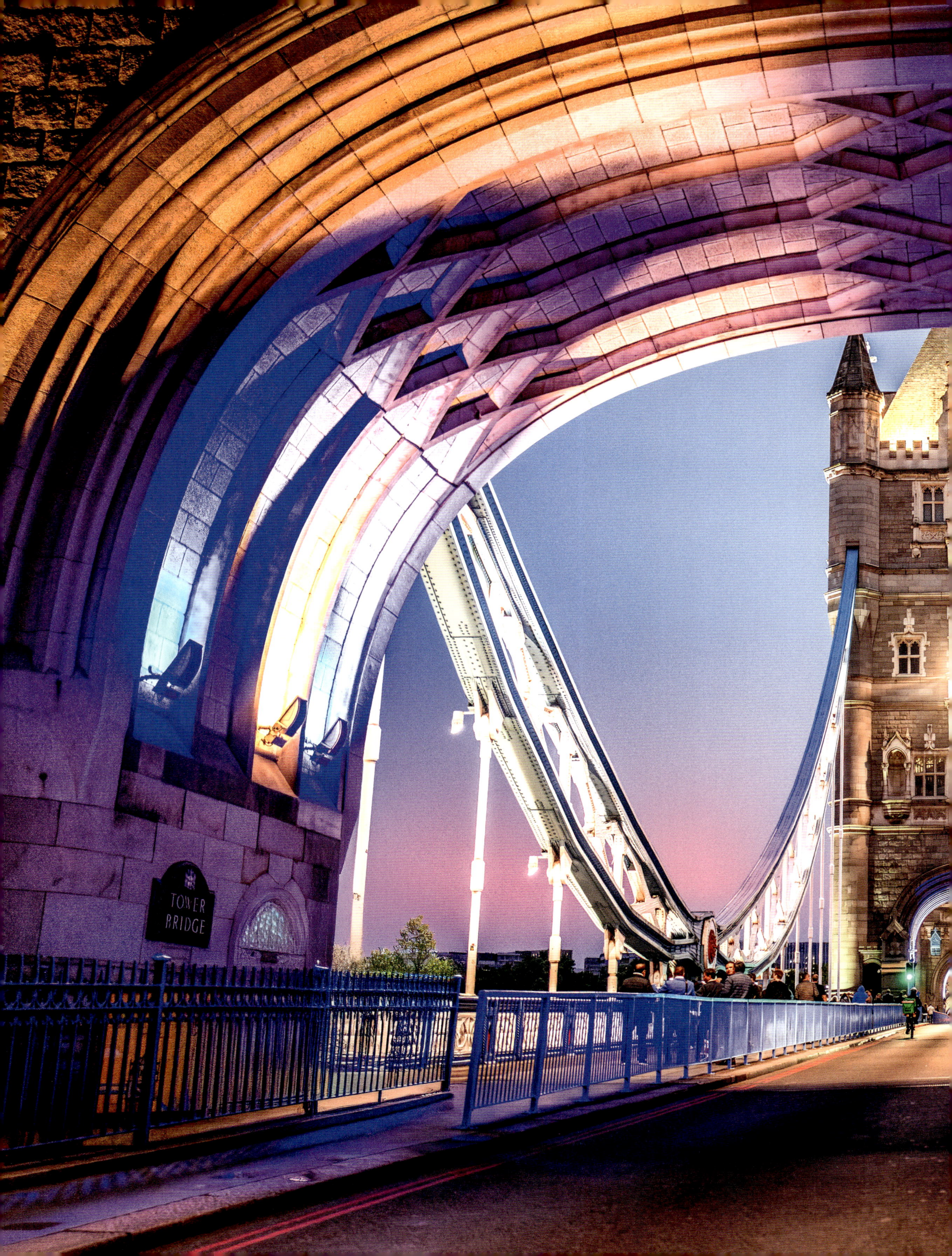
TOWER
BRIDGE

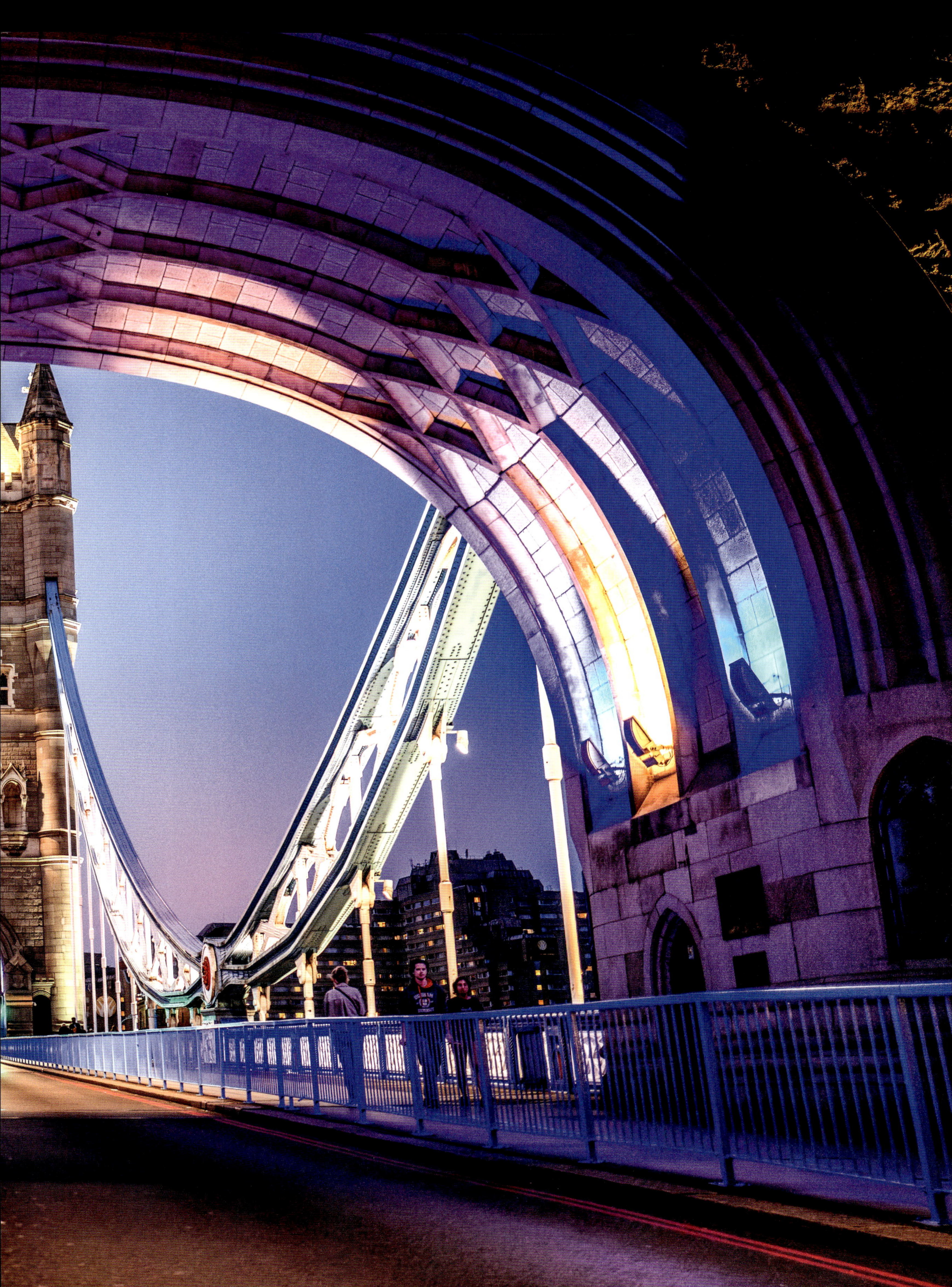

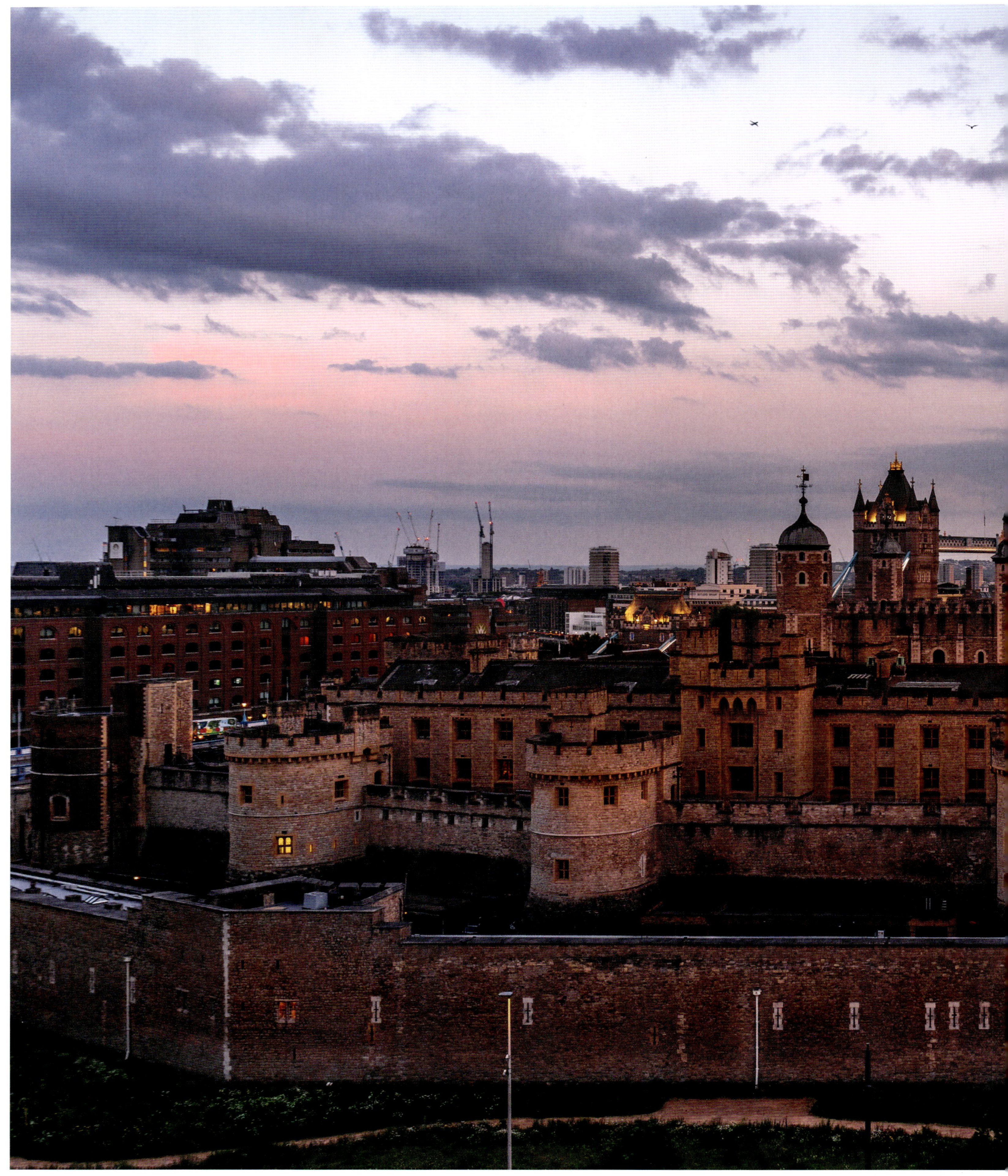

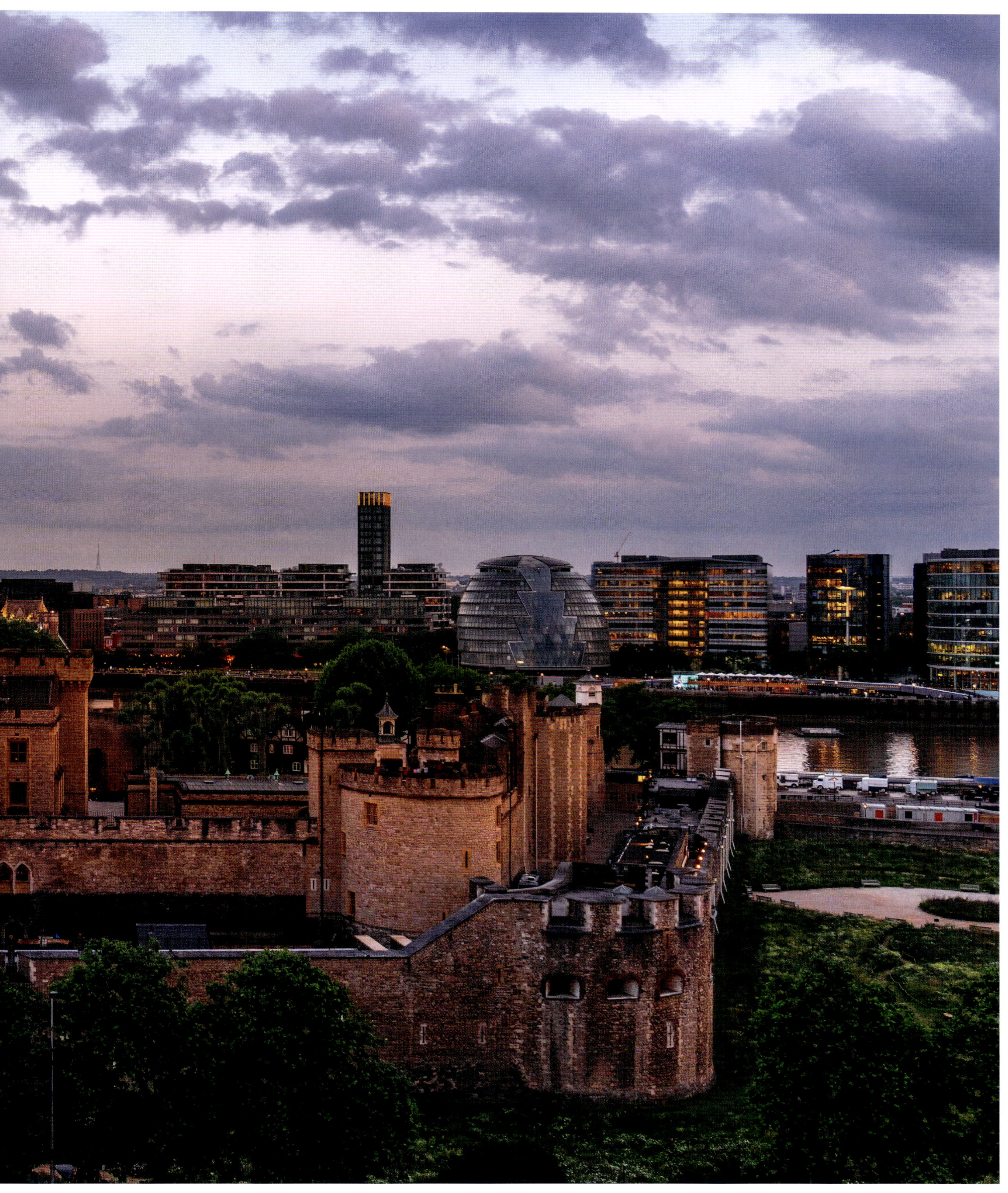

Pages 144–145: Southwark Bridge and the Shard at sunset. At 1,016 feet (310 meters) tall, the skyscraper was Europe's tallest building for a few months in 2012.

Pages 154–155: Tower Bridge framed through an illuminated stone archway, offering a dramatic view from below. This iconic London landmark, completed in 1894, is built in the Victorian Gothic style and features both bascule and suspension bridges.

Previous pages and opposite: The Tower of London at dusk. Throughout its long history, this World Heritage Site has served as a prison, London's first zoo, a military fortress, and the secure home of the Crown Jewels.

Seiten 144–145: Southwark Bridge und der Shard bei Sonnenuntergang. Mit 310 Metern war der Wolkenkratzer 2012 zwei Monate lang das höchste Gebäude Europas.

Seiten 154–155: Ein effektvoller Blick auf die Tower Bridge durch einen beleuchteten Steinbogen von unten. Dieses ikonische Wahrzeichen Londons aus dem Jahr 1894 im neugotischen Stil ist eine kombinierte Klapp- und Hängebrücke.

Vorherige und diese Seite: Der Tower of London bei Sonnenuntergang. Im Laufe seiner langen Geschichte diente das UNESCO-Weltkulturerbe als Gefängnis, Londons erster Zoo, Militärfort und sichere Aufbewahrungsstätte der Kronjuwelen.

Pages 144–145 : Southwark Bridge et « The Shard » (le tesson de verre). Culminant à 310 mètres, ce gratte-ciel a été le plus haut édifice d'Europe pendant quelques mois en 2012.

Pages 154–155 : Spectaculaire vue en contre-plongée de Tower Bridge dans l'encadrement d'une arche en pierre illuminée. Cet emblème de Londres construit en style victorien en 1894 se compose d'un pont suspendu et d'un pont basculant.

Cette page et la précédente : La tour de Londres au crépuscule. Au fil de sa longue histoire, ce monument classé au patrimoine mondial a servi de prison, de premier zoo à la ville, de forteresse et de lieu sécurisé où sont conservés les joyaux de la Couronne.

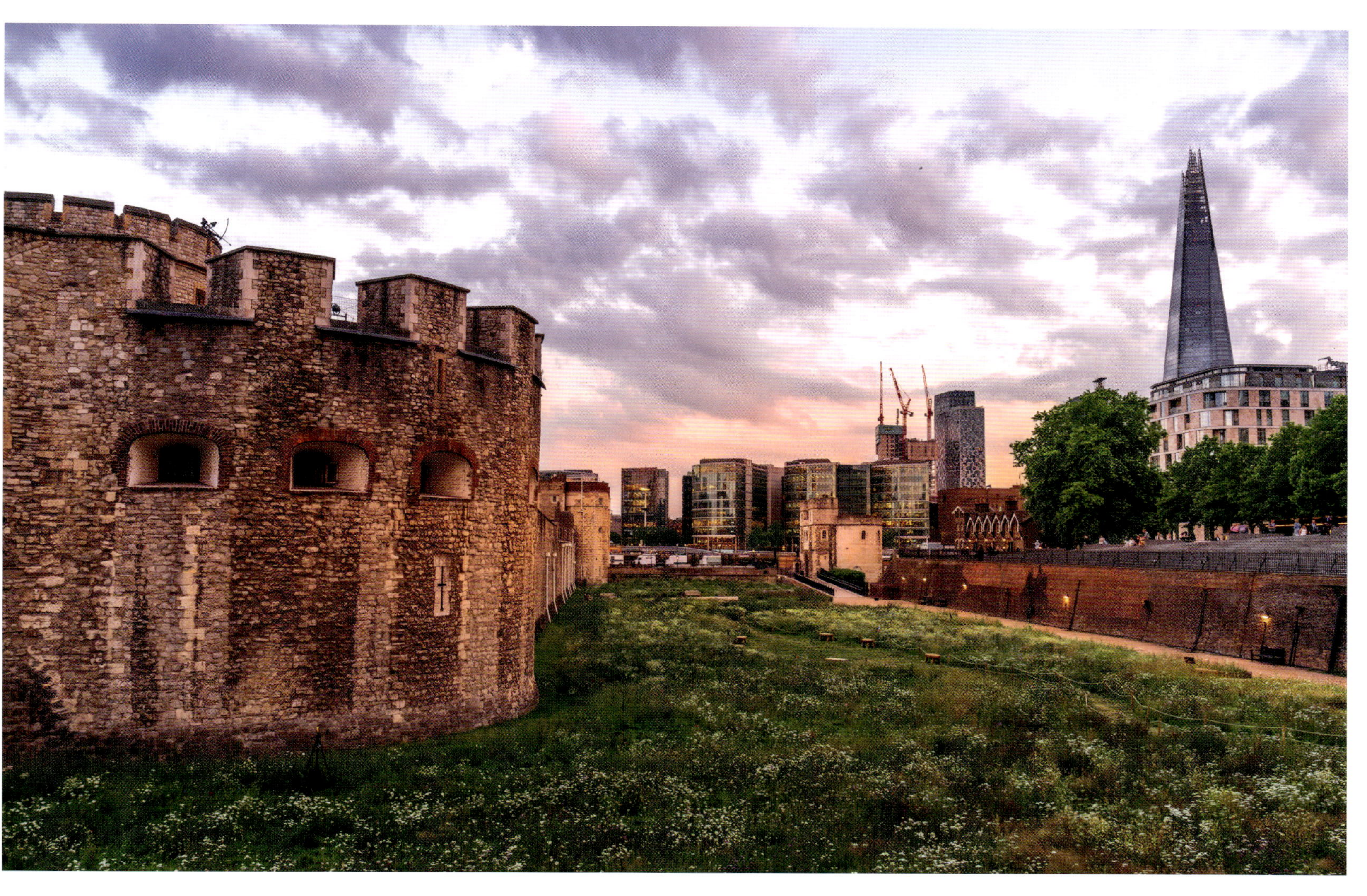

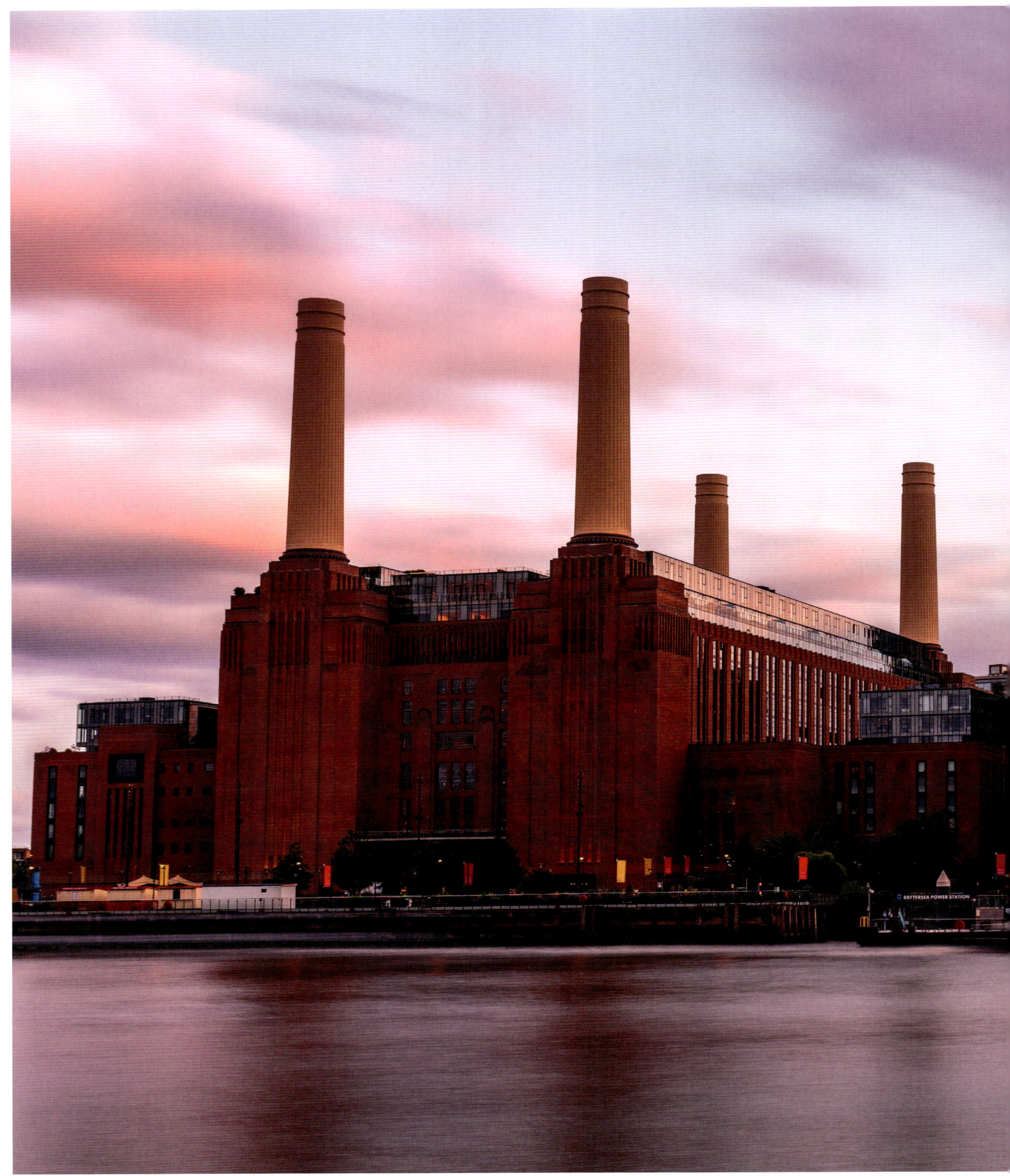
BATTERSEA POWER STATION

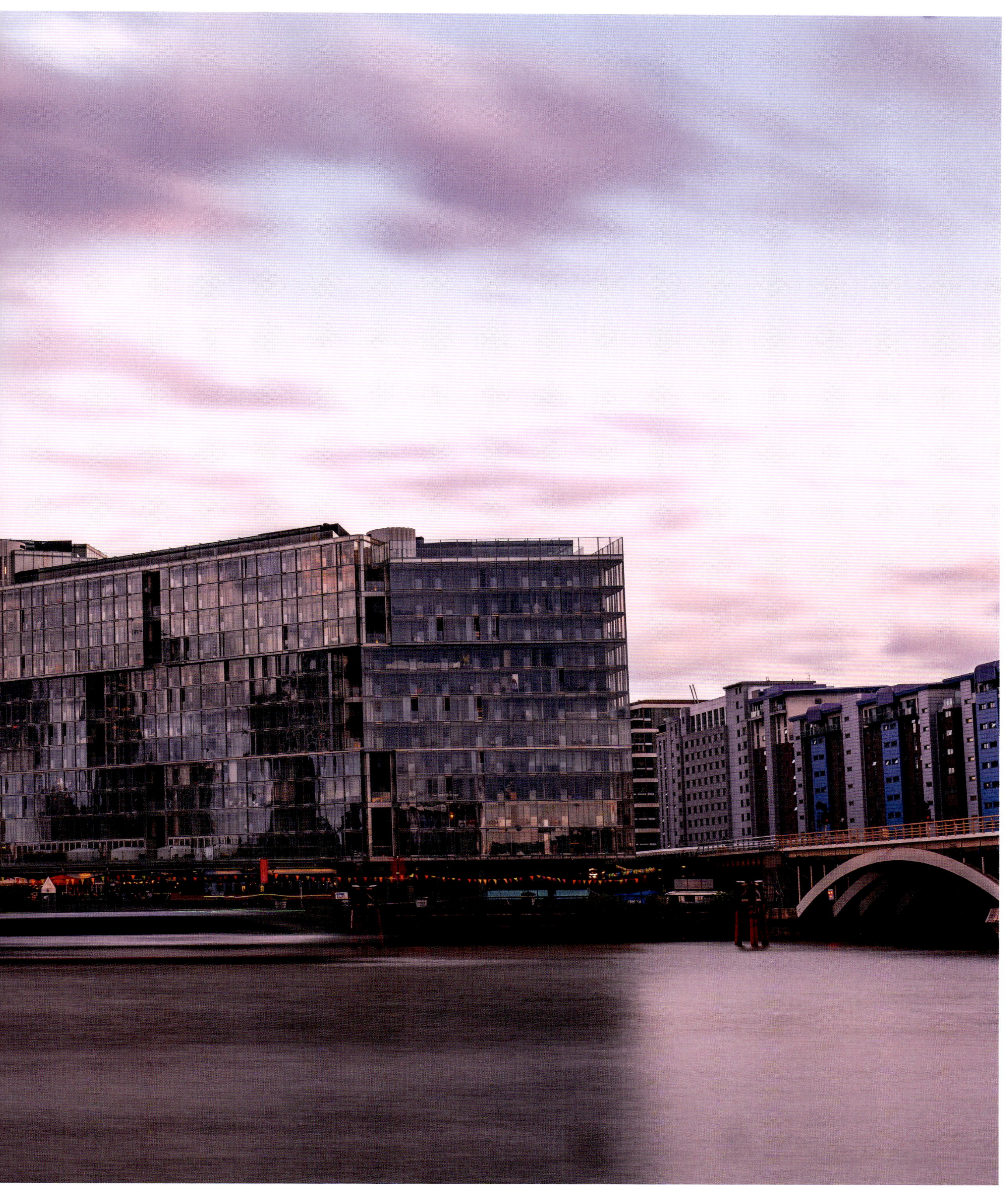

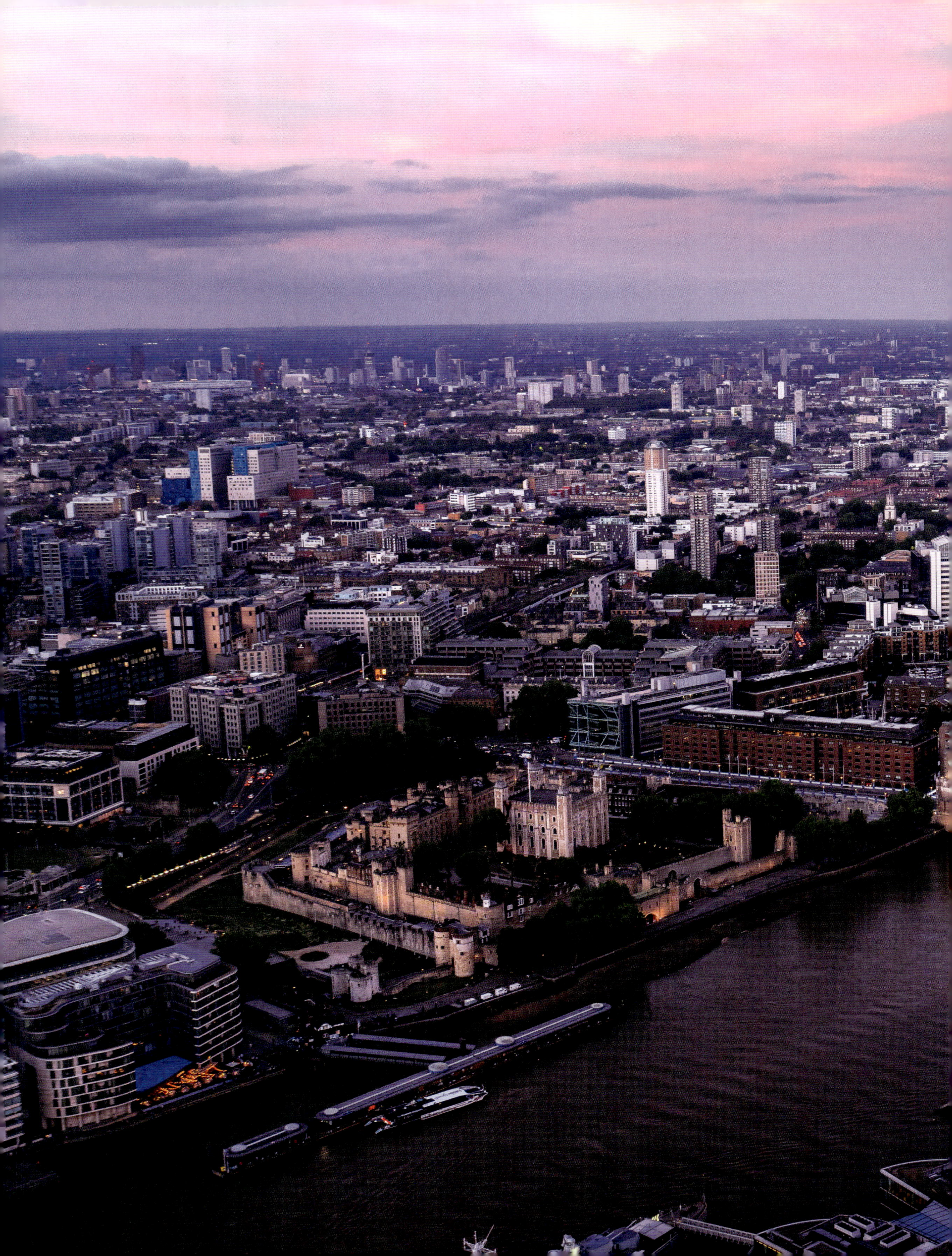

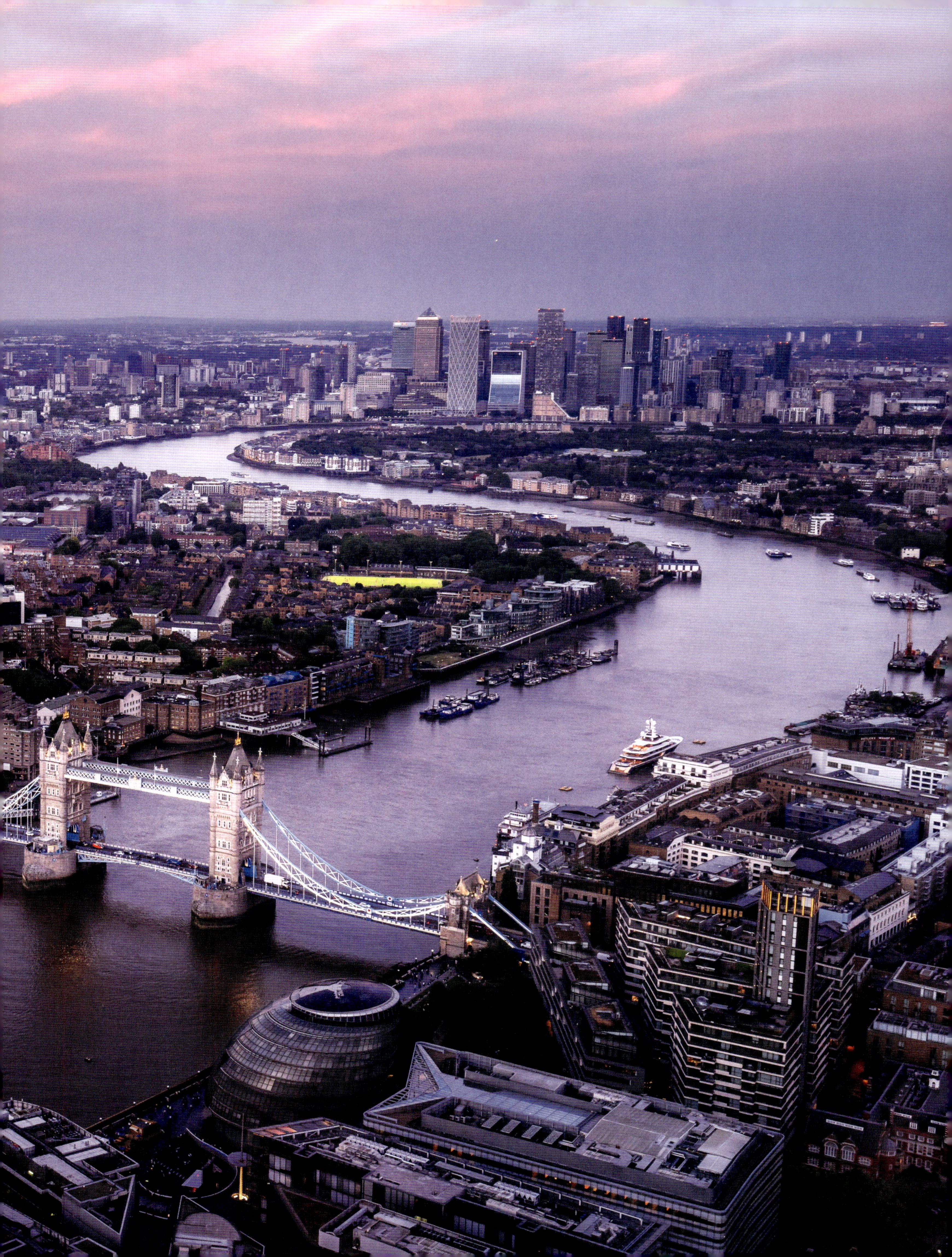

10 – 11

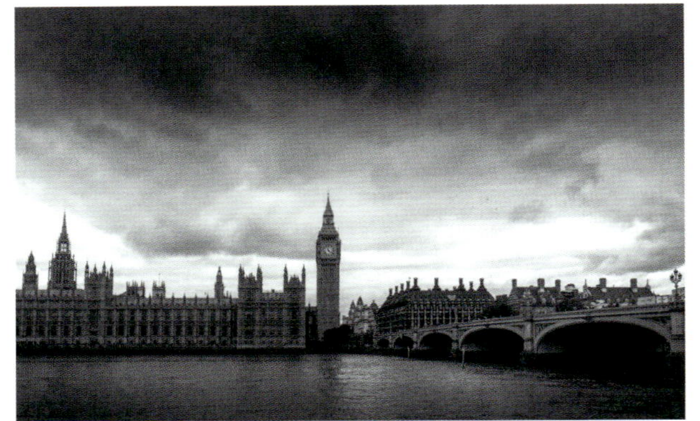

12 – 13

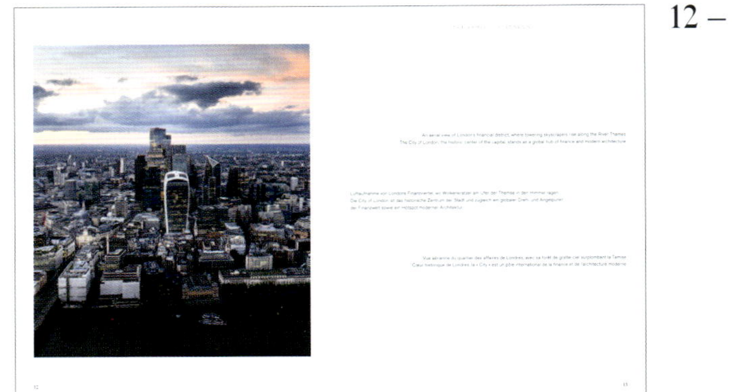

14 – 15

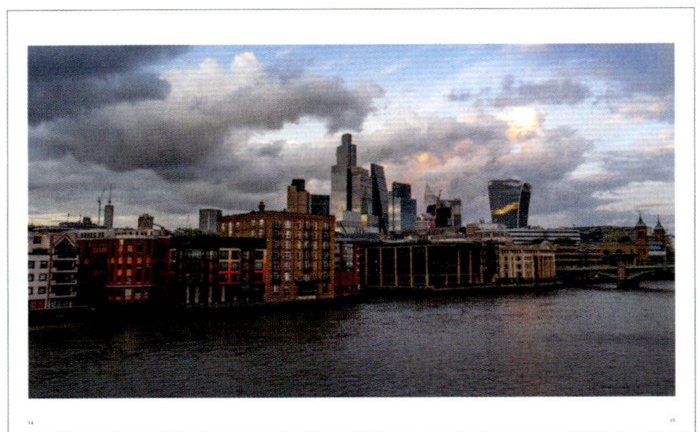

16 – 17

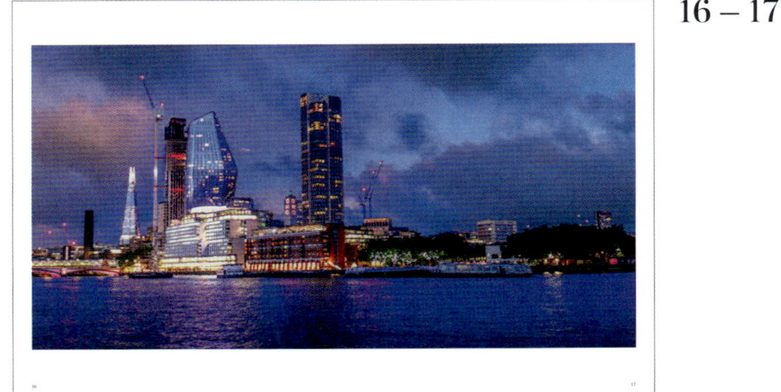

18 – 19

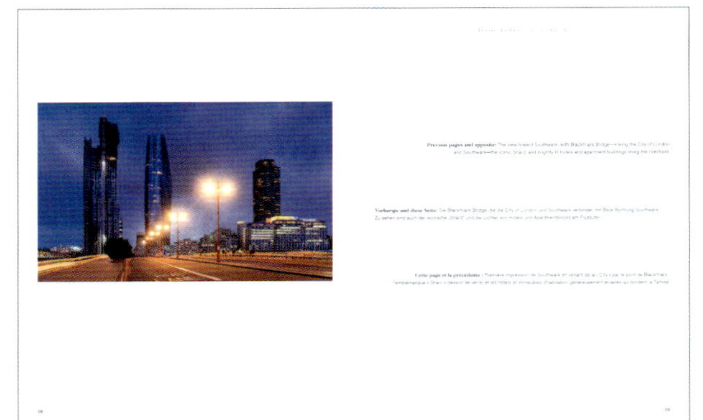

20 – 21

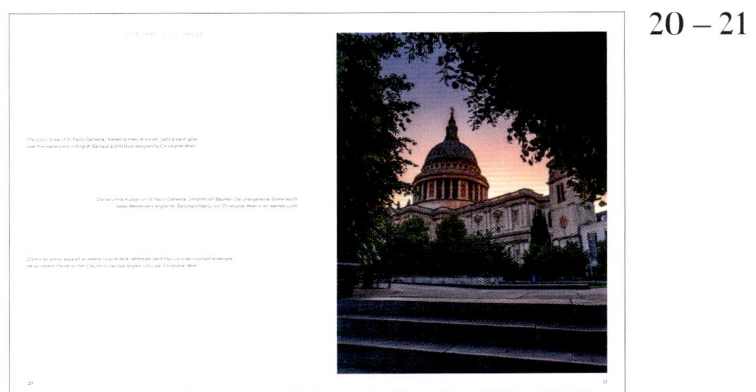

22 – 23

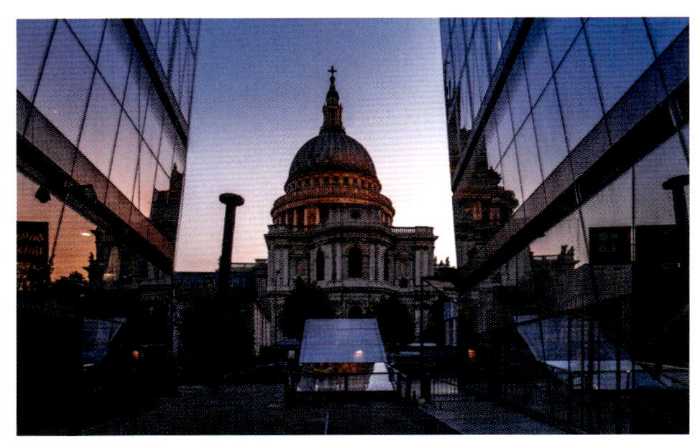

24 – 25

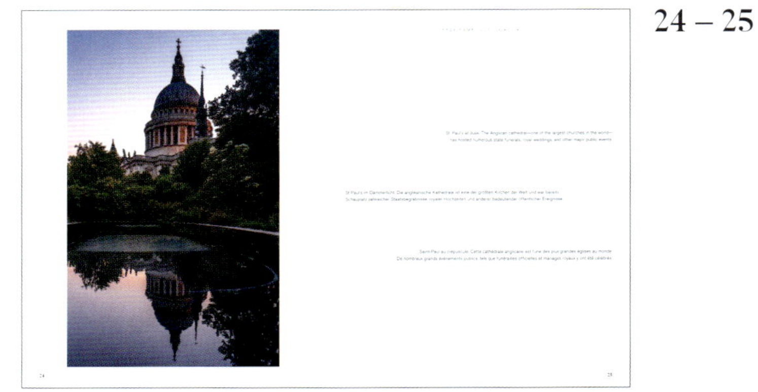

26 – 27

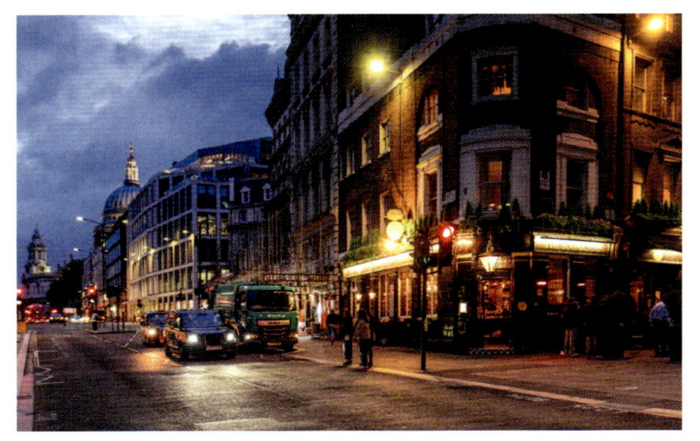

28 – 29

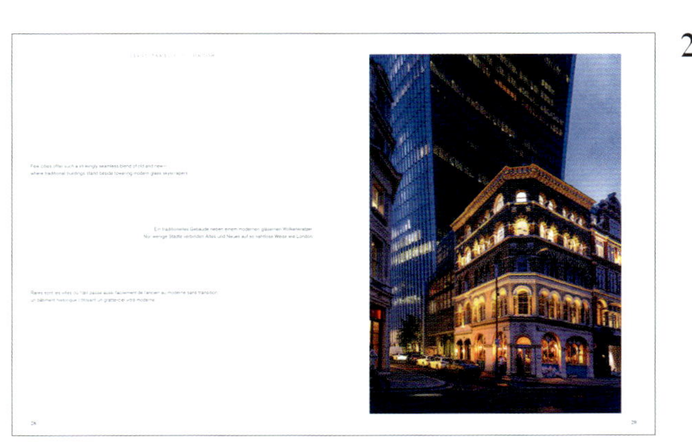

30 – 31

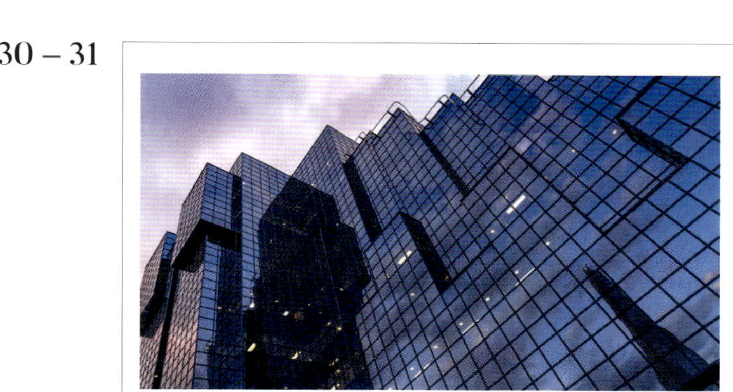

32 – 33

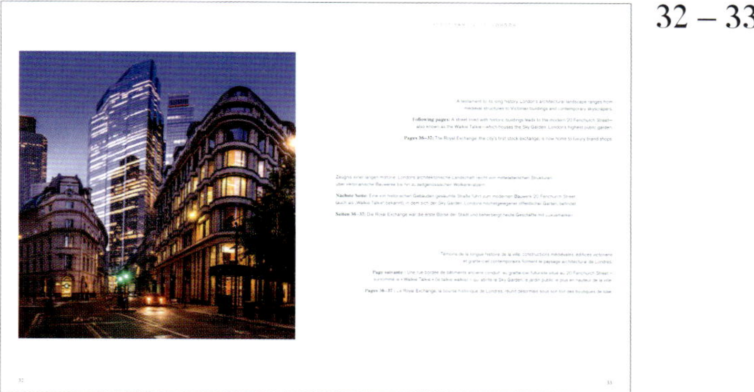

34 – 35

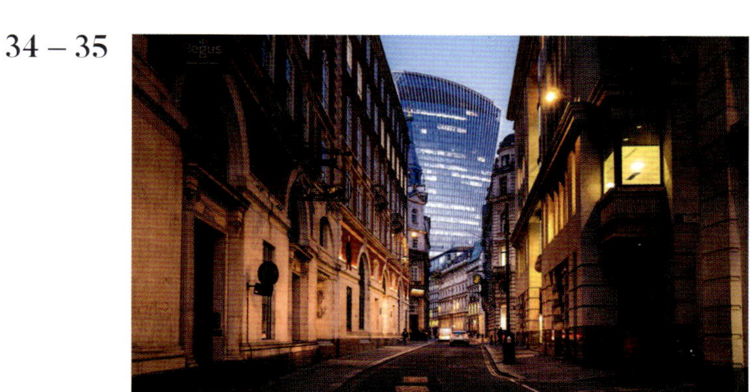

36 – 37

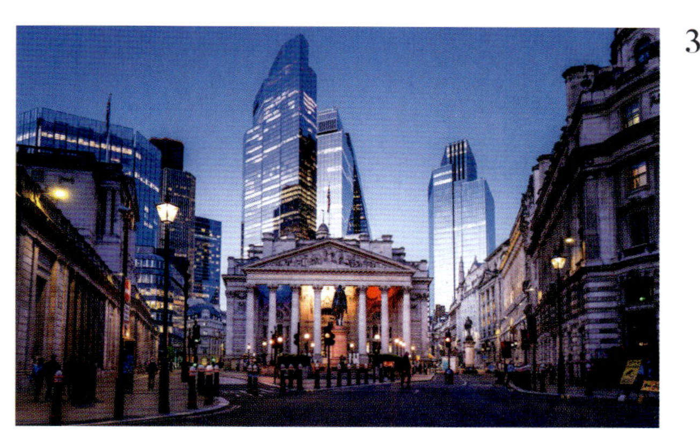

38 – 39

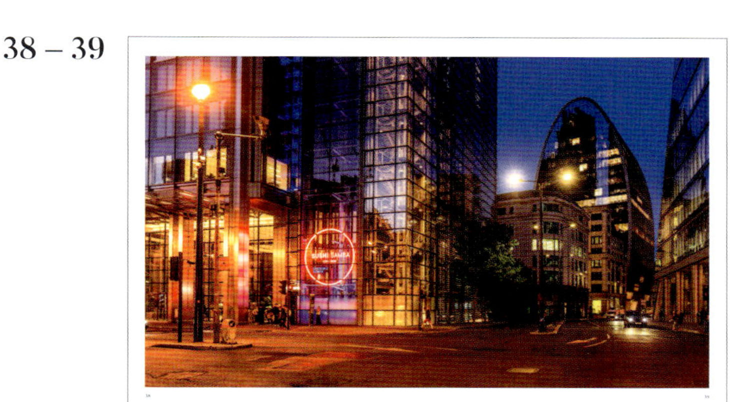

40 – 41

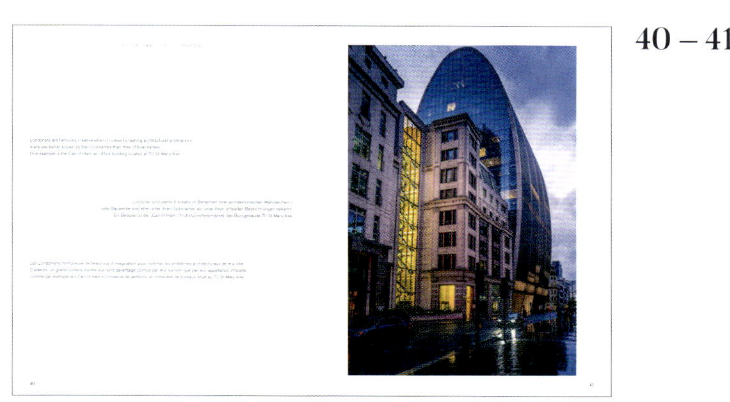

42 – 43

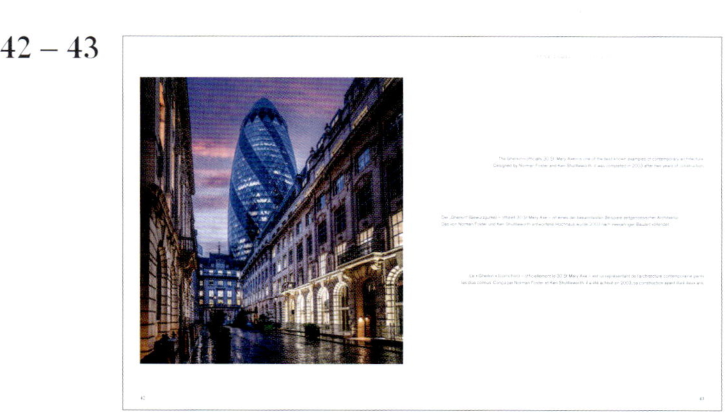

44 – 45

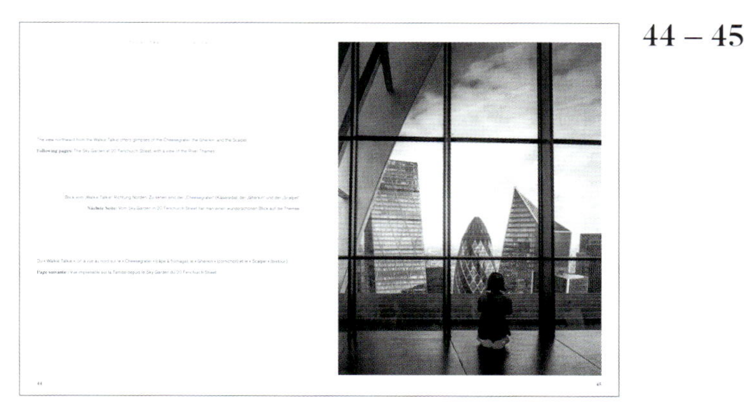

46 – 47

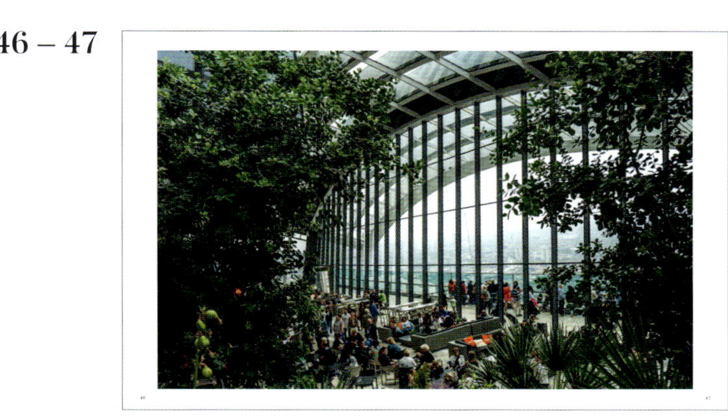

48 – 49

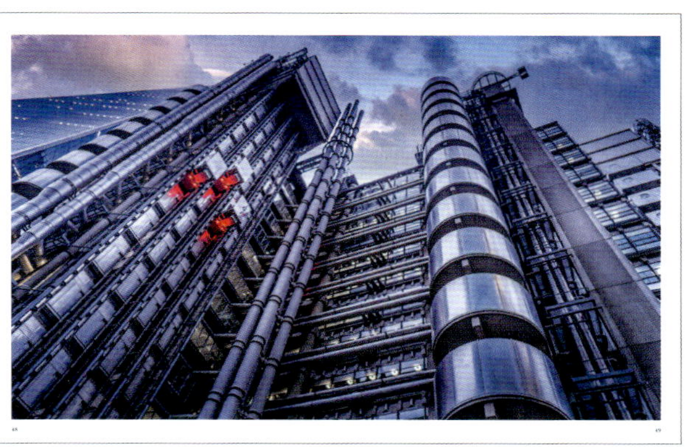

50 –51

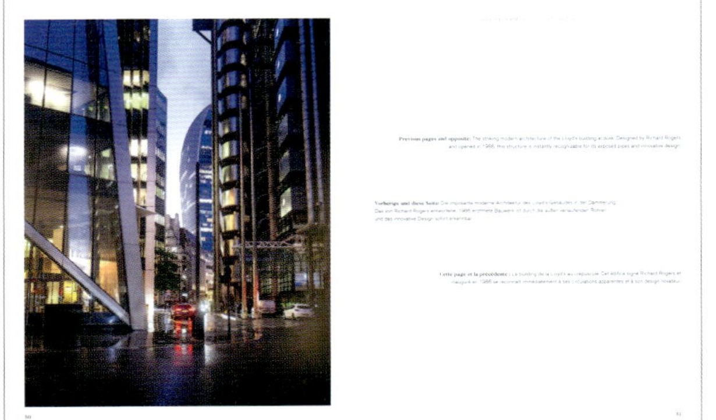

52 – 53

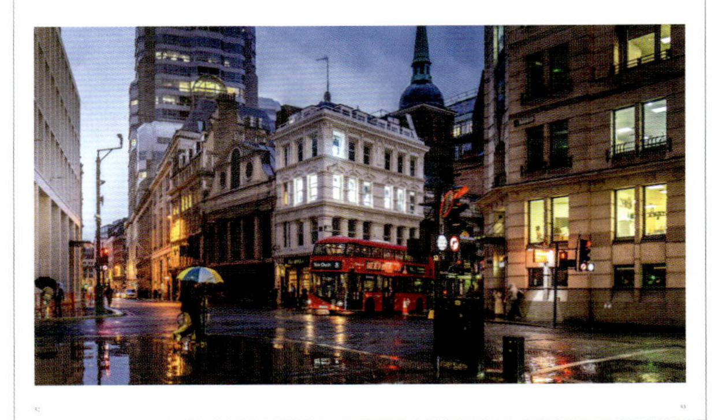

54 – 55

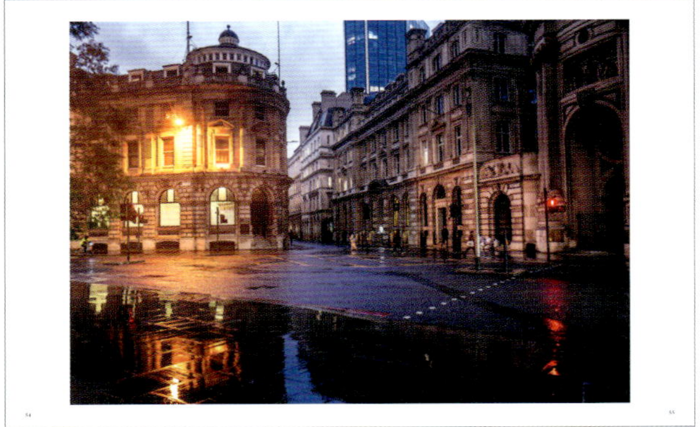

56 – 57

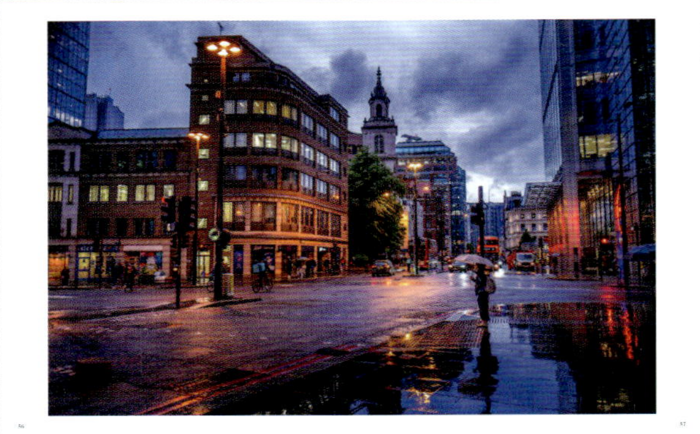

58 – 59

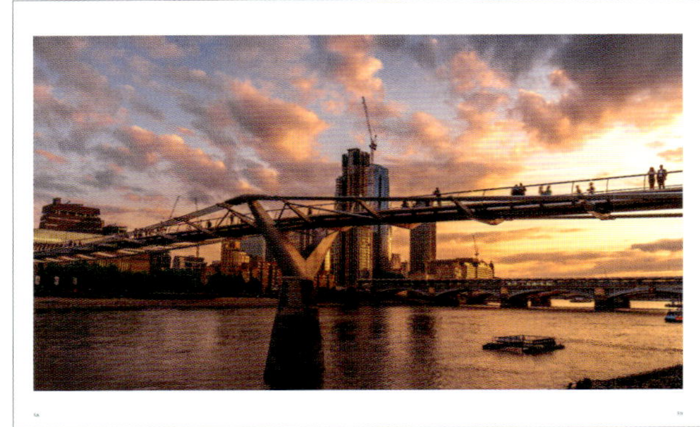

60 – 61

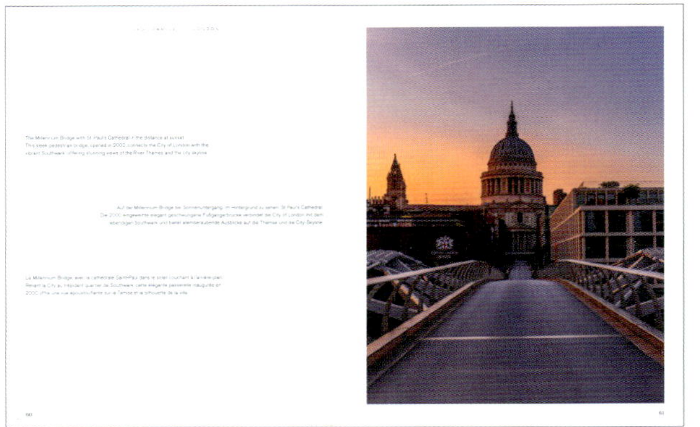

62 – 63

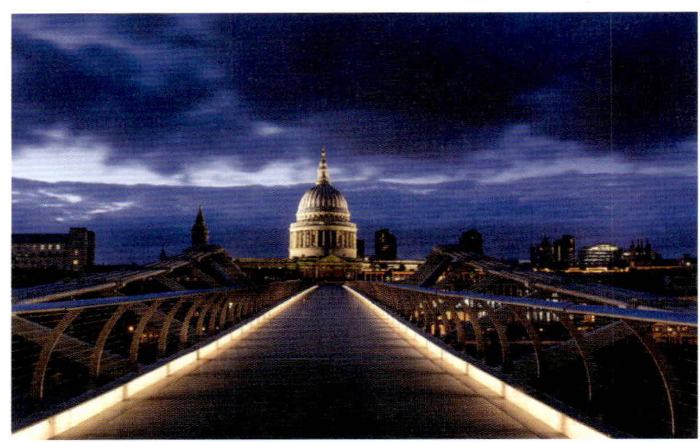

64 – 65

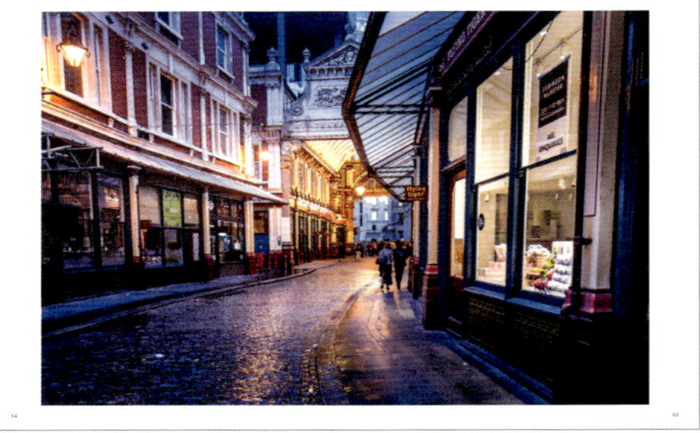

66 – 67

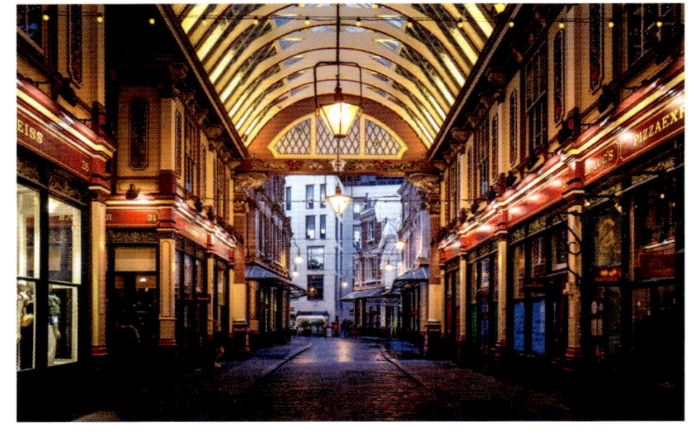

68 – 69

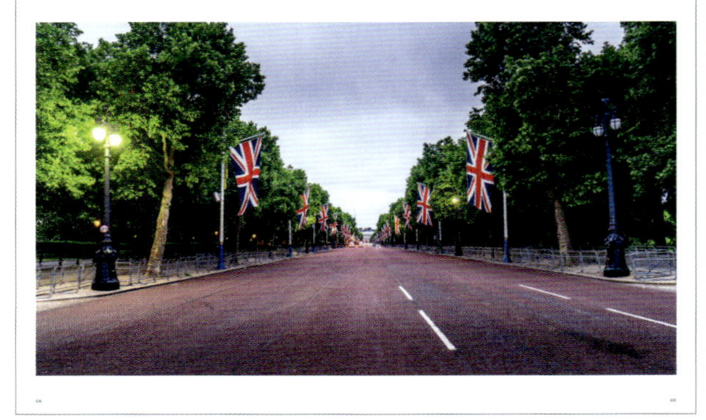

70 – 71

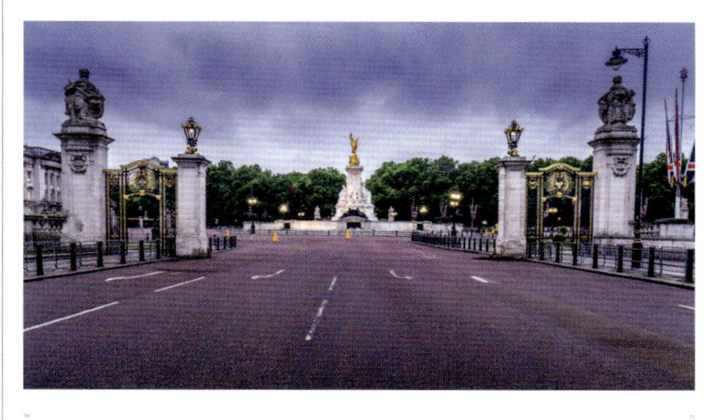

72 – 73

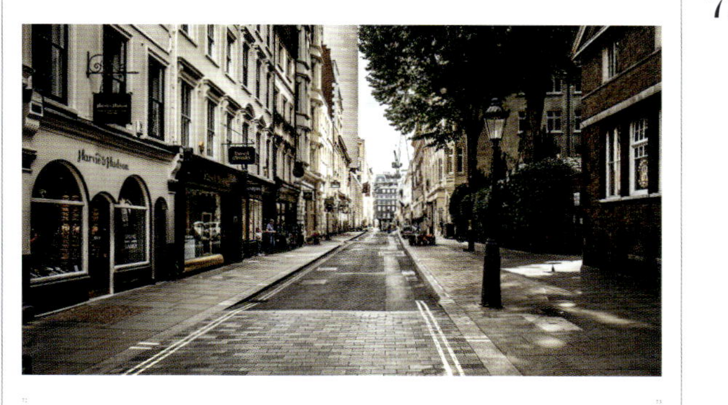

74 – 75

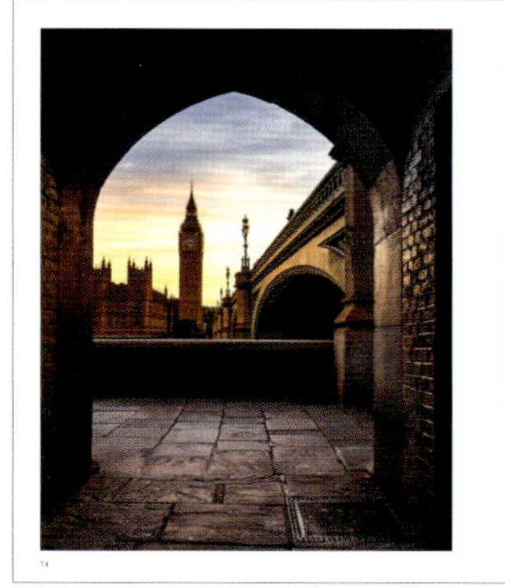

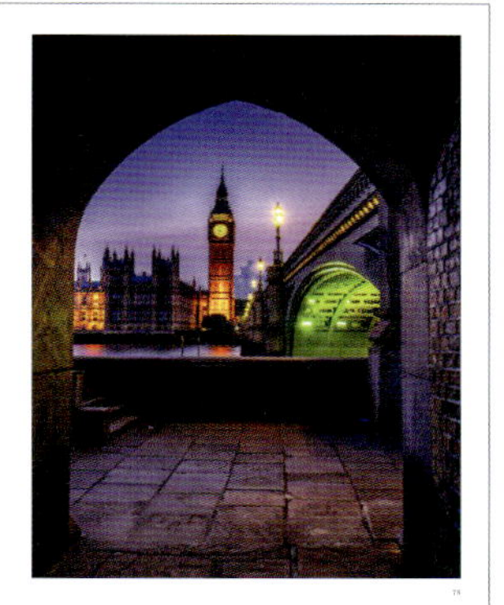

76 – 77

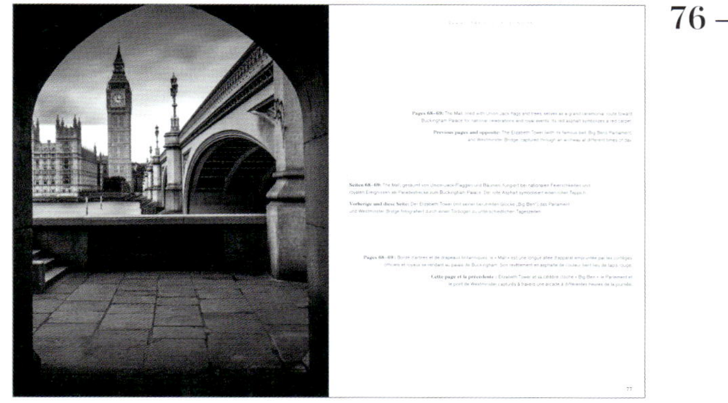

78 – 79

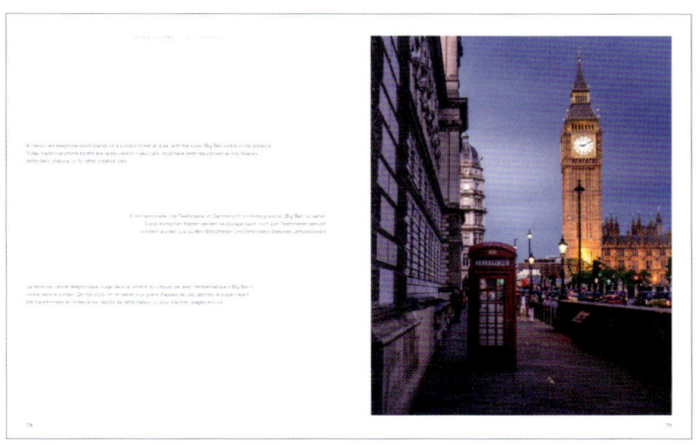

80 – 81

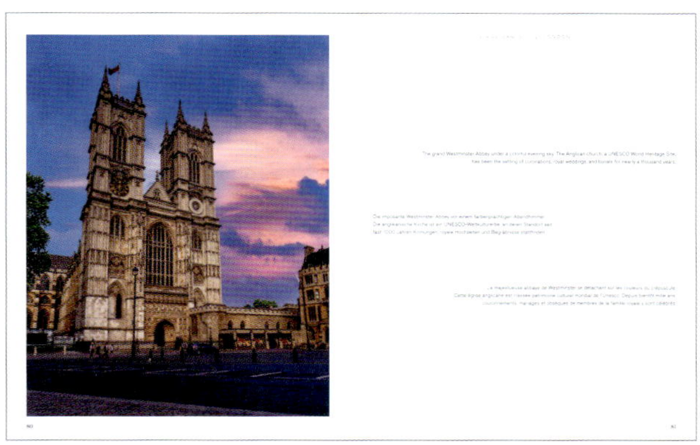

82 – 83

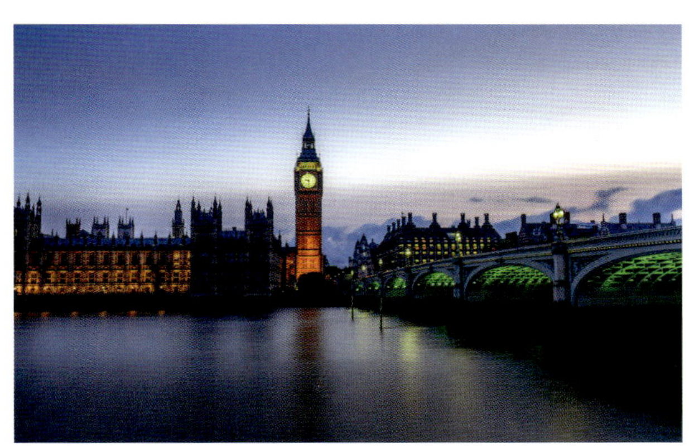

84 – 85

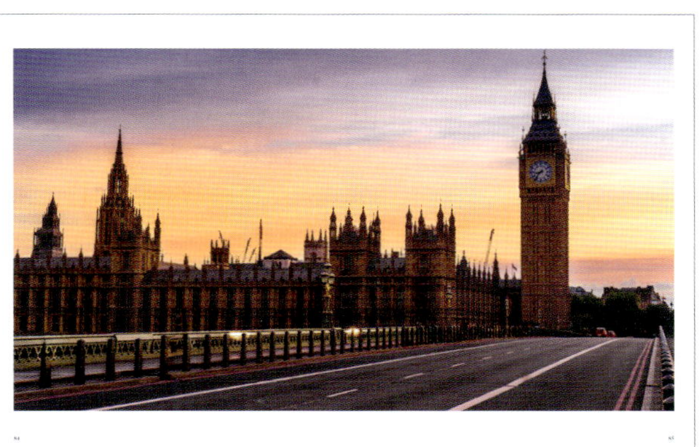

86 – 87

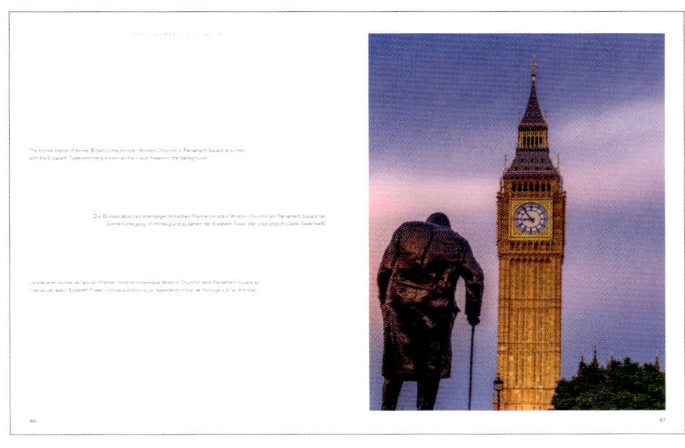

88 – 89

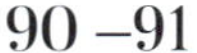

90 –91

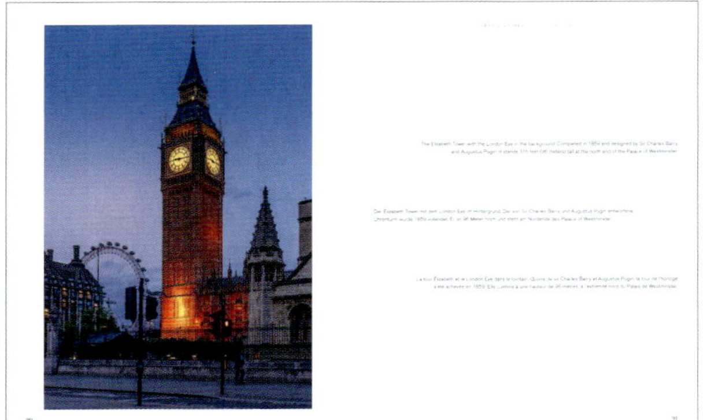

92 – 93

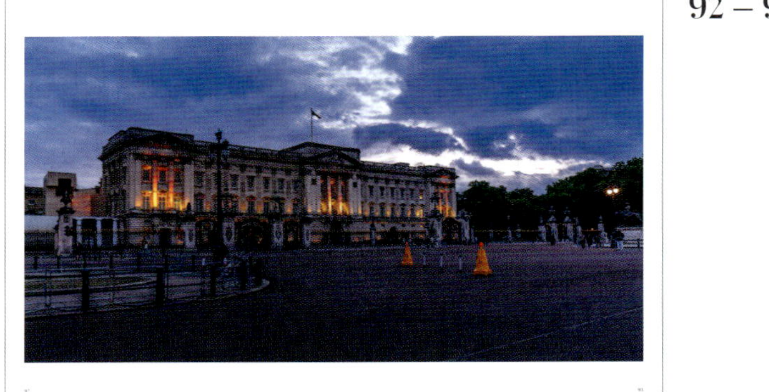

94 – 95

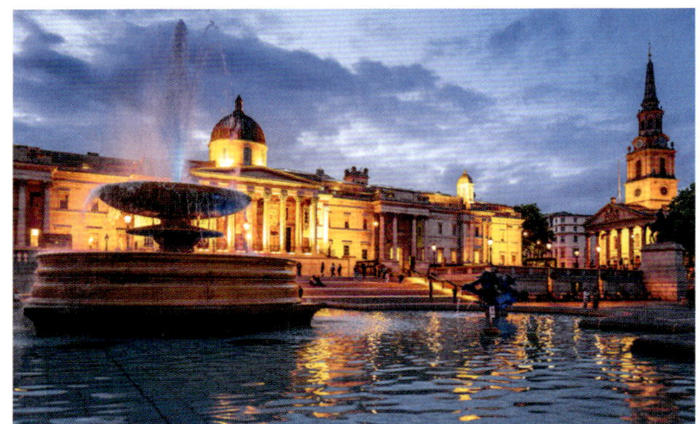

96 – 97

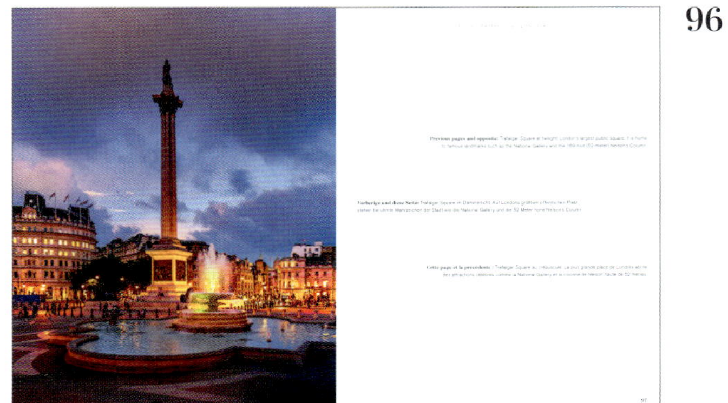

98 – 99

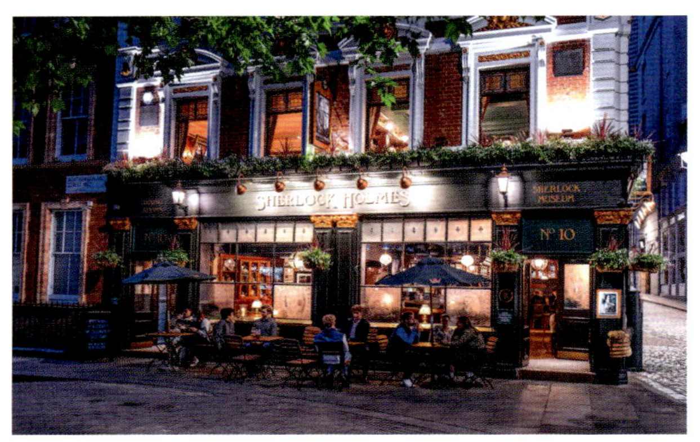

100 – 101

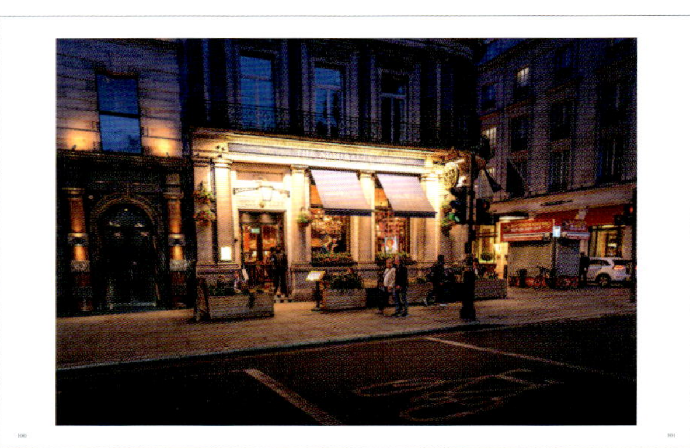

102 – 103

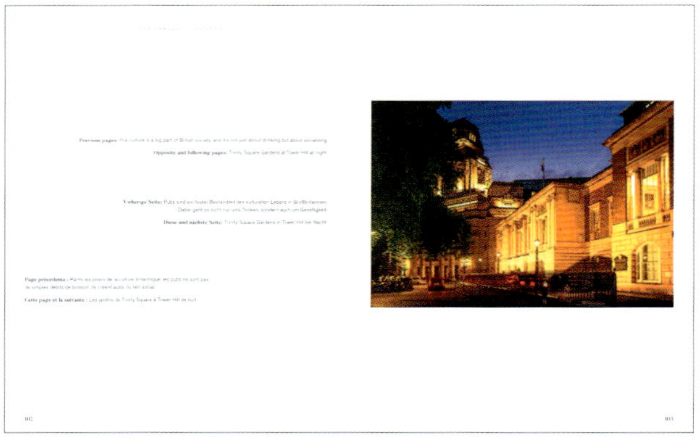

104 – 105

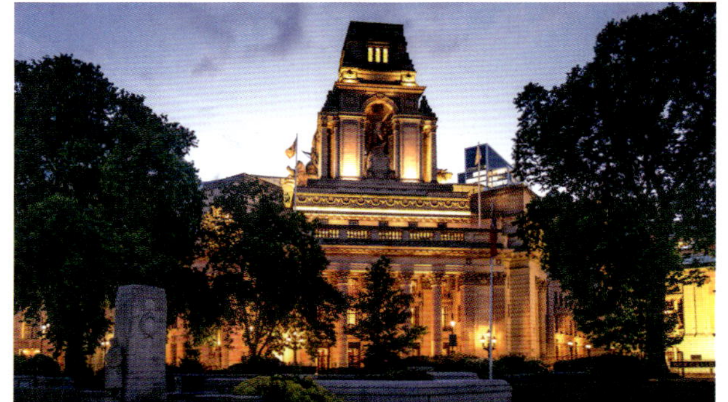

106 – 107

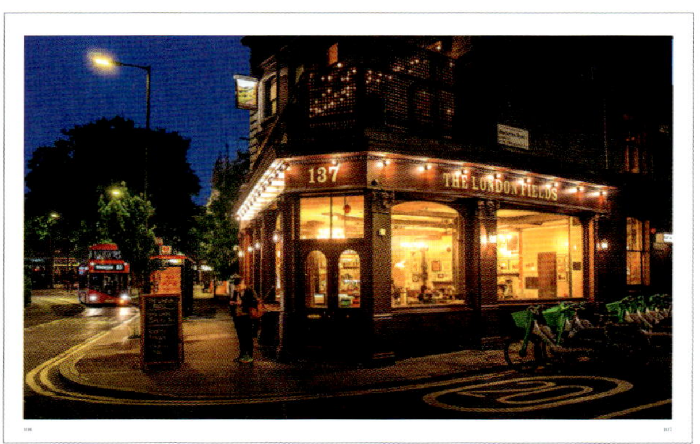

108 – 109

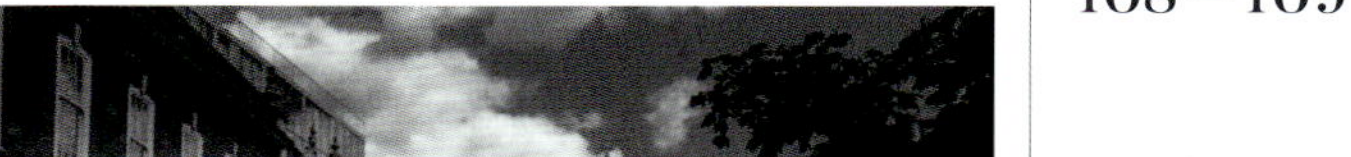

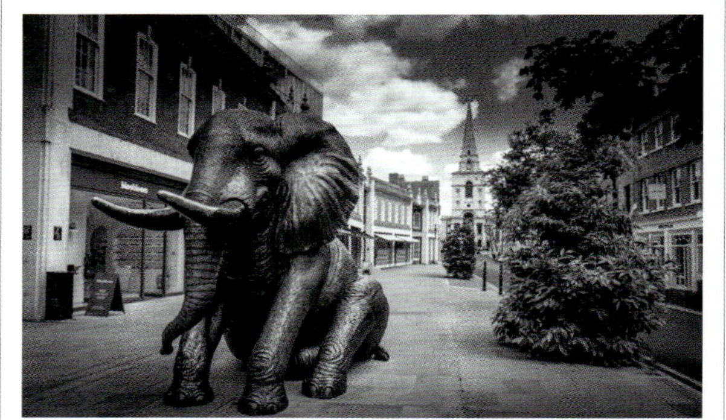

110 – 111

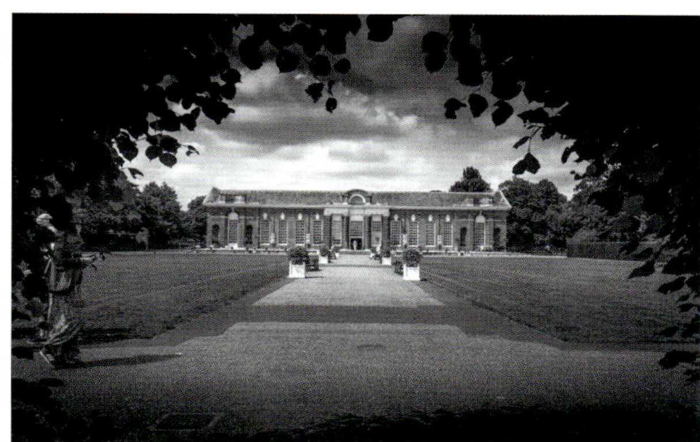

112 – 113

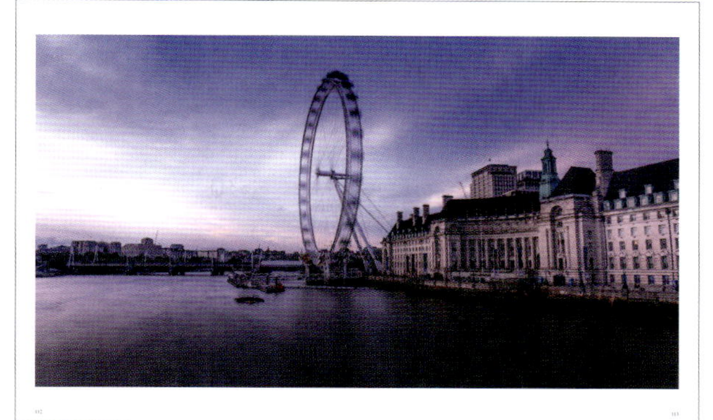

114 – 115

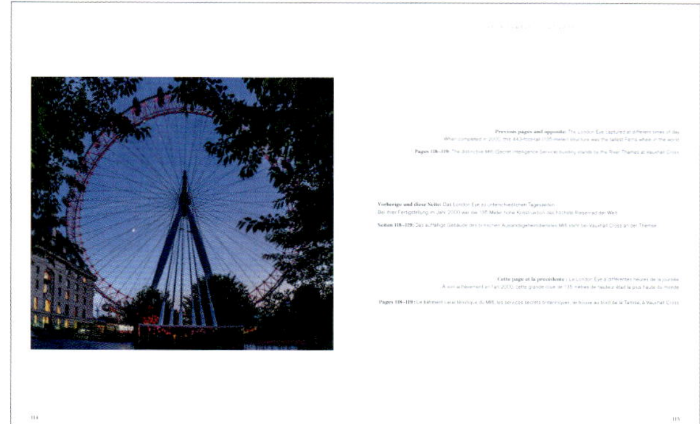

116 – 117

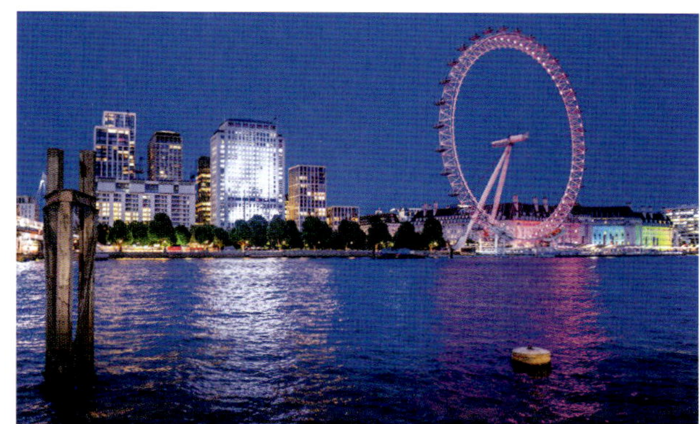

118 – 119

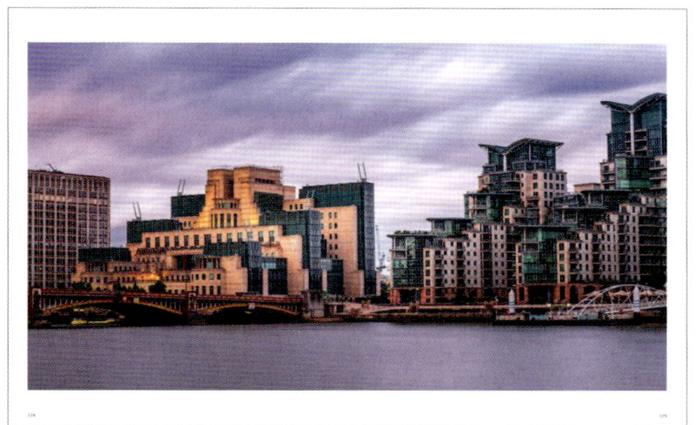

120 – 121

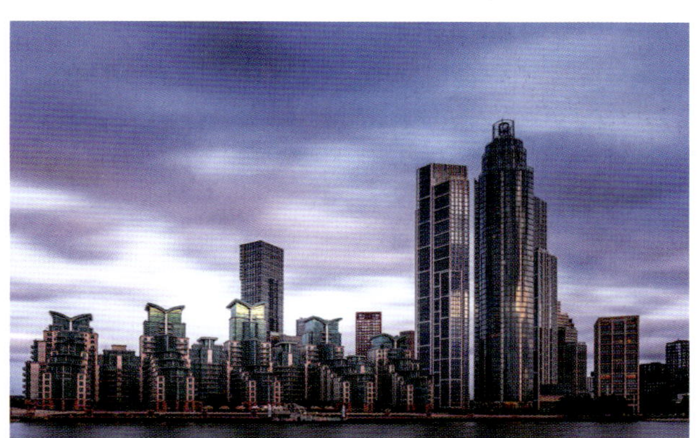

122 – 123

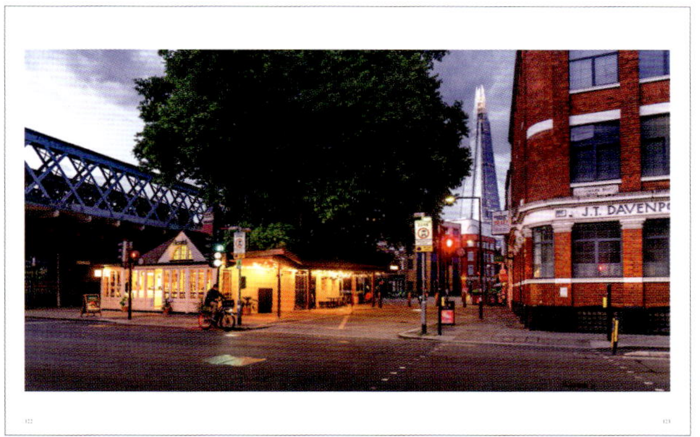

124 – 125

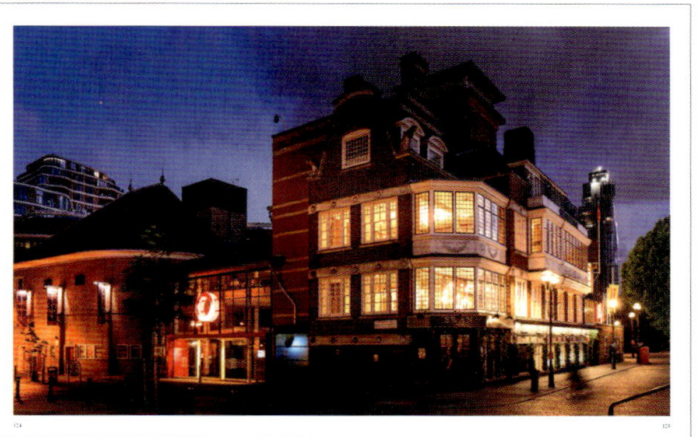

126 – 127

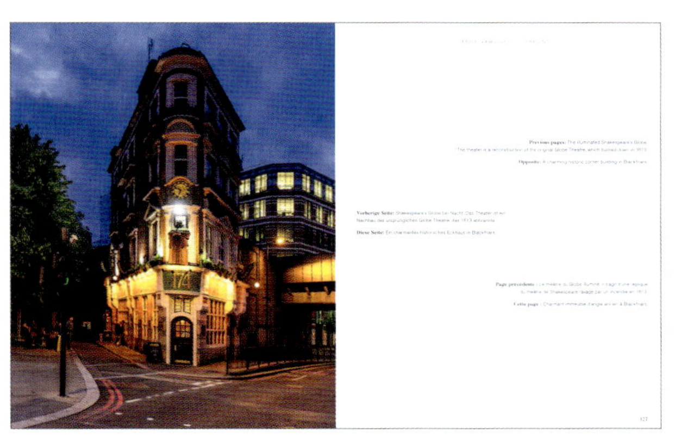

128 – 129

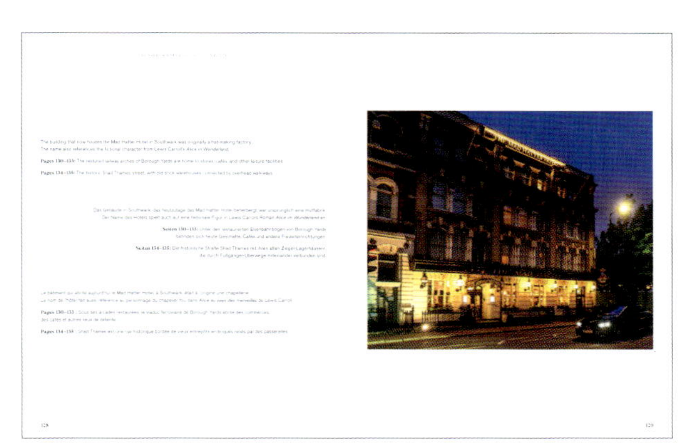

130 – 131

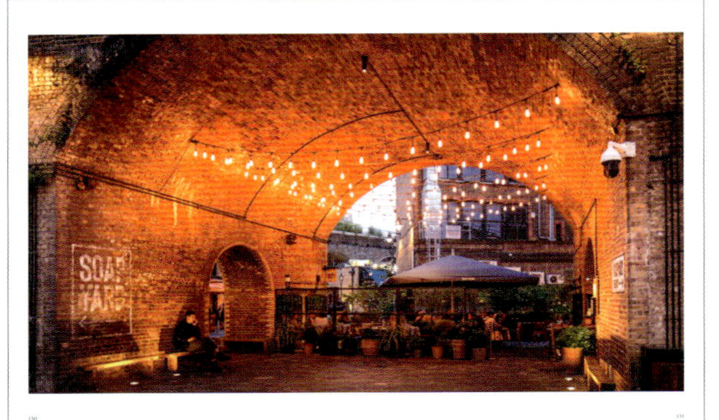

132 – 133

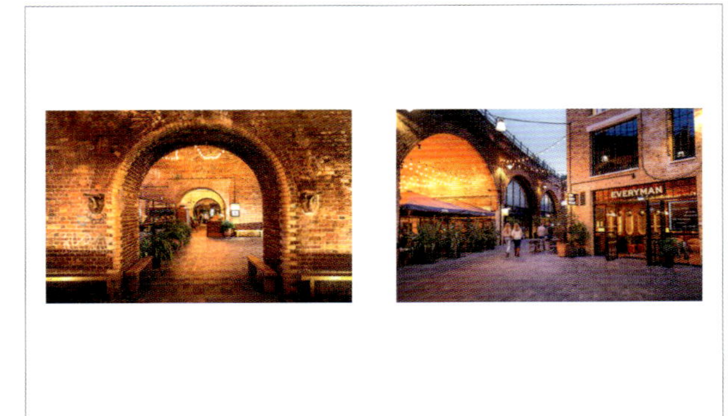

134 – 135

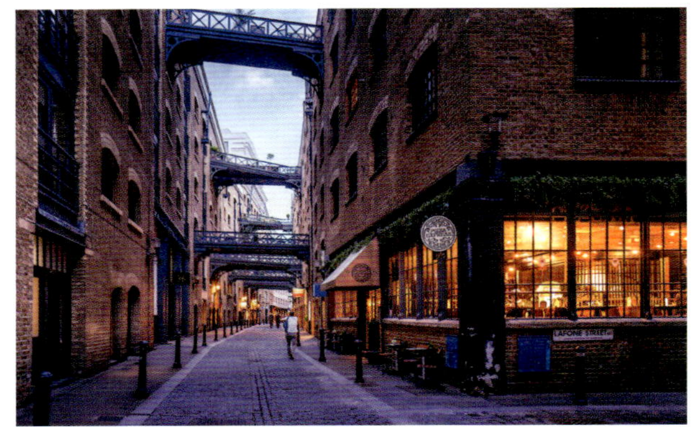

136 – 137

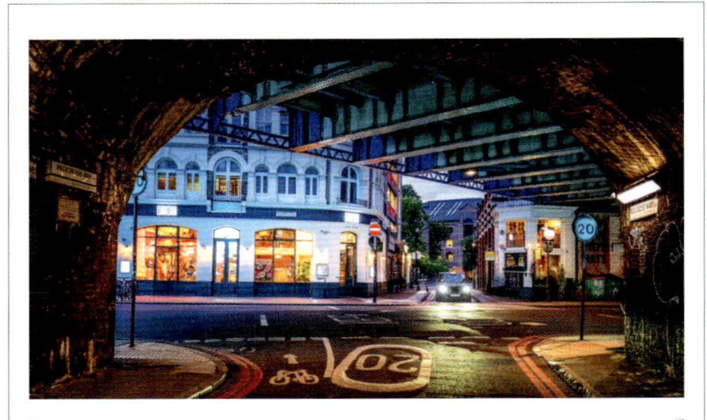

138 – 139

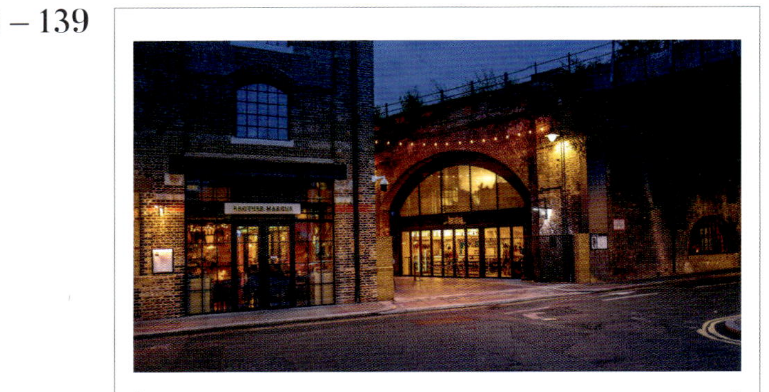

140 – 141

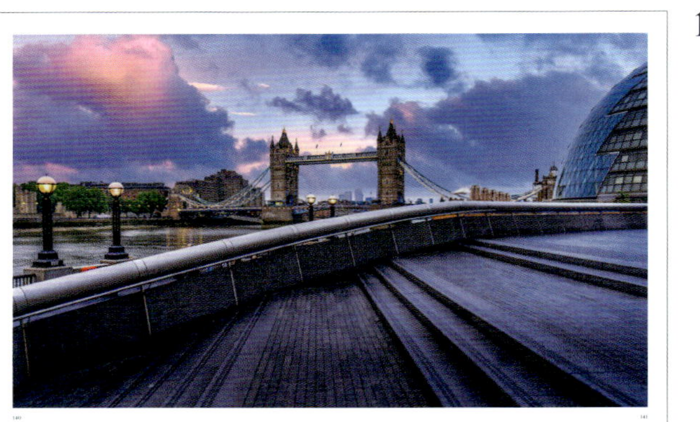

142 – 143

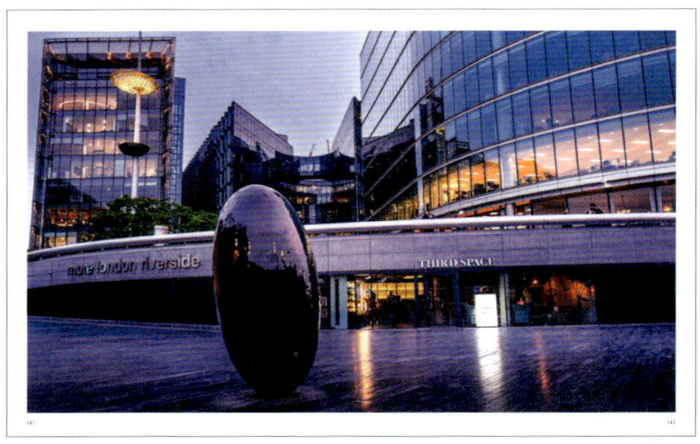

144 – 145

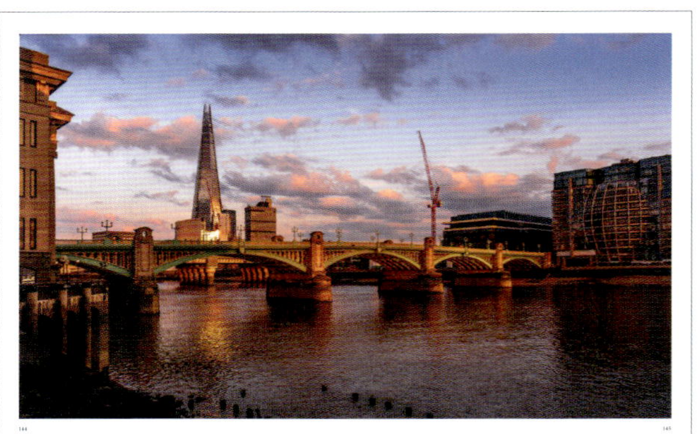

146 – 147

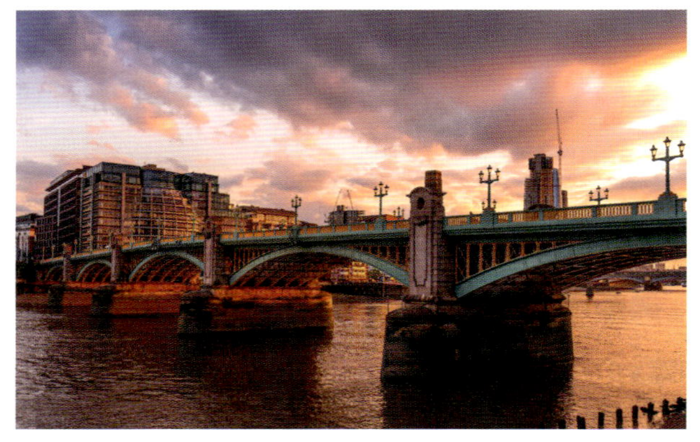

148 – 149

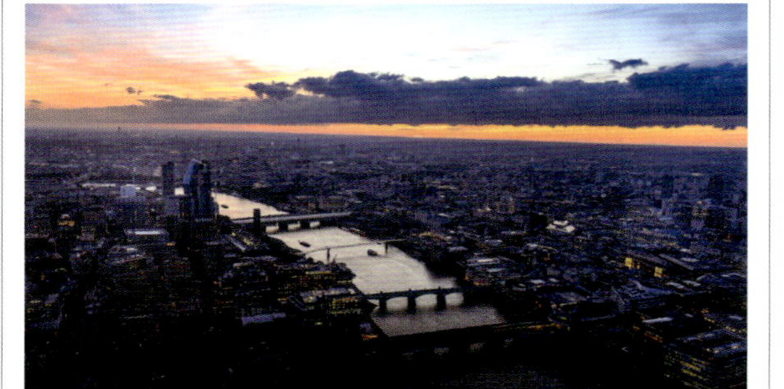

150 – 151

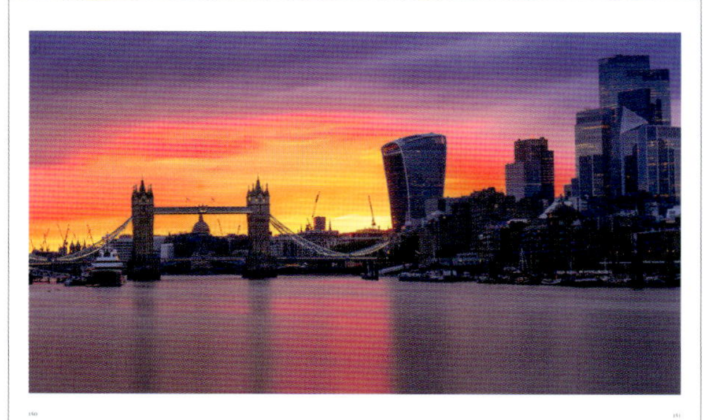

152 – 153

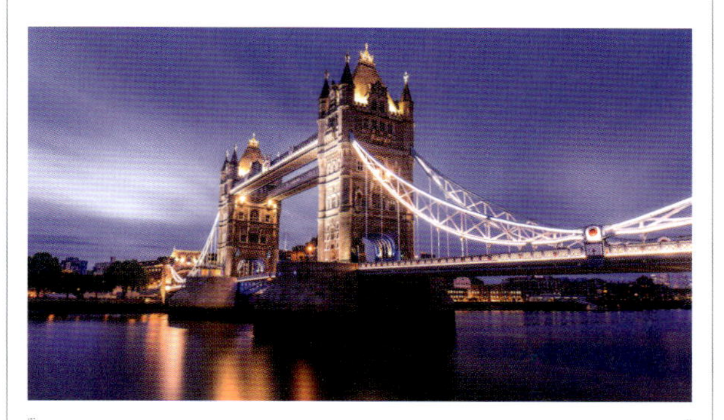

154 – 155

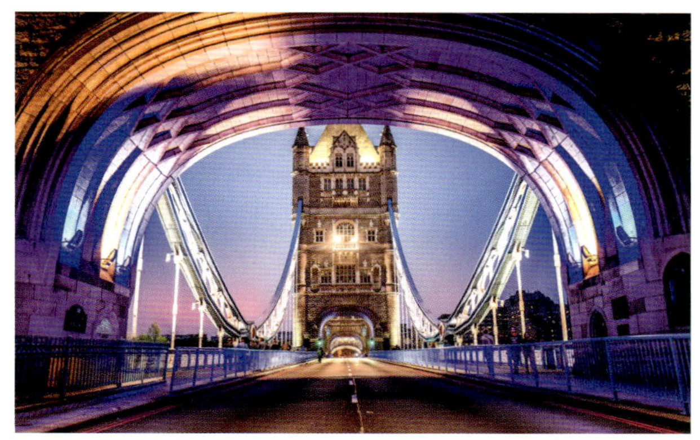

156 – 157

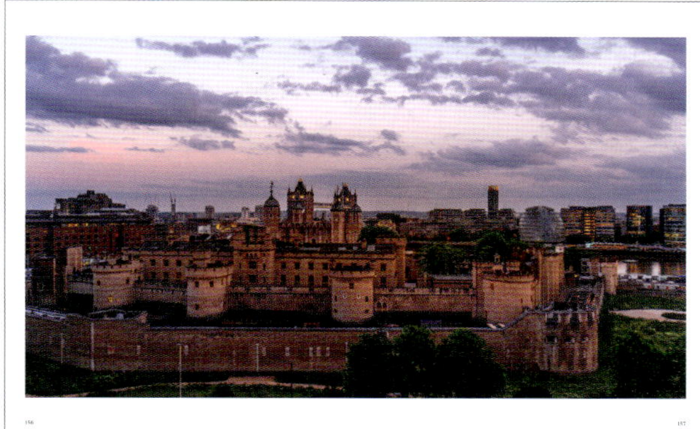

158 – 159

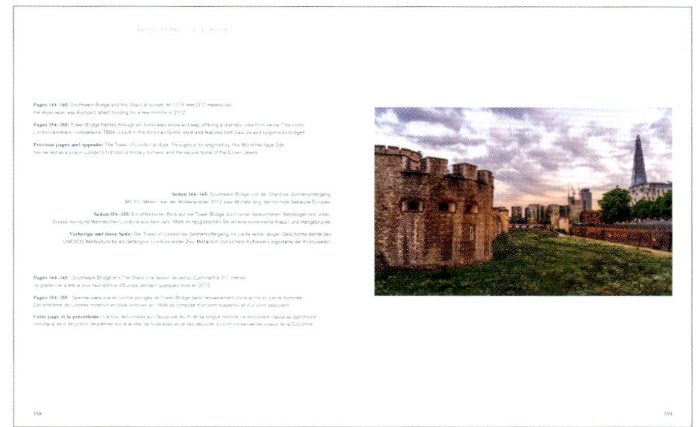

160 – 161

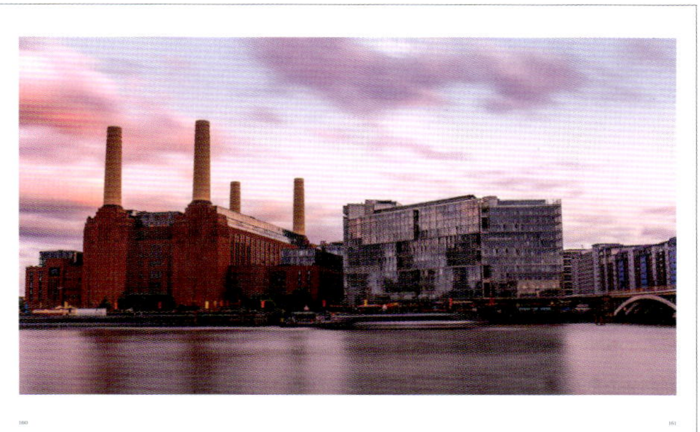

162 – 163

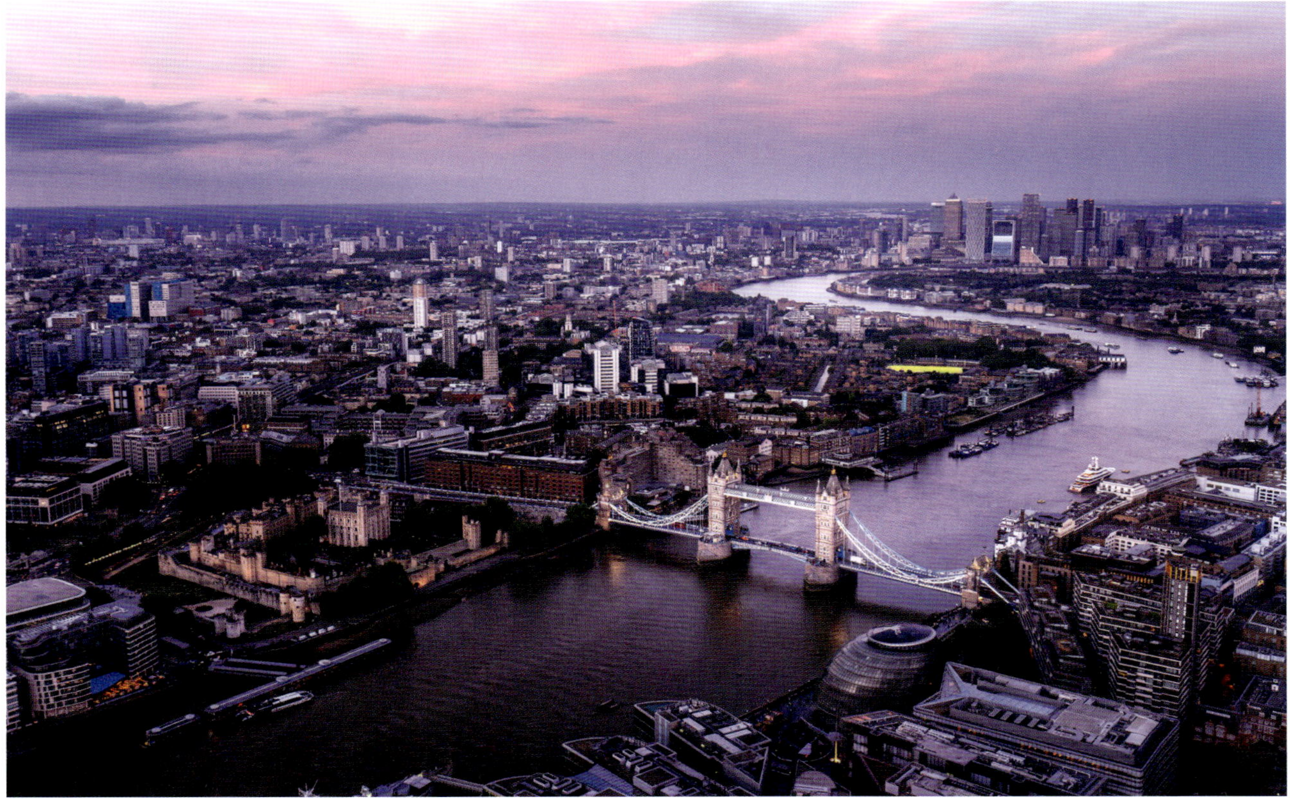

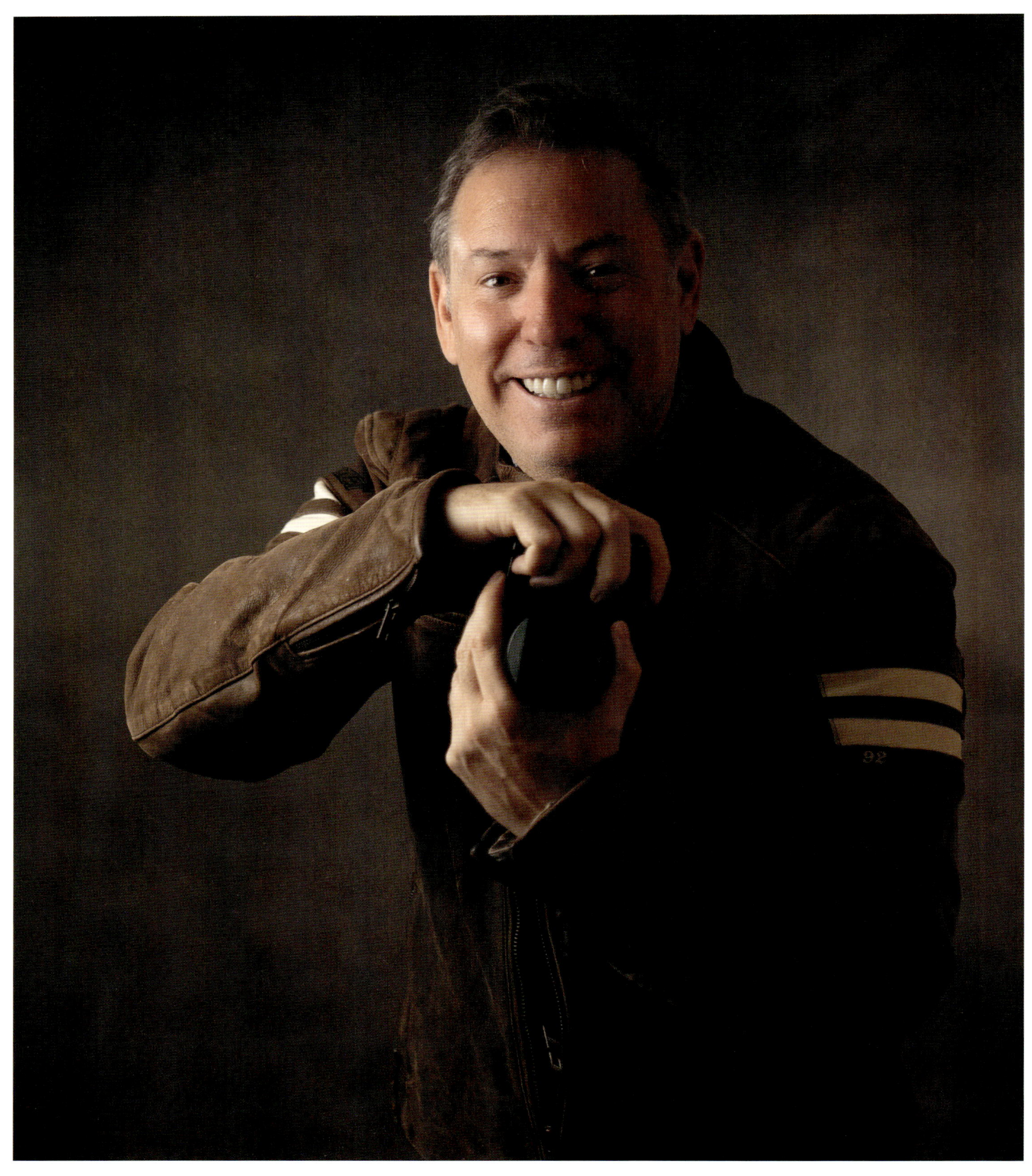

Self-portrait | Selbstporträt | Autoportrait

SERGE RAMELLI

Serge Ramelli has been a professional photographer for the past 15 years, and his work is exhibited in 120 galleries around the world. In 2025, he became the official photographer of the city of Las Vegas. From a very young age, he was passionate about movies and how images can portray the world. Popular films like *Gladiator*, *Saving Private Ryan*, *Indiana Jones*, and *Star Wars* inspired him to show the world in its most beautiful and cinematic light.

He served as vice president of sales for an agency in Paris from 2004 to 2010. After work, he would take photos of Paris with the idea of capturing a cinematic look for his own pleasure. In 2010, he quit his job to become a full-time photographer and never looked back. Since then, he has published many books with teNeues featuring Paris, New York, Los Angeles, Venice, Barcelona, and now London.

Serge Ramelli arbeitet seit 15 Jahren als professioneller Fotograf. Seine Bilder werden in 120 Galerien weltweit ausgestellt, 2025 wurde er zum offiziellen Fotografen der Stadt Las Vegas ernannt.

Schon sehr früh entdeckte Serge seine Leidenschaft fürs Kino und dafür, wie Bilder die Welt darstellen können. Erfolgsfilme wie *Gladiator*, *Der Soldat James Ryan*, *Indiana Jones* und *Star Wars* inspirierten ihn dazu, die Welt auf kinematografische Weise von ihrer schönsten Seite zu zeigen.

Von 2004 bis 2010 war er stellvertretender Vertriebsleiter einer Agentur in Paris. Nach der Arbeit fotografierte er Paris mit dieser Idee eines filmischen Looks im Kopf zu seinem Privatvergnügen. 2010 kündigte er seine Anstellung, um hauptberuflich als Fotograf zu arbeiten, und hat diesen Schritt nie bereut.

Seitdem hat Serge bei teNeues zahlreiche Bücher mit Bildern von Paris, New York, Los Angeles, Venedig, Barcelona und jetzt London veröffentlicht.

Serge Ramelli est photographe professionnel depuis 15 ans, ses travaux sont exposés dans 120 galeries de par le monde. En 2025, il est devenu photographe officiel de la ville de Las Vegas.

Depuis sa tendre enfance, il est fasciné par le cinéma et la manière dont les images peuvent représenter le monde. Des grands succès du grand écran tels que *Gladiateur*, *Il faut sauver le soldat Ryan*, *Indiana Jones* et *La Guerre des étoiles* ont été sa source d'inspiration pour montrer le monde sous son jour le plus beau et le plus cinématographique.

Il a été directeur commercial pour une agence web parisienne de 2004 à 2010. À ses heures de loisir, il prenait pour son propre plaisir des photos de Paris dans une optique cinématographique. En 2010, il a quitté son poste pour se consacrer entièrement à la photographie, une décision qu'il n'a jamais regrettée.

Depuis, il a publié aux éditions teNeues de nombreux livres mettant à l'honneur Paris, New York, Los Angeles, Venise, Barcelone et maintenant Londres.

DARIUS STEVENS WILHERE

Darius Stevens Wilhere is an Earth-based writer-director who can occasionally be found in London—window shopping on Bond Street, location scouting with espresso in hand to find frames from iconic Bond films, or enjoying a glass of something stronger while listening to The Clash at Gordon's Wine Bar and soaking in the World War II–era underground bunker atmosphere.

Darius Stevens Wilhere ist ein auf der Erde lebender Autor/Filmemacher, der gelegentlich in London vorzufinden ist. Dort bummelt er auf der Bond Street, sucht mit einem Espresso in der Hand nach Locations aus ikonischen James-Bond-Filmen, genießt zum Sound von The Clash einen Drink in Gordon's Wine Bar und taucht in die Atmosphäre eines Luftschutzbunkers aus dem Zweiten Weltkrieg ein.

Darius Stevens Wilhere est un citoyen de monde, auteur et réalisateur que l'on peut parfois rencontrer à Londres, faisant du lèche-vitrines sur Bond Street, ou en repérage un petit noir à la main pour dénicher des lieux de tournage des films de James Bond ou encore en train de siroter une boisson plus forte en écoutant The Clash dans l'atmosphère d'abri antiaérien de la Seconde Guerre mondiale du Gordon's Wine Bar.

THANK YOUS

I would like to thank my wife, Karen Ramelli, for making this book. She has an amazing eye, and many times she has helped me find the perfect composition. I would like to thank Charlie and Kate Wakley for helping to find the best locations in London.

I would like to thank all my mentors:

- L. Ron Hubbard for his guidance with the Art Series
- Scott Kelby for teaching me photography some 20 years ago

To all the great filmmakers who gave me a life purpose:

- Steven Spielberg
- Ridley Scott
- George Lucas
- Robert Zemeckis

To my four children, Marine, Anthony, Alexi, and Mickael—you are the best kids a dad could ever dream of.

IMPRINT

London
Serge Ramelli

Foreword by Darius Stevens Wilhere

Editorial Management by Nadine Weinhold
Design by Iris van Kempen
Color Separation by Robert Kuhlendahl
Production by Alwine Krebber
Copyediting by Victorine Lamothe (English),
Nadine Weinhold (German), Mireille Onon (French)
Translation by Ronit Jariv (German), Christèle Jany (French)

Printed in the Czech Republic by Finidr
Hergestellt in Europa

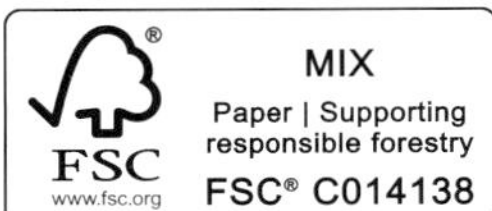

Published by gestalten, Berlin 2025
ISBN 978-3-96171-699-9

1st printing, 2025

For more information, and to order books, please visit www.teneues.com and www.gestalten.com

Die Gestalten Verlag GmbH & Co. KG
Mariannenstrasse 9–10
10999 Berlin, Germany
hello@gestalten.com

Düsseldorf Office
Waldenburger Straße 13
41564 Kaarst, Germany
verlag@teneues.com

teNeues Press Department
press@gestalten.com

Bibliographic information published by the Deutsche Nationalbibliothek. The Deutsche Nationalbibliothek lists this publication in the Deutsche Nationalbibliografie; detailed bibliographic data is available online at www.dnb.de

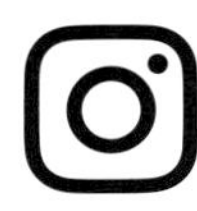

https://instagram.com/teneuespublishing

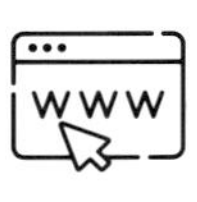

www.teneues.com